INDIA
SUSTAINING REFORM, REDUCING POVERTY

THE WORLD BANK

OXFORD
UNIVERSITY PRESS

OXFORD
UNIVERSITY PRESS

YMCA Library Building, Jai Singh Road, New Delhi 110 001

Oxford University Press is a department of the University of Oxford.
It furthers the University's objective of excellence in research, scholarship,
and education by publishing worldwide in

Oxford   New York
Auckland   Cape Town   Dar es Salaam   Hong Kong   Karachi
Kuala Lumpur   Madrid   Melbourne   Mexico City   Nairobi
New Delhi   Shanghai   Taipei   Toronto

With offices in
Argentina   Austria   Brazil   Chile   Czech Republic   France   Greece
Guatemala   Hungary   Italy   Japan Poland   Portugal   Singapore
South Korea   Switzerland   Thailand   Turkey   Ukraine   Vietnam

Oxford is a registered trade mark of Oxford University Press
in the UK and in certain other countries

Published in India
By Oxford University Press, New Delhi

ISBN-13: 978-0-19-566830-8
ISBN-10: 0-19-566830-8

Printed at Pauls Press, New Delhi 110 001
Published by Manzar Khan, Oxford University Press
YMCA Library Building, Jai Singh Road, New Delhi 110 001

INDIA
SUSTAINING REFORM, REDUCING POVERTY

ACKNOWLEDGEMENTS

This report was prepared by a team led by Mark Baird and Manuela Ferro, under the overall guidance of Sadiq Ahmed and Michael Carter, and with advice from Stephen Howes and Ijaz Nabi. The peer reviewers were Nick Stern, Shankar Acharya, Suman Bery, and Pranab Bardhan.

Major contributors to the report were Brian Pinto and Farah Zahir on fiscal policy, Robert Beschel and Vikram Chand on civil service reform, Jeffrey Hammer on human development, Priya Basu on the investment climate for industry and services, Dina Umali-Deininger on agriculture and rural development, Bhavna Bhatia on the power sector, James Hanson on the financial sector, Anthony Bottrill on the external sector, Kruti Bharucha on social outcomes, Luis Constantino on decentralization, Esperanza Lasagabaster on pensions, Gloria Kessler on the environment, Zhi Liu on roads, and Garry Pursell on trade policy. A background paper on fiscal management was prepared by National Institute of Public Finance and Policy (NIPFP) in New Delhi. Bhaskar Naidu and Kruti Bharucha provided statistical support. Administrative support was provided by Shunalini Sarkar and Shahnaz Rana. The DPR team visited India in February 2003 and received valuable comments on the draft report from the Government of India in June 2003.

This report was edited by Bruce Ross-Larson, Elizabeth McCrocklin, and Christopher Trott of Communications Development Inc., Washington, D.C.

CURRENCY AND EQUIVALENT

Currency Unit = Indian Rupee
US$ 1 - INR 46.28

FISCAL YEAR

April 1 - March 31

ACRONYMS

AIDS	Acquired Immuno-Deficiency Syndrome		ILO	International Labour Organization
APDRP	Accelerated Power Development and Reform Program		IMF	International Monetary Fund
			IT	Information Technology
CAG	Comptroller and Auditor General		MOP	Muriate of Potash
CENVAT	Central Value-added Tax		MRP	Maximum Retail Price
CII	Competitiveness of India Inc.		NER	Net Enrolment Rate
CRISIL	Credit Rating and Information Services of India Limited		NGO	Non Governmental Organization
			OECD	Organisation for Economic Co-operation and Development
DAP	Di-ammonia Phosphate		PDS	Public Distribution System
EIU	Economist Intelligence Unit		RBI	Reserve Bank of India
EPF	Employee Provident Fund		RFI	Rural Finance Institution
EPS	Employee Pension Scheme		SEB	State Electricity Board
EU	European Union		SME	Small and Medium-scale Enterprise
FDI	Foreign Direct Investment		SSP	Single Phosphate
FICCI	Federation of Indian Chambers of Commerce and Industry		TFP	Total Factor Productivity
			TPDS	Targeted Public Distribution System
GDP	Gross Domestic Product		VAT	Value-added Tax
HIV	Human Immunodeficiency Virus		WHO	World Health Organization
ICAR	Indian Council of Agricultural Research		WTO	World Trade Organization

INDIA: SUSTAINING REFORM, REDUCING POVERTY

TABLE OF CONTENTS

FIGURES

TABLES

BOXES

STATISTICAL ANNEX

STATISTICAL APPENDIX

INDIA: SUSTAINING REFORM, REDUCING POVERTY

EXECUTIVE SUMMARY

India continued to make good progress in increasing incomes and improving living standards over the past decade. After the setback associated with the 1991 balance of payments crisis, economic growth picked up, income poverty continued to decline, and many social indicators, in particular literacy, continued to improve (table 1). These developments were supported by the wide-ranging reforms launched in 1991 to open and deregulate the economy. Even though the pace of reforms has slowed since the mid-1990s, the cumulative changes have been substantial, improving the investment climate. More sectors have been opened to private activity. Trade policy and the exchange rate regime have been further liberalized. And capital markets have been reformed.

Assessing Development Outcomes

Development progress has been steady, but uneven across indicators of living standards. While poverty and education indicators have improved, those for maternal and under-five mortality have not. The new threat of HIV/AIDS is spreading quickly. And unemployment, though still low by international standards, has increased. Progress has also been

Table 1. Progress on Social Indicators, 1980-2000

Indicator	1980s		1990s		2000
Poverty					
Poverty incidence (%)	44.5	-8.5	36.0	-9.9	26.1
Adjusted poverty incidence (%)					28.6
Education					
Overall literacy rate: 7+ years (%)	44	+8	52	+12	65
Female literacy rate as a percent of male literacy rate (%)	53	+8	61	+10	71
Net enrollment rate (NER): grades 1-5 (%)	47	+4	51	+26	77
Female NER as a percent of male NER: grades 1-5 (%)	70	+10	80	+1	81
Health					
Life expectancy at birth (years)	56	+4	60	+1	61
Infant mortality rate 0-4 years (per 1000 live births)	115	-36	79	-11	68
Maternal mortality rate (per 100,000)	n.a.		424	+116	540
Prevalence of HIV (million people)	n.a.		3.5	+0.5	4.0
Sanitation					
Access to improved water source (%)	n.a.		68	+10	78
Households with toilet facility (%)	n.a.		30	+6	36

n.a. Reliable data not available.

Source: Table 1.4.

Box 1. Who are India's Poor?

Pervasive in India, poverty is becoming more concentrated in the country's lagging states and rural areas. More than half of India's poor now live in Bihar, Madhya Pradesh, Orissa, and Uttar Pradesh-more than two-thirds in rural areas. In rural areas, the poverty incidence is highest amongst agricultural workers, many of them small-scale farmers or casual laborers. And people of scheduled castes and scheduled tribes are far more likely to be poor than those of other social groups, because low status and gender barriers still operate as social obstacles that block or exclude them from opportunity.

India's poor suffer from lower incomes-and from lower access to and quality of such public services as basic health, education, and infrastructure, all low in quality. Often lacking the leverage to ensure that state institutions serve them fairly, the poor must pay for education and health services that others receive for free. Studies by India's Public Affairs Center indicate that the wealthy and middle classes are more likely to resolve their complaints at a lower cost. Corruption is often a highly regressive tax, with the poor paying a higher proportion of their incomes than do the wealthy and the middle class.

Source: World Bank.

uneven across regions. There is evidence of divergence in per capita incomes across states, with richer states increasing incomes faster than poorer ones. As a result, poverty has become concentrated in the country's slower growing states (box 1).

Recent growth trends also give reason for concern (table 2). Economic growth slowed from an annual average of 6.7% over the five years from 1992/93 to 1996/97, to 5.5% for 1997/98 to 2001/02. Offsetting strong growth in services was a

Table 2. Macroeconomic Trends Over the Past Two Decades

Indicator	1980s	1992/93-1996/97	1997/98-2001/02	2002/03[a]
GDP growth (% a year)	5.6	6.7	5.5	4.4
Agriculture	3.4	4.7	1.8	-3.1
Industry	7.0	7.6	4.5	6.1
Services	6.9	7.5	8.1	7.1
Investment rate (% of GDP)	22.0	23.3	22.5	22.1
Public	10.0	8.0	6.6	6.3
Private	12.1	15.3	15.9	15.7
Inflation (Wholesale Price Index, % a year)	8.0	8.7	4.9	2.5
General government deficit (% of GDP)	8.1	7.2	9.3	10.4
Current account balance (% of GDP)	-2.1	-1.2	-0.7	1.0
External reserves (months of goods and services imports, end of period)	3.3	5.9	7.0	11.0

a. Estimated.

Source: Table 1.1.

slowdown in industrial growth and a marked decline in agricultural performance. In 2002/03, growth slowed even more-to an estimated 4.4%, due to the impact of poor rains on agricultural output in several states.

The slowdown in growth was accompanied by a slowdown in investment, especially in the private sector. Firms borrowed and invested heavily in the mid-1990s, building capacity for demand from continuing high growth rates and continuing reforms that would generate high returns. Meanwhile, trade reforms left some sectors more open to competition, while facing "behind the border" constraints to increasing productivity. As the pace of reforms slowed, interest rates rose, and the expected demand failed to materialize, many firms found themselves saddled with excess capacity and debt.

The fiscal position of the general government (center plus states) also deteriorated. The overall budget deficit rose from around 7% in 1997/98 to more than 10% in 2002/03, due to a significant increase in government consumption and continued low revenue mobilization. Higher public debt and higher interest rates also added to the debt service burden. As a result, resources available for public investment became tighter, with consequences for infrastructure development.

But there were some pluses as well. Prudent monetary policy helped contain inflation and strengthen the balance of payments. Rapid growth of information technology (IT) service exports, sluggish domestic demand for imports, and higher remittances turned the current account balance into surplus. With modest capital inflows, external reserves rose to more than $80 billion, almost a year of imports.

With more than a billion people and one-third of the world's poor, India needs rapid growth to reduce poverty and create enough jobs to sustain

income increases for its population. In its Tenth Five-Year Plan, the government targets an average growth rate of 8% a year for 2002/03-2006/07. But macroeconomic vulnerabilities and structural impediments limit India's prospects for accelerating growth and reducing poverty, as the Tenth Plan and the most recent Economic Survey recognize. India's development policy challenges can be grouped into two broad areas:

✦ Improving the management of public resources, by reducing budget deficits, reallocating spending to more productive investments, and enhancing the quality of service delivery.

✦ Improving the investment climate and raising productivity in industry, services, agriculture, and rural development.

Policy Agenda: Managing Public Resources

Fiscal Policy

The general government (center plus states) fiscal deficit has averaged more than 9% of GDP over the past six years, the Ninth Plan year plus 2002/03 (figure 1). About 60% of this deficit is at the center and 40% at the state level, where much of the recent

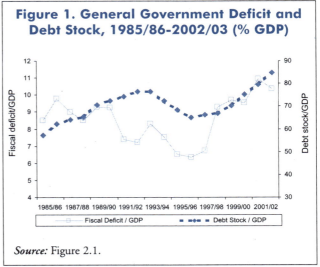

Figure 1. General Government Deficit and Debt Stock, 1985/86-2002/03 (% GDP)

Source: Figure 2.1.

deterioration in the fiscal situation has occurred. Of particular concern is the sharp increase in revenue deficits, which doubled from less than 3% in the late 1980s to more than 6% of GDP over the past six years. Falling revenues-and rising expenditures on interest payments, subsidies, civil service salaries and pensions, administration, and defense-have crowded out development spending, with negative implications for long-run growth and welfare.

These fiscal deficits have largely been financed by borrowing, with a strategic shift toward long-term rupee debt after the 1991 crisis. General government debt rose from 58% of GDP at the end of March 1986 to 85% of GDP by the end of March 2003 (see figure 1). Including the debt of public enterprises, total public debt is now 95% of GDP, with contingent liabilities from loss-making public enterprises adding another 12% of GDP. With high primary deficits (more than 3% of GDP) and interest rates close to growth rates, the burden of public debt is expected to continue rising-unless there is a concerted effort to adjust the fiscal position of the center and state governments, in a progressive and phased manner over the next few years.

On the surface, these fiscal indicators are worse than those faced in 1991-and worse than in many other countries that actually suffered a macroeconomic crisis. But the risk of crisis in India today is mitigated by the country's strong external position. Rising external reserves and low levels of short-term external debt give the country a very comfortable cushion to counter any speculative attack. Further reducing the risk of a speculative attack is: a pliant financial system (willing to hold large amounts of domestic government debt), limited capital account convertibility, and a flexible exchange rate. So India is not vulnerable in the short term to the type of collapse suffered by Russia and Argentina.

Even so, the Tenth Plan is right to be concerned about the consequences over the medium term of leaving the current fiscal situation unchecked. What has emerged in effect is a mixture of "loose fiscal, tight monetary" policy that has helped to keep inflation low and the external accounts strong. But this has been at the expense of growth and welfare. Growing interest payments have crowded out public investment, and high real interest rates have constrained private investment. Even though interest rates have declined over the past 18 months, public debt dynamics have continued to worsen.

There is a lively debate in India today about whether the large fiscal deficit is a serious problem or not, given the external reserves and food stocks. Indeed, some see a fiscal stimulus as desirable to counter the slowdown in private sector activity. But the arguments for a fiscal stimulus are not convincing when public debt levels are so high and interest rates may well start to rise from their current low levels. And to the extent that the recent increase in external reserves has reflected capital inflows driven by one-off events related to September 11, 2001, it would be risky to slow fiscal reform on a gamble that such flows will continue indefinitely. Nor would it be prudent to assume that India can simply grow out of its fiscal problem. To the contrary, analysis in the Tenth Plan suggests that a sizable fiscal adjustment will be required to generate the level of public savings, and provide space for the level of public and private investment, needed to generate 8% growth.

Based on this analysis, fiscal reforms are needed in the following areas:

✦ **Taxes.** The Tenth Plan targets an increase in tax revenues from 8.1% of GDP in 2001/02 to 10.3% of GDP by 2006/07. Achieving this goal rests on several key assumptions, including a strong recovery in manufacturing growth (the sector with the highest tax buoyancy) and extending the tax base to the booming services. The Kelkar Committee reports on direct and indirect taxes essentially endorse the above approach, requiring that lower tax rates be complemented with the elimination of exemptions, bringing services and agriculture into the tax net, and using information technology to improve tax administration. These reforms deserve the highest priority in view of the substantial decline in the tax ratio during the 1990s and the positive impact that a stronger tax effort would have on reducing primary and revenue deficits in the future.

♦ **Subsidies.** Financial losses of the power sector reached an alarming Rs.332 billion in 2001/02, about 1.4% of GDP. Recent studies show that the poor do not benefit from cheap electricity, either in urban or rural areas, providing little social justification for continuing losses. So, the financial and social case for reform is strong (box 2). Similarly, food and fertilizer subsidies totaled Rs.352 billion in 2002/03, also about 1.4% of GDP. These subsidies have distorted the cropping

---

Box 2. Urgent Need for Reforms in Power Distribution

Reform of power distribution is essential for both fiscal sustainability and faster growth by providing more efficient supply and quality of power services to industry, farmers, and rural areas. Under the framework of the new Electricity Act (2003), reforms are urgently needed in the following areas:

Tariffs. Ensuring that tariffs on average cover costs and yield a reasonable rate of return for the utility-and that regulatory systems have suitable mechanisms and sufficient independence to assure this over time. Achieving phased but time-bound reduction of the cross subsidy paid by industries and services, and improving cost recovery through consumption-based tariffs charged to agriculture and residential consumers.

Subsidies. Ensuring that where, for policy reasons, the government wishes to subsidize power, subsidies are clearly delineated, targeted and funded, within fiscally sustainable levels. Developing alternative mechanisms to deliver subsidies while enabling the utilities to operate on a commercial basis. Moving from present flat-rate tariffs to consumption-based tariffs for agriculture water pumping.

Restructuring, commercialization, and sector governance. Separating State Electricity Boards into generation, transmission, and distribution businesses. Ensuring that the unbundled utilities have independent boards, financial autonomy, and skilled management with full control over operations and labor force. Reducing transmission and distribution losses, including theft, and improving operational and managerial efficiency in power distribution and supply.

Privatizing distribution. Accelerating privatization of the commercially viable segments of the distribution business to lock in the gains from improved operational and managerial efficiencies. Targeting a broader range of potential investors and actively mitigating the perceived policy and regulatory risks.

Strategies for rural areas. Developing approaches to shift from the present form of subsidy for electricity consumption to innovative models of provision of capital subsidy for improving access in rural areas and for the poor. Facilitating new entry for timely and cost-effective provision of electricity services.

Competition. Opening electricity trading by industries with self-generation, along with other power suppliers, by providing open access to transmission and distribution networks in a phased manner along with the elimination of cross-subsidies over an agreed time frame.

Source: World Bank.

and investment decisions of farmers, contributing to natural resource degradation. Proposals for reforms in these areas-and for reallocating funds to more productivity-enhancing public investments-are outlined in the section on agriculture and rural development. Petroleum subsidies, which totaled Rs.63 billion in 2002/03, or 0.3% of GDP, are also to be phased out over the medium term.

* **Financial sector.** Indian banks have one of the highest ratios of government debt to deposits in the world. Financial institutions (including insurance and provident funds) that invested heavily in long-term government paper have been making trading profits as interest rates continued to fall. But they now face risks from rising interest rates. Moreover, state provident funds have also invested heavily in bonds issued by special purpose vehicles and guaranteed by state governments. The growing risk that these guarantees will be called is reflected in the widening spread on state guaranteed bonds relative to central government securities. It is thus encouraging to note that both the Reserve Bank of India and the Government of India are working to establish a clear and transparent framework for guarantees. Returns on provident funds and small savings should also be linked to market benchmarks.

* **Fiscal management.** The central government needs to lead by example-by cutting its revenue deficits and providing the right incentives for fiscal adjustment at the state level. Fiscal discipline at the center is likely be reinforced (but not guaranteed) by the new Fiscal Responsibility and Budget Management Bill, which mandates the elimination of the center's revenue deficit by March 2008. Three states have passed similar acts to limit their own deficits, and others are following suit. The center can also help improve fiscal management at the state level by: enforcing global caps on borrowing (both on-budget borrowing and off-budget borrowing through special-purpose vehicles); simplifying the borrowing regime for states by allowing them to borrow responsibly from markets within their global gaps while phasing out borrowing from captive sources; further expanding the volume of center-to-state transfers linked to reforms and performance; breaking down artificial distinctions between plan and non-plan expenditures; and consolidating centrally sponsored schemes, with greater flexibility for states to allocate the funds according to their needs and priorities.

The government debt projections illustrate the importance of generating primary fiscal surpluses to stabilize or reduce the debt-to-GDP ratio (figure 2). Without reforms, the debt-to-GDP ratio continues to rise to 107% by the end of the Tenth Plan period. Under the reform scenario-with lower primary deficits (falling to 0.7% of GDP by 2006/07) and higher economic growth (rising to 8% in 2006/07)-the debt-to-GDP ratio is brought down to 95%. With lower interest payments and subsidies, the reform scenario also frees up more resources for spending on priority programs

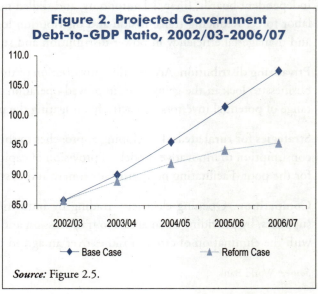

Figure 2. Projected Government Debt-to-GDP Ratio, 2002/03-2006/07

Source: Figure 2.5.

(including operations and maintenance, social services, and basic infrastructure). Both these trends-lower primary deficits and better expenditure composition-would be good for growth and poverty reduction. Without reform, the risks of crisis would steadily build with higher and less sustainable debt levels over the medium term.

Delivery of Public Services

Sustained growth is the most powerful driver of poverty reduction. But poverty reduction also requires investment in human development-for health and education are the most important assets of the poor, allowing them to both contribute to and benefit from growth through higher-paying employment. In addition, when incomes fall below minimum standards, the poor and vulnerable need access to effective social safety nets. Better delivery of social services thus requires increasing the level and (more important) the quality of public expenditures in these areas. And this in turn requires improving the governance and productivity of India's civil service. On the positive side, a variety of reforms already being implemented at the center, state, and local levels could be quickly scaled up and disseminated across the country. There is also a growing social demand for good governance. These developments present a real opportunity to raise the performance of the civil service and enhance service delivery. The key is to push ahead with implementation.

In aggregate numbers, the Indian civil service is not particularly overstaffed in comparison with other countries. But there is a pronounced imbalance in skills mix. Staff profiles need to be revisited to reduce the number of administrative and support personnel (particularly at lower grades) and increase the number of staff involved in front-line service delivery, including rural schools and health clinics. In addition, reforms are needed to reduce the fragmentation of bureaucratic structures and responsibilities. Such reforms would improve coordination, shorten delivery times, and generate overall efficiency gains.

There is also a pressing problem of affordability. The Fifth Pay Commission awards in 1996/97 significantly increased spending on civil service wages, especially at the state level. Beyond the fiscal burden, these high salary awards are questionable since the public sector is now paying a substantial premium over the private sector in many job categories (table 3). Recent experience suggests it may be wise to hold off on holding periodic pay commissions. Instead, the Government of India and state governments could opt for limited annual wage increases, or even pursue a freeze for 2-3 years, followed by a limited relaxation for skilled positions. Alternatively, a permanent pay commission could be established to continually analyze and recommend compensation, in consultation with the states. Whatever system is adopted, more weight should go to local market comparators in determining salary levels.

The costs of the civil service are raised further by burgeoning pension liabilities at both the center and state levels. In response, the Government of India recently announced a plan to establish a fully funded defined contribution scheme for new civil servants. This will force the payment of pension liabilities as they accrue, creating a more transparent and financially viable scheme. But since this reform will apply only to new civil servants, it will contain pension costs only over the longer term. Indeed, in the short to medium term, fiscal outlays may rise, as the government has to meet the combined costs of the old and new schemes. Further reforms may therefore be needed, including changes in eligibility criteria, a possible shift of younger civil servants to the new plan, and opening the new scheme to private sector workers. These reforms could well serve as a model for the states to reform their own pension plans, setting a benchmark for reforming other pension schemes (including the Employee Provident Fund and the Employee Pension Scheme) over the medium term.

Table 3. Ratio of Average Wages in the Public and Private Sector

Selected occupations	1993/94	1999/2000
Professional, technicians, and related workers	1.5	1.7
Engineers	1.1	1.3
Engineering technicians	1.3	1.3
Physicians and surgeons	1.7	2.0
Nurses	2.0	2.0
Teachers	1.8	2.0
Administrative, executive, and managerial workers	1.3	1.4
Clerical and related workers	1.6	1.7
Stenographers, typists, and others	1.7	2.1
General clerks (receptionist, office attendants, and others)	1.5	1.7
Service workers	2.3	2.5
Sweepers, cleaners, building caretakers	1.8	1.9
All	1.9	2.3

Source: Table 3.2.

As a general rule, recent wage gains were not compensated by any commensurate increase in the overall quantity and quality of government services. To the extent that qualitative improvements have been made, they have often relied heavily on the application of information technology to streamline and re-engineer business processes. But even when IT has made many functions redundant, civil servants and powerful unions have often extracted pledges of no job losses as the price of allowing the innovations to go ahead. As a result, many line departments find themselves in a precarious position, with a growing proportion of their non-plan resources being taken up by salaries, over which they have very limited control. Another fundamental problem haunting India's civil service is the failure to use staff productively, pushing the cost structure of many government functions significantly higher than in the private sector.

The burden of weak administration falls particularly heavily on the poor, who suffer from skewed government spending, limited access to services, and employee indifference. Civil service reform is thus an essential element of any poverty reduction program. An effective program of civil service reform will have to include measures that achieve the following three objectives:

✦ **Improve access to information.** Citizen charters are one vehicle to empower the public in dealings with service providers. It is important, however, that such charters be developed in consultation with major stakeholders and widely disseminated. NGOs can also help in collecting raw data, transforming it into usable information, and disseminating it to a wider audience. Several states are using IT to improve access to information and speed up decisionmaking. While there is evidence that computerization by itself seems to have an important effect on reducing corruption, the most successful initiatives combine computerization with extensive business re-engineering. The Government of India and a number of states are promoting greater transparency by adopting Right to Information legislation.

✦ **Strengthen accountability.** Internal audit procedures need to be strengthened, with clear sanctions for corrupt or incompetent officers. But the key is to strengthen "external" accountability-to the public. The recent experience of the Lok Ayukta (Ombudsman) in Karnataka seems to be generating good results. Independence and adequate budgets are keys to the success of such initiatives. In addition, a comprehensive anti-corruption strategy should include: a radical overhaul and simplification of the procedures for imposing major and minor penalties; expanded "whistleblower" protection; and publication of property and tax returns of senior officials. Each state should be asked to pass the Corrupt Public Servants (Forfeiture of Property) Act, which has already been drafted by the Law Commission.

✦ **Reduce political interference.** This topic is sensitive because the right to transfer civil servants is clearly vested within the political leadership under Article 310 of the Constitution. Yet few would disagree that this power is often abused by both civil servants and politicians. The result in such states as Uttar Pradesh has been a reduction of average tenure for key senior service positions to less than a year. Compounding this problem has been the relative absence of effective transition mechanisms. Recent successful reform efforts show the value of having an empowered and dedicated manager in place for several years. Karnataka has gone one step further and limited civil service transfers, with transfer data posted on a public website and more objective cadre management committees to approve transfer requests.

Weaknesses in service delivery are of special concern in the social sectors: education, health, and social safety nets. While India has made substantial progress toward better social indicators over the past two decades, the rates of improvement have not been sufficient to achieve the targets set in the Tenth Plan or even the less ambitious Millennium Development Goals. Indeed, progress in health indicators has been slowing precipitously.

Public spending on health and education in India has risen over the past decade, largely due to the sharp increase in wages awarded by the Fifth Pay Commission in 1997. International comparisons suggest that India's spending on health and education is in line with other countries at similar incomes-though with a more dominant role for the private sector in health, and distribution of public spending in education skewed toward the secondary and tertiary levels. While additional funding would help, better outcomes depend on improving the quality of services. As one indication, absentee rates for teachers and medical providers are very high in India, especially in the poorer states (table 4). Since absentee workers are on the payroll, it is no surprise that public money does not translate directly into better outcomes.

The root cause of poor quality services is that governments do not focus on social outcomes. One way to increase the focus on outcomes is to generate and disseminate information about progress in service delivery. Parents, patients, and beneficiaries should know what they are entitled to and have a place to lodge complaints when services are not received. Providers and policymakers should know (and be constantly learning) what works. One critical role of the central government, when states have the primary responsibility for health and education, is to be an independent source for measuring outcomes. Over time, such measures could be used to hold states accountable for improvements-perhaps by conditioning fiscal transfers on progress.

Table 4. Absence Rates from Primary Facilities, 2003 (%)

State	Primary School Teachers	Primary Health Care Workers
Andhra Pradesh	31	n.a
Assam	31	58
Bihar	26	58
Gujarat	21	52
Haryana	19	35
Karnataka	23	43
Kerala	18	n.a
Orissa	14	35
Punjab	18	n.a
Rajasthan	23	39
Tamil Nadu	17	n.a
Uttar Pradesh	26	42
Uttaranchal	25	45
West Bengal	21	43

n.a. Reliable data not available.

Source: Table 3.3.

There are two deep problems in the health sector: a lack of realism concerning the public sector's role in the health system, and a lack of priorities for the public sector's possible contribution. Most health care is now given in the private sector and, for the poor, by very poorly or untrained practitioners. But there is no way to expand free publicly supplied medical care to replace these private practitioners. Instead, the government should aim to improve the private market, by providing training, public information and accreditation; over time, public financing of private provision could be increased. Government programs should focus on ways to improve health outcomes, including programs outside the health sector (such as those for clean water and sanitation).

Within the health sector, the highest priority for public funds is to combat communicable diseases. Disease control has large externalities, disproportionately benefiting the poor. Relative to medical care, most of these activities are also much easier to administer. The largest emerging problem in communicable disease control is the increase in HIV infections and AIDS cases. While estimates vary, there is no dispute that the infection is spreading rapidly. The primary focus of policy should be on prevention. There are many competing needs for public health infrastructure, and it is important that HIV/AIDS programs neither undercut the resources to deal with such killers as tuberculosis, malaria, and diarrhea-nor get marginalized.

Progress in education has been much greater than in health. This reflects the greater opportunities for communities and parents to monitor and evaluate school performance. Even so, there are large variations across states and income groups, and overall progress is insufficient to attain the Tenth Plan goals. To accelerate progress in elementary education, the Government of India has launched the Sarva Siksha Abhiyan (Education for All) program. It aims at providing eight years of schooling for all children in the 6-14 age group by 2010. Achieving this goal, which is also formalized in the 86th Constitutional Amendment, will require additional public resources and improvements in how they are used. Making schools more accountable to the community is critical, possibly by giving parents the right to hire and fire teachers through local school committees (as tried in Madhya Pradesh). Localities must be allowed the freedom to find their best solutions, while higher levels of government provide measures of attendance, learning outcomes, and other information to evaluate progress.

Many observers of the Indian administration have argued that decentralization and local empowerment will be essential in improving the quality of service delivery at the village level. The most visible achievement of the 73rd and 74th Amendments to the Constitution, ratified in 1992, has been the high degree of political decentralization. But progress on the fiscal and administrative aspects of decentralization has been much more modest and hesitant. In response, India now needs to move from the decentralized patchwork it has created, toward an intergovernmental framework that leads to better service delivery without increasing fiscal pressures.

Good fiscal management would suggest reallocating public funds from central and state schemes into a well-designed fiscal framework for local governments-to guarantee their autonomy and accountability, while helping them to match resource allocations with local preferences. It would also suggest creating incentives for local governments to collect a share of their revenues from local taxpayers (say, through land taxes). Flows of funds from the center and state governments should be dependent on good performance and resource mobilization at the local level.

Policy Agenda: Improving the Investment Climate

Industry and Services

A wide range of structural reforms stimulated investment and growth in industry and services in the early 1990s-then momentum in industry slowed in the second half of the decade, especially in manufacturing. Despite recent signs of recovery, the manufacturing sector in India still accounts for only 17% of GDP, compared with 35% in China and 25-35% in the South East Asian economies. Furthermore, India's penetration of world markets in industrial products has not increased much over the past decade, and foreign direct investment (as a share of GDP) is lower than in China and many emerging markets. As a result of these trends, growth in manufacturing employment has averaged only about 2% a year since the mid-

1990s, most in the unorganized sector. The organized manufacturing sector provides only about 7 million jobs today. Compare that with a total labor force of around 406 million, with just under a million workers coming out of agriculture every year.

Against this background, the Tenth Plan calls for faster growth in the industrial sector to create 100 million or so new jobs over the next decade. The Plan notes that sustained industrial growth and employment will require a step up in domestic investment, particularly private investment, coupled with higher productivity. International comparisons indicate that India has intrinsic advantages, such as a large local market and skilled workforce, which should allow it to emerge as a major hub for manufacturing and labor-intensive service industries. At the same time, recent studies on the investment climate show that the performance of India's industrial and service sectors continues to be constrained by three key factors: product market distortions, inefficiencies in factor markets, and infrastructure bottlenecks. The success in achieving the ambitious targets set in the Tenth Plan will depend crucially on progress in these areas.

Product market distortions. Inadequate follow-through on key reforms to create a level playing field for investment, both domestic and foreign, inhibits industrial performance. So does slow progress in trade policy reforms. Tariff protection in India is still substantially higher than in most other developing countries (table 5). The government has many well-justified concerns about the policies of other countries that restrict its exports. And it is one of the most active developing countries in raising these concerns in international fora, such as the World Trade Organization (WTO).

India has some bargaining leverage to gain concessions from other countries. But it should also use the WTO process to advance domestic reforms and protect them from local pressure

Table 5. Customs Duty Rates in India and Other Developing Countries

Country	All goods	Agriculture	Manufacturing
India 2001/02 (CD only)	32.3	41.7	30.8
India 2002/03 (CD only)	29.0	40.6	27.4
India 2002/03 (CD+SAD)a	35.0	47.1	33.3
India 2003/04 (CD+SAD)a	32.7	46.8	30.7
Pakistan 2001/02	20.4	21.8	20.2
Pakistan 2002/03a	18.2	13.9	18.3
Brazil 2000	14.1	12.9	14.3
China 2000	16.3	16.5	16.2
Indonesia 2000	8.4	6.3	8.9
Thailand 2000	16.6	39.9	14.6
South Korea 2000	12.7	47.9	6.6
105 developing countries (1996-2000)	13.4	17.4	12.7

Note: Unweighted average rates. CD=Customs Duty. SAD=Special Additional Duty.

a. Estimated.

Source: Table 4.2.

groups. In particular, the government should move aggressively to reduce import tariffs to a single rate (say, 10%) over the next three to four years and phase out remaining tariff exemptions, specific tariffs, and anti-dumping duties. It should also remove other product market distortions by eliminating the remaining preferential policies for small players, reducing indirect tax distortions by full and uniform implementation of the new value-added tax across states, and phasing out remaining limits on foreign direct investment (FDI), including the ban on FDI in the retail sector.

While the "License Raj" has been largely eliminated at the center, it still survives at the state level, along with a pervasive "Inspector Raj". Starting a business in India requires 10 permits (6 in China), and the median time taken is 90 days (30 in China). Complaints of delays, corruption, and harassment are common. To reduce the costs of investment related to delays and corruption, all procedures for the entry and exit of firms need to be simplified and expedited-for example, through "single window" clearances.

Inefficiencies in factor markets, coupled with a weak bankruptcy framework, further constrain the industrial and services sectors:

+ Restrictions on the hiring and firing of workers are identified as one of greatest challenges of doing business in India. Any registered firm wishing to retrench labor can do so only with the permission of the state government, which is rarely granted. The government has recently announced its intention to raise the limit for seeking permission from 100 to 300 workers. But to become effective, this requires enactment of legislative changes by parliament. The government should also consider amending the Contract Labor Act to allow the use of contract labor for all activities-not just for temporary activities.

✦ High real interest rates are often cited as another major impediment to industrial performance in India. Large, creditworthy borrowers have benefited from the recent decline in interest rates. But the lack of access to adequate, timely credit on competitive terms continues to constrain small and medium-size enterprises (SMEs). In response, banks should make efforts to introduce new technologies for SME credit and to train and motivate branch managers to provide loans to commercially viable SMEs. The government can help by facilitating the establishment of well-functioning credit information bureaus/credit registries for small borrowers, updating land and property records for small loans, and promoting collateral substitutes.

✦ Problems with the use and transfer of land also affect the performance of larger firms. Indeed, some 90% of land parcels in India are reportedly subject to disputes over ownership, which take decades to settle in court. And obsolete tenancy and rent control laws keep a large part of urban real estate off the market. The central government has already abolished the Urban Land Ceiling Act, which previously made changes in land use very difficult. But only a few states have repealed their corresponding Urban Land Ceiling Acts.

✦ Outdated bankruptcy procedures make industrial restructuring almost impossible. But this could change when the recently enacted Amendments to the Companies Act are put into effect, providing a framework for liquidating firms outside the court process. The repeal of the Sick Industries Companies Act is essential for this framework to become effective. The recently passed law on the enforcement of creditors' rights should also help accelerate industrial restructuring.

Severe infrastructure bottlenecks continue to constrain India's industrial sector performance.

Access to reliable power at reasonable cost is a prime concern for most Indian businesses. Not only does industry receive irregular and low quality power, but it is also charged tariffs much above the cost of supply, reducing the competitiveness of firms. As a result, a large majority of Indian firms operate their own (captive) generators, undermining utility finances. Small industries, unable to afford captive generation, often have to go without power. Power reforms are now widely accepted as fundamental to improving industrial performance. Urgent priorities are to rationalize power tariffs, depoliticize tariff-setting, and implement a phased reduction in cross-subsidies that operate against industrial consumers. Time-of-day tariffs need to be introduced for industries with peak and off-peak rates.

The foregoing measures need to be accompanied by steps to improve the financial and operational performance of the power utilities by unbundling and commercializing State Electricity Boards, ensuring independent regulation, and improving sector governance. Privatization should be accelerated to lock in operational and managerial efficiencies. The strategy for privatizing distribution should consider focusing on the commercially viable segments of the network, while developing alternate strategies for improving services and targeting subsidies in rural areas. The new Electricity Act (2003) establishes the legal framework for power sector reform and restructuring. But the key will be its implementation. The government can support reforms at the state level by imposing rigorous policies on payments to central generation and transmission utilities, rewarding progress in reducing State Electricity Board losses, and improving governance under the Accelerated Power Development and Reform Program.

Speedy, reliable door-to-door transport services are also critical to India's manufacturing competitiveness. India has one of the most extensive transport systems in the world, but it suffers from severe capacity and quality constraints. The Tenth Plan proposes road upgrading programs for 10,000 kilometers, along with access-controlled expressways in high-volume corridors. Meeting the Tenth Plan targets will require a significant increase in funding from the private sector. In part, this can be addressed through better cost-recovery from users. Much can also be gained in the short to medium term by strengthening the financial performance and accountability of road agencies and state public works departments.

Indian Railways continues to be a patient that resists any bitter medicines, despite the many prescriptions available. Reforming the sector will require large-scale financial restructuring, involving the shedding (or even ring-fencing) of noncore assets or businesses. Government policy also needs to address price distortions resulting from the long practice of cross subsidization from freight to passenger services, which causes excessively high freight tariffs, preventing Indian Railways from serving the nonbulk, high-margin transport market. In the ports sector, total berth capacity is no longer a serious constraint. But the low productivity of port equipment and labor continues to cause delays in turnaround and to increase costs for cargo and containers, especially in older ports.

The government is keen to promote greater private participation in the provision and funding of infrastructure. In the long run, this requires action to address the policy problems that underlie investor concerns by raising prices to cost-covering levels and establishing a sound legal and regulatory framework. In the short run, various public-private partnerships involving subsidies, risk-bearing, and other forms of government assistance may help attract private investment and close financing gaps. But they can also risk simply postponing the day of reckoning, imposing serious costs on taxpayers. So they should be seen as temporary measures at best, to be entered into with caution.

Agriculture and Rural Development

Promoting more rapid agricultural and rural growth is a major priority for the government. Although agriculture contributes only about a quarter of GDP today, its importance in the economic, social, and political fabric of India is far greater. About 75% of India's poor live in rural areas, and a large proportion of the rural poor depend on agriculture for employment. Total factor productivity in agriculture declined between the 1980s and 1990s due to the slowdown in productivity gains from the earlier adoption of high-yielding varieties, the decline in public investments in the agriculture sector, and increasing natural resource degradation due to the existing incentive framework.

Looking forward, better agricultural performance will require rebalancing government expenditures from subsidies towards more productivity-enhancing public investments and removing the remaining restrictions on domestic trade to improve the investment climate for farmers, while supporting a regulatory framework that ensures fair competition. Developing the nonfarm sector will also be essential to provide employment opportunities in rural areas and support the growth of agriculture.

The government's foodgrain policy has led to mounting buffer stocks and food subsidies in recent years. In response, the government established a high-level committee to develop a long-term foodgrain policy-with the primary goal of self-sufficiency. The committee's proposals to remove the rice levy and all restrictions on foodgrain trade (except in emergencies) will improve incentives for the private sector. But other key proposals raise concerns. The shift in the underlying principle of the proposed policy from food security to self-sufficiency, which also ties farmers to low-value rice and wheat production, will come at the cost of efficiency. The continuing large role envisioned for the public sector in foodgrain markets will crowd out private participation. And the reversion to an untargeted public distribution scheme is likely to bring back the earlier problems of subsidies being captured by nonpoor families and result in higher food subsidies.

Perhaps the most contentious issue in foodgrain policy is the Minimum Support Price (MSP) for rice and wheat. Steady increases in the MSP in recent years have encouraged more production, leading to larger government procurement. Strong political pressure from states where the largest procurement takes place has stalled government efforts to contain increases in the MSP. The proposal to limit the MSP to cover cash costs plus the returns to family labor, land, and capital is a step in the right direction. But in the longer run fostering competitive markets would ensure remunerative returns to farmers. For this, the MSP should be complemented by other schemes in providing a safety net for farmers (such as Targeted Public Distribution System and employment schemes).

The government's agricultural policy of the last three decades has relied on subsidizing key inputs to promote faster production growth and ensure food security. But there is also broad recognition that the rapidly rising subsidies are fiscally unsustainable-and crowding out productivity-enhancing public investments in rural infrastructure, irrigation, and technology upgrading. Power and water subsidies, to the extent they encourage inefficient water use, are also leading to salinity, water logging, and declining groundwater tables in many areas. And fertilizer subsidies, concentrated largely on urea, have distorted input use. The priorities are as follows:

◆ *Fertilizer.* In 2001/02 the government announced its policy to rationalize fertilizer pricing and to implement the recommendations of the Expenditure Reforms Commission for a phased program of price

increases and complete decontrol of urea by April 2006. Since then, several reform actions have been implemented. Continuing commitment to the proposed timetable will significantly reduce fertilizer subsidies over the next few years.

◆ *Water.* The government's national water policy promotes the adoption of a comprehensive and integrated approach to planning and managing water resources. It gives priority to delivering good quality water services, making demand-driven investments in rehabilitation and maintenance of infrastructure through greater participation of users in managing systems, and recovering at least operations and maintenance costs to ensure the longer term financial and fiscal sustainability of operations. To encourage full adoption of these reforms at the state level, the government recently introduced an incentive program to encourage recovery of operations and maintenance costs.

◆ *Power.* The large subsidy on the price of electricity to farmers has contributed to the financial crises of State Electricity Boards. This undermines the boards' ability to undertake required investments and maintain day-to-day operations, resulting in deteriorating power services to consumers, including farmers. The incidence of subsidies is also heavily regressive. India should move to a more transparent and targeted subsidy mechanism. For this to work, it is indispensable that there be recovery of at least operating costs, universal metering of consumption, payment discipline, and greater efficiency of electricity providers.

Product and factor markets. While progress in economic and trade reforms has helped to improve the incentive framework for agriculture over the past decade, the sector is still hampered by the continuing overregulation of domestic trading activities for major agricultural commodities. On the positive side, the government has temporarily lifted several key regulations such as storage, transport and credit control in recent years. But the overhang of their possible re-introduction discourages both local and foreign investments. Moreover, some state governments have not lifted the associated state controls. This inevitably raises marketing margins, putting downward pressure on farm prices and raising costs to consumers, reducing the competitiveness of exports.

Agricultural import tariffs have increased in recent years to an unweighted average (including the special additional duty) of about 47%, compared with an average nonagricultural import tariff of about 31%. With a few exceptions, India is no longer explicitly taxing or using licensing, export bans, or quotas to deliberately restrict agricultural exports and depress domestic prices, as it did in the past. But since 2001 it has been exporting stocks of rice and wheat accumulated by the Food Corporation of India at prices far below prevailing domestic prices. It is questionable whether these subsidized exports are in India's long-term interests in a more open international agricultural market. India should also consider reducing its WTO agricultural tariff bindings, mostly now at 100% or more, as an external constraint on domestic lobbies pressing for high tariffs.

Access to land. The distribution of land ownership in India has become less skewed since the 1970s, with a rising share owned by marginal and smaller farmers. The trend towards landlessness has also been arrested. But regulations aimed at increasing the security of tenure for tenants have had unintended adverse effects, leading to large-scale self-cultivation by landlords or the adoption of wage labor contracts. Where their implementation was incomplete, they may also reduce land access and equity.

There is now a growing consensus, reflected in government policy statements, about the need to revisit and reformulate current tenancy legislations. In considering tenancy reform, it is critical to draw lessons from states that do not have tenancy restrictions. For some states, the benefits from relaxing tenancy laws are likely to be higher than in others, due to the more advanced commercialization of agriculture (and significant amounts of informal leasing) and stronger political commitment to reform. These states could serve as a starting point for pilots, and yield important insights for policy debate and tenancy reforms in other states.

The Department of Land Resources introduced a scheme in the mid-1990s to pilot computerization of land records in selected districts nationwide. Some states have not only scaled up the program statewide-they have also implemented the program in partnership with the private sector. These initiatives have reportedly contributed to more efficient and faster service, while reducing the opportunities for corruption through greater transparency. Over the longer term, the focus will have to shift to a more holistic approach to improving land administration systems at the state level. To be successful, the systems would have to meet several other key standards of performance, including security, costs, fairness, and sustainability.

Access to rural credit. India has a wide network of rural finance institutions, but many of the rural poor remain underserved or left out of the formal financial system. A key factor constraining better access to rural credit relates to inefficiencies in the formal rural finance institutions. The government should aim to improve the performance of the regional rural banks and rural credit cooperatives by enhancing regulatory oversight and supervision, reducing government control and ownership, and strengthening the legal framework for loan recovery and the use of land for collateral.

Other priorities for improving access to rural credit include:

+ Liberalizing interest rates by removing the existing "cap" for small loans (it has the perverse effect of rationing credit available to small rural borrowers).

+ Improving credit information on rural households, by designating an agency that could take the lead in collecting and disseminating information on micro borrowers.

+ Facilitating the scaling-up and sustainability of existing low-cost microfinance models, such as the self-help group bank linkage model and the Grameen bank replicators.

+ Removing legal and regulatory obstacles to the development of innovations that can help reduce the costs and risks associated with rural finance.

Productivity-enhancing investments. Greater emphasis on productivity-enhancing investments will be critical to raising agricultural growth and developing the rural nonfarm sector. But to be effective, new investments need to be matched by improvements in the quality of public spending, particularly through a sharper focus on operations and maintenance, which also involves significant institutional reforms. If anything, the growth rate is likely to slow down over time, as the deteriorating fiscal situation and the sluggish progress on the reform agenda worsen the investment climate. Sectoral priorities are as follows:

+ *Research and extension.* India's public agricultural research and extension system is one of the largest in the world. But the efficiency and effectiveness of these services have been called into question. There is a need for a more regionally differentiated research strategy, and greater coordination between the public and private sectors. Similarly, the top-down, crop-focused approach to agricultural extension has become outmoded and ineffective in meeting the needs of farmers. The public extension system needs to become more demand-driven, with stronger synergies between public and private extension efforts.

+ *Rural roads.* Most government programs for rural roads are designed to address the immediate rural accessibility problem, without a carefully designed policy and institutional framework to ensure the sustainability of these investments. Additional funds should be allocated for rural road maintenance, with more coordination by the Ministry of Rural Development. Community participation offers significant potential for mobilizing local support to generate resources, acquire land, and tailor rural road programs to local needs.

+ *Rural electrification.* India's rural electrification program has focused on extending the grid supply to villages and remote areas. But access by rural households remains low, and power-based economic activities in the electrified villages is minimal. The government plans to accelerate the rural electrification program over the coming decade. This needs to be matched by a more conducive policy environment, with adequate incentives for service providers and more effective targeting of subsidies to poorer farmers and rural consumers. Decentralized generation should be encouraged, as reforms are put in place to privatize the commercially viable parts of the sector.

Development Prospects and Risks

Continuing progress in poverty reduction will require both higher growth and improved delivery of health, water, sanitation, and education services. Many of these goals are reflected in the Tenth Plan, which projects an average growth rate of 8% a year and rapid progress across a range of social indicators. But the plan period started with a slowing of growth to an estimated 4.4% in 2002/03. Some of the slowdown was due to external factors on agricultural output, including the impact of flooding in some areas and drought in many

Table 6. Macroeconomic Projections: Baseline and Reform Scenarios

Indicator	Ninth Plan 1997/98-2001/02	Baseline Scenario 2002/03-2006/07	Reform Scenario 2002/03-2006/07
Real GDP growth at factor cost (% a year)	5.5	5.0	6.5
Agriculture, forestry and fishing	1.8	1.5	2.2
Industry	4.5	5.3	7.1
Services	8.1	6.4	8.0
Investment (% of GDP)	22.5	20.5	27.7
Public	6.6	6.4	7.3
Public, general government	3.1	3.0	3.7
Private	15.9	14.1	20.4
Consumption (% of GDP)	78.8	80.5	73.5
Public	12.5	12.0	12.4
Private	66.3	68.5	61.1
General Government (% of GDP)			
Fiscal deficit	9.3	11.8	10.3
Primary deficit	3.5	3.6	2.2

Source: Table 6.1.

others. While some recovery in growth is expected in 2003/04, as the external environment improves, this bounceback is unlikely to be sustained-without a major push to reinvigorate the reform agenda. In the absence of major external or domestic shocks, current policies in India are likely to translate into a continued growth slowdown, averaging around 5% a year over the Tenth Plan period (table 6).

By contrast, a comprehensive reform program would allow India to achieve growth of 8% a year by the end of the Tenth Plan period, with positive impacts on employment and poverty reduction (box 3). Reforms to reduce fiscal imbalances at the center and in the states would create space for increased private investment. Improvements in the composition of expenditure-with less spending on civil servants'

wages and pensions, subsidies and interest payments, and a shift towards operations and maintenance and investments in key infrastructure-would further "crowd in" private investment. Improvements in the investment climate, through the removal of remaining bottlenecks in product and factor markets, and in key infrastructure areas, would increase the productivity of both public and private investment across the economy, including India's poor rural areas. More effective delivery of health and education services, as well as social safety nets, would help accelerate social progress, empowering India's citizens to both contribute and benefit from faster economic growth.

Accelerating growth and poverty reduction in India cannot be achieved without accelerating growth in India's lagging states. If the trends of the past few years continue, the richer states would have to grow at nearly 10% a year to reach an all-India average of 6.5% during the Tenth Plan period. This is rather unlikely. So, implicit in the envisaged reform scenario is a special effort to correct fiscal imbalances, reallocate public resources to priority programs, improve public service delivery, and strengthen the investment climate in lagging states. Primary responsibility for these reforms lies with the state governments. But the central government can also catalyze and set the pace for reform at the state level.

Of particular importance for poverty reduction and rural incomes are policies to increase agricultural productivity. In the short run, the removal of subsidies to foodgrains could reduce agricultural output in a few states that benefit most from them. But these are also states where significant agricultural diversification can take place. More important-this reform would free resources for agricultural research and development and rural infrastructure. Simultaneously, faster growth in industry and continuing rapid growth in services can provide jobs for the labor force released from agriculture.

India's large fiscal imbalances pose a serious threat to sustained growth and development over the medium term. The persistence of current fiscal trends will, at best, limit growth and job creation. And slower growth would, in turn, speed the deterioration in debt dynamics. If this negative cycle continues, a full-fledged fiscal crisis cannot be ruled out.

It is politically easy to downplay this risk, hoping that faster growth and lower interest rates will eventually solve the fiscal problem. But experience suggests it would be unwise to sit back and wait for such a virtuous circle to emerge. Instead, the central and state governments will have to be proactive in reducing the fiscal deficit, shifting expenditures into more productive areas and removing structural impediments to higher private investment and productivity. The sooner the roadmap for these reforms is put in place, and concrete action taken to show commitment to follow through, the more manageable will be the adjustment path, and the quicker the payoff in faster growth and poverty reduction.

There are other potential risks. Domestically, Indian politics are often distracted by general or state elections and tensions with neighboring countries. Externally, the global recovery is expected to be slow. While India is still a relatively closed economy, and therefore somewhat protected from global trends, it does suffer from a loss of market share to its major competitors, especially China, where reforms have moved ahead much faster. And the inflow of remittances into India and other countries in the region may well slow down, as the impact of one-off events weakens. So, it would be risky to gamble that the recent strength in the balance of payments will continue, providing a counterweight to the deteriorating fiscal situation.

India can be proud of its development record over the past two decades. That record reflects the emergence of a much wider consensus about the importance of opening up the Indian economy to competition. The results in faster growth and poverty reduction are impressive. But India has still fallen behind its main competitors in East Asia. And poverty remains a reality for many Indians, especially those in the poorer states of the North and East. The government is right to set ambitious targets for growth and social development during the Tenth Plan. The key now is to implement the policy and institutional changes to achieve these goals. Sustained progress will no doubt be difficult, especially in the politically charged areas of labor, power, and agricultural reform. But those changes also promise high returns for poverty reduction.

Box 3. Summary of Priority Reforms

Fiscal Policy

✦ Progressively reduce the primary deficit at the center and in states by completing tax reforms (eliminating exemptions, bringing services into the tax net, and implementing a uniform state value-added tax), reducing power sector losses, and phasing out petroleum subsidies.

✦ Reduce financial sector risks by implementing the new securitization law, linking returns on provident funds and small savings to market benchmarks, and establishing a clear framework for managing state government guarantees.

✦ Improve fiscal management by imposing greater fiscal discipline on state borrowing and transfers, breaking down artificial distinctions between plan and non-plan expenditures, and consolidating centrally sponsored schemes.

✦ Improve the composition of public expenditures, by reducing the share spent on wages, pensions, interest payments, and agricultural subsidies, and increasing investment and operations and maintenance for priority social, infrastructure and agriculture programs.

Delivery of Public Services

✦ Reduce administrative fragmentation and reform civil service pay policy and pensions. Improve the performance of the civil service and quality of service delivery by improving public access to information, strengthening accountability, and reducing political interference.

✦ Refocus health, education, and social safety net programs on outcomes. The central government can be an independent source for measuring progress toward agreed goals.

✦ Improve the private market for health care through training, public information, and accreditation. Priorities for public funds are to provide clean water and sanitation, and to combat communicable diseases (including HIV/AIDS prevention).

✦ Support the education-for-all goals by providing more public resources and improving resource use in elementary education. Schools should be more accountable to communities and have more local autonomy to find the best solutions.

✦ Develop a well-designed fiscal framework for local governments to guarantee their autonomy and accountability. Flows of funds from the center and states should depend on good local fiscal performance and resource mobilization.

Investment Climate for Industry and Services

✦ Speed up trade reform by reducing average import tariffs and phasing out tariff exemptions, specific tariffs, and antidumping duties. Remove other product market distortions by eliminating preferential policies for small players, implementing a full and uniform value-added tax, and phasing out remaining foreign direct investment restrictions.

- Reduce inefficiencies in factor markets by easing restrictions on hiring and firing of workers, improving access to credit for small and medium-size enterprises, addressing problems in the use and transfer of land, and updating bankruptcy procedures.

- Ensure access to reliable power at reasonable costs by rationalizing power tariffs and improving the financial and operational performance of State Electricity Boards.

- Address capacity and quality constraints in transport by improving public sector performance (for roads and rail), mobilizing private investment (including better cost recovery for roads), phasing out price distortions (for rail), and improving the efficiency of existing capacity (for ports).

Agricultural Policy and Rural Development

- Put in place a market-based foodgrain policy that protects the poor through targeted safety nets, while mitigating drastic supply shocks through a cost-effective and well-managed price stabilization mechanism.

- Reduce input subsidies that are fiscally unsustainable and distorting input use. Savings should be used to fund more productive investments in agricultural research and extension, rural roads, and rural electrification.

- Reduce regulation of domestic trading activities for major agricultural commodities and eliminate remaining trade policy distortions, including subsidized exports of rice and wheat.

- Improve access to land by revisiting current legislation on land tenancy and building on successful initiatives to improve land administration. Devise market-based solutions to improve rural access to a larger range of financial services at lower cost.

Source: World Bank.

CHAPTER 1

INTRODUCTION: ASSESSING DEVELOPMENT OUTCOMES

India made good progress in increasing incomes and improving living standards over the past decade. After the 1991 balance-of-payments crisis, economic growth picked up, income poverty continued to decline, and many social indicators continued to improve. These developments were supported by wide-ranging reforms launched in 1991 to open and deregulate the economy. Even though the pace of reform has slowed since the mid-1990s, the cumulative changes have so far been substantial, improving the investment climate. More sectors have been opened to private activity. Trade policy and the exchange rate regime have been further liberalized. And capital markets have been reformed.

Development progress has been steady but uneven. Poverty and education indicators improved, particularly for females. But maternal and under-five mortality have hardly improved. And unemployment, though still low by international standards, has increased in rural areas and among educated youth. Aggregate outcomes at the all-India level mask sharp and increasing inequalities in income and social development levels across the country, with large parts of the heavily populated northern and eastern states remaining particularly poor and undeveloped.

Economic growth slowed after 1997/98, from an annual average of 6.7% between 1992/93 and 1996/97 (Eighth Plan period), to 5.5% between 1997/98 and 2001/02 (Ninth Plan). Growth slowed further in 2002/03, to an estimated 4.4%, due to the impact of poor rains on agricultural output. And fiscal performance deteriorated at the center and in the states, with rising deficits and worsening public expenditure compositions limiting the prospect for accelerating growth and poverty reduction.

India starts the twenty-first century with a per capita income around half that of China and Indonesia, countries that were at comparable stages of development in 1970 (figure 1.1). In its Tenth Five-Year Plan for 2002/03-2006/07, the Government targets an average growth rate of 8% a year. Accelerating poverty reduction requires setting India on a higher growth path. This chapter reviews the development outcomes of recent years. The remainder of the report proposes policies to accelerate development in India.

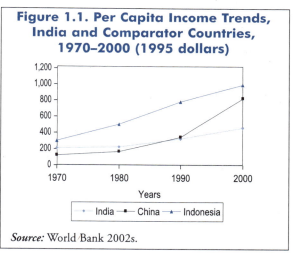

Figure 1.1. Per Capita Income Trends, India and Comparator Countries, 1970–2000 (1995 dollars)

Source: World Bank 2002s.

Poverty Outcomes and Economic Performance

Income poverty declined in the 1990s, broadly in line with earlier trends (figure 1.2).[1] As a result, the share of the population living below the

---

[1] The conventional definition of poverty equates it with income or expenditure levels. In India, the Planning Commission defines poverty as the level of per capita consumer expenditure sufficient to provide an average daily intake of 2,400 calories per person in rural areas and 2,100 calories per person in urban areas, plus a small allocation for basic nonfood items. This report relies on income poverty estimates from the National Sample Survey's quinquennial rounds ("thick samples" of 1983, 1987/88, 1993/94, and 1999/2000).

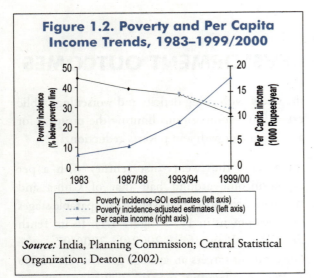

Figure 1.2. Poverty and Per Capita Income Trends, 1983–1999/2000

Poverty incidence-GOI estimates (left axis)
Poverty incidence-adjusted estimates (left axis)
Per capita income (right axis)

Source: India, Planning Commission; Central Statistical Organization; Deaton (2002).

poverty line declined from nearly half in the early 1980s, to a little over a quarter in 1999/2000 (26% according to Government of India official estimates or 28.6% according to alternative estimates).[2] Internationally comparable poverty estimates also show a decline in the proportion of people living on less than $1 a day, from 46% in the early 1990s to 39% in 1999/2000.[3]

Most of the reduction in income poverty has been driven by economic growth, with higher average consumption per capita (Deaton and Drèze 2002). Although India's per capita growth rates never reached East Asia's, the acceleration of growth in the 1980s and 1990s translated into a near

doubling of per capita income over those two decades, a one-third increase in the 1990s alone (see figure 1.2).[4] Growth has reduced poverty, but the pattern of growth was also decisive (Ravallion and Datt 1995). Rural consumption growth reduced poverty in both rural and urban areas. Urban growth benefited the urban poor somewhat, but had no impact on rural poverty. Economic growth has also been a key determinant for the improvement in some social indicators, particularly in poor states, where the private sector provides education and health services to a large share of the population.

Macroeconomic performance. Overall, India's economy performed well in the 1980s and even better after the reforms of the early 1990s (table 1.1). Inflation remained low, and external balances improved. GDP growth accelerated, from only 3.5% a year in the 1960s and 1970s, to nearly 7% a year between 1992/93 and 1996/97.[5] Growth was led by industry and services in the 1980s and by services in the 1990s (table 1.2). Agriculture, forestry, and fishing expanded slowly throughout the two decades. The structure of the Indian economy changed considerably as a result, with the share of agriculture declining to one-fourth of total output and the share of services increasing to nearly half. But recent trends give cause for concern.

---

2   Changes in the questionnaire design of the 55th Round (1999/2000) of the National Sample Survey render the official poverty estimates for that year not strictly comparable to those from previous rounds. Several researchers attempted to correct for the changes in the survey methodology. Most estimates (Sundaram and Tendulkar 2002; Deaton 2002; Ravallion and Datt 2002a) point to a 5-10 percentage point reduction between 1993/94 and 1999/2000. Based on the national accounts, Bhalla (2002) contends that conventional poverty measures overstate India's poverty and understate recent progress. However, there are conceptual and measurement differences that lead to discrepancies in the per capita income growth rates implied by the Central Statistics Office's national accounts statistics and the National Sample Survey Office's household level statistics.

3   Poverty estimated using internationally comparable poverty estimate for the mid-1990s, based on an international poverty line of $1 per day with adjustments for purchasing power across countries (Ravallion and Datt 2002b).

4   Econometric analysis (Ravallion and Datt 1996, 2002a) using 23 surveys over 1958-91 and private consumption per capita data from the national accounts reveal an elasticity of -1.2, obtained by regressing the log of the headcount poverty index against the log of private consumption per capita.

5   A recent study by the Reserve Bank of India (RBI 2002c) identified two regime shifts in India's GDP growth series over the past two decades, which caused increases in the trend growth rate of GDP. The first occurred in 1981/82, in the wake of an oil shock and a severe drought. The second break occurred in 1990/91 as a result of the structural reforms and stabilization that followed the balance of payments crisis.

First, fiscal aggregates of the general government (center plus states) deteriorated after 1997/98, with the overall budget deficit expanding from 7% of GDP to more than 10% by 2002/03. Why the deterioration? A decline in revenue mobilization, and a significant increase in government consumption, driven by wages and pensions of civil servants, food subsidies, and debt service. The effects of nuclear tests, tight monetary policy to keep inflation low, and higher interest rates worldwide, contributed to higher interest costs. As a result, resources available for public investment were constrained, with adverse consequences for infrastructure development and, to less extent, social programs. Interest rates have declined since, primarily because of low investment demand in India and the current low interest rates worldwide for government and prime borrowers. But the public debt burden remains high, and small and medium-scale enterprises continue to face high interest costs. Except in the 1991 crisis, when fiscal policy clearly encouraged macroeconomic stability and growth, it can be argued that fiscal policy has kept growth below potential.

Second, economic growth decelerated, to 5.5% on average between 1997/98 and 2001/02, and to 4.4% in 2002/03 (see table 1.1). Output from agriculture, which performed poorly throughout the 1990s, contracted by 3.1% in 2002/03. Industrial growth slowed markedly between 1997/98 and 2001/02, and expanded at average rates below those of the 1980s. The exception is services, which continued to expand rapidly.

Sectoral output performance. *Agricultural output* expanded slowly in the 1980s and 1990s. Growth slowed further after 1997, partly a result of extensive droughts in many states and flooding in

Table 1.1. Macroeconomic Trends Over the Past Two Decades

	1980s	1990s	1992/93-1996/97[a]	1997/98-2001/02[b]	2002/03[c]
GDP growth (% a year)	5.6	5.8	6.7	5.5	4.4
Agriculture, forestry, and fisheries	3.4	3.0	4.7	1.8	-3.1
Industry	7.0	5.8	7.6	4.5	6.1
Services	6.9	7.6	7.5	8.1	7.1
Investment rate (% of GDP)	22.0	23.0	23.3	22.5	22.1
Private	10.0	7.8	8.0	6.6	6.3
Public	12.1	15.2	15.3	15.9	15.7
Inflation (Wholesale Price Index, % a year)	8.0	8.1	8.7	4.9	2.5
General government deficit (% of GDP)	8.1	7.8	7.2	9.3	10.4
Current account balance (% of GDP)	-2.1	-1.4	-1.2	-0.7	1.0
External reserves (months of goods and services imports, end of period)	3.3	5.6	5.9	7.0	11.0

a. Eighth Plan period.

b. Ninth Plan period.

c. Estimated.

Source: Central Statistical Organization.

Table 1.2. Sectoral Shares of GDP, Factor Cost, 1980/81 and 2001/02
(%)

Sector	1980/81	2001/02
Agriculture, forestry, and fishing	38	25
Industry	26	26
Services	36	49
Total	100	100

Source: Central Statistical Organization.

others. Two other factors contributed to the slowdown. First was the dwindling impetus from the green revolution that increased productivity increases in Punjab, Haryana, Andhra Pradesh, and western Uttar Pradesh. Second was the limited public investment in agricultural infrastructure. Instead, an increasing share of public resources for agriculture was spent on the minimum support price for foodgrains. This program has given farmers little incentive to diversify. It has filled government storage facilities with grain stocks while keeping the market price for foodgrains artificially high. Slow agricultural growth is a concern not so much because of its contribution to India's overall output or food security-but because of the sector's importance in the country's economic, social, and political fabric. Agriculture still provides employment to a large share of India's population and an even larger share of the poor.

Industrial growth slowed sharply after the mid-1990s. Following liberalization in the early 1990s, investment and industrial output expanded rapidly. But because demand failed to expand as rapidly as expected, and with greater competition from imports, industry was left with excess capacity. Simultaneously, the domestic policy environment did not support productivity increases. Infrastructure bottlenecks and distortions in product and factor markets, combined with lower external demand and rising interest rates, led to a slowdown in industrial investment and growth after 1997/98. Industry has only recently begun to show signs of recovery, with the index of industrial production suggesting a recovery, particularly in capital goods.

Growth of the services sector has been strong and broadly based. One of the reasons is the rapid expansion of information technology, which has turned India into one of the world's leading providers of software (box 1.1). But other services have also expanded, such as transport, trade, and financial services. The national accounts also reflect an increase in the value added by public administration. But if GDP estimates are corrected for the "spurious" addition to growth caused by the use of the wage bill to estimate the value added of government services, annual GDP growth between 1997/98 and 1999/2000 would have been lower by about half a percentage point (Acharya 2002a).

Investment. Previously enabling phases of acceleration and stability in periods of slowdown (RBI 2001a), investment declined markedly after 1997/98, raising concerns about future growth.[6] Public investment was clearly crowded out by expanding public consumption and debt service. Several economists agree that the slowdown of public investment in the 1990s contributed to the slowing of private investment, as there appears to be a crowding-in phenomenon between certain types of public and private investments (Sundarajan and Thakur 1980 and RBI 2001a).

Private investment slowed for several reasons. Following the high growth rates of the early 1990s, firms invested and borrowed heavily in the mid-1990s, building capacity for a continuing

---

[6] Given the low openness of India's economy, external demand has played a small role in influencing business cycles.

Box 1.1. India's Success in Information Technology

India has emerged as a leader among developing countries in providing cross-border information services. Although the information technology (IT) industry in India has been around for more than three decades, its takeoff into a major software business is recent, with Bangalore, Hyderabad, Chennai, Mumbai, and Pune emerging as competitive IT hubs. Some critics assert that India's "new economy" has little to offer to the majority of Indians who are not engineers-and that it is essentially an export enclave. Others point out that India cannot live off IT services alone.

There is some truth to these assertions, but India's new economy, beyond making an increasing contribution to GDP and exports, also sets an example. It grew from $1 billion (or 0.3% of GDP) in 1990/91, to $9.6 billion (or 2% of GDP) in 2001. And the share of IT (mainly software) in total exports jumped from 1% in the early 1990s to 18% in 2001. Several factors contributed to this takeoff. The skilled English-speaking workforce coming out of India's engineering schools and earning lower wages than European and US counterparts. The low dependence of IT on physical infrastructure. And introducing current account convertibility and easing controls and regulations in the early 1990s.

IT-enabled services are also expanding rapidly in India, such as back-office operations, remote maintenance, accounting, public call centers, medical transcription, insurance claims, and other bulk processing. Such services have the potential for broader job creation than IT itself.

Source: *The Economist*; World Bank.

expansion in domestic demand. Businesses invested on the expectation that the pace of regulatory and infrastructure reform and investment would remain rapid-and thus contribute to higher productivity investment. Meanwhile, trade reform left some sectors more open to competition, while they still faced behind-the-border constraints to improving productivity. As the pace of reform slowed, interest rates rose, and the expected demand from high overall growth rates failed to materialize, many firms found themselves saddled with excess capacity and debt.

External sector. India's integration into the global economy increased in the 1990s. The real depreciation of the rupee after the 1991 crisis promoted exports, and the reduction of import barriers allowed more foreign goods into the country. Exports of goods and nonfactor services rose from 7.5% of GDP in 1990/91 to 10.5% in 2001/02.

The balance of payments has strengthened considerably in recent years. The performance of merchandise exports has been somewhat erratic-as the stimulus from the steep real depreciation of the rupee in the early 1990s faded, replaced by upward pressure. Sluggish domestic demand growth, however, has more than offset the impact of gradual relaxation of import barriers, and import growth has been modest in recent years. The trade deficit has thus roughly halved since 1999/2000-from around $12 billion to around $6 billion in 2002/03. Exports of IT services have increased sharply, and remittances have edged up. The current balance, which swung into a deficit of 3.4% of GDP in 1990/91, has shifted to a small surplus.

Capital inflows picked up strongly in response to the reforms of the early 1990s but have since been more modest. Foreign direct investment and equity inflows have eased from their peaks, and borrowing from both official and private creditors has typically been more moderate. The external debt has risen only modestly, falling from almost 40% of GDP in the early 1990s to around 23%. The combination of an improving current balance and even modest capital inflows has been enough to allow a substantial buildup of reserves, from $17 billion in 1995/96 to more than $80 billion today-equivalent to almost 12 months of imports.

The external sector continues to play a modest role, and India remains much more closed than other large Asian economies, where exports account for much larger shares of GDP-29% in China, 34% in Indonesia, and 41% in the Republic of Korea. India's share of world merchandise exports edged up from 0.5% in 1990 to 0.7% in 2001, but remains relatively modest for the size of the economy. The Government's cautious approach to opening the economy further in recent years reflects a desire to avoid a repetition of the balance-of-payments crisis of the early 1990s. Fiscal imbalances are re-emerging. And domestic vested interests, concerned about their ability to compete against foreign companies, resist further trade liberalization.

Unemployment. Jobless rates in India are not high by international standards, but recent trends have raised concern, as reflected in the Tenth Plan (table

Table 1.3. Unemployment Rates, India and Comparator Countries, Selected Years (%)

Country	Year	Unemployment Rate
India	1999/2000	4.4
China	1996	3.0
Indonesia	1998	5.5
Brazil	1998	9.0
Pakistan	2000	5.9

Source: ILO 2001.

1.3). Unemployment rates based on National Sample Survey data have been traditionally low in India.[7] But all measures show an increase in unemployment between 1993/94 and 1999/2000, explained almost entirely by an increase in unemployment in rural areas (figure 1.3 and statistical annex table A21). Disaggregated

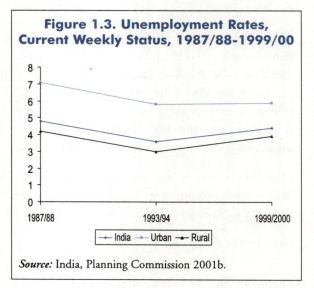

Figure 1.3. Unemployment Rates, Current Weekly Status, 1987/88-1999/00

Source: India, Planning Commission 2001b.

unemployment figures in the rural sector suggest that this deceleration in rural employment growth is due to a decline in employment in agriculture and the low capacity of rural industry and services to absorb the labor released from agriculture. The share of employment in the organized sector remains low, and unemployment rates are high among certain population groups, such as urban educated youth, and in certain states, such as Kerala, Tamil Nadu, and West Bengal.

Social Outcomes

Social progress in India has been uneven. Education indicators have improved markedly, but progress in health has been mixed (table 1.4). For the first time since independence, the absolute number of illiterates in India declined-between 1991 and 2001. Literacy

---

7   The National Sample Survey Organisation provides four different measures of unemployment, which capture different facets of the labor market situation: Usual Principal Status, Usual Principal and Subsidiary Status, Current Weekly Status, and Current Daily Status.

Table 1.4. Progress on Social Indicators, 1980-2000

Indicator	1980s	1990s	2000
Poverty			
Poverty incidence (%)	44.5	36.0	26.1
Adjusted poverty incidence (%)	n.a.	n.a.	28.6
Demographics			
Population (millions)	685	846	1,027
Rate of population increase (%)	2.4	2.2	n.a.
Overall sex ratio, ages 0-4 (females per 1,000 males)	978	955	927
Education			
Overall literacy rate: 7+ years (%)	44	52	65
Female literacy rate as a percent of male literacy rate (%)	53	61	71
Net enrollment rate (NER): lower primary (%)	n.a.	71	77
Net enrollment rate (NER): upper primary (%)	n.a.	70	74
Female NER as % of male NER: lower primary (%)	n.a.	84	90
Female NER as % of male NER: upper primary (%)	n.a.	78	86
Dropout rate, grades 1-5 (%)	54	45	40
Health			
Life expectancy at birth (years)	56	60	61
Infant mortality rate 0-4 years (per 1,000 live births)	115	79	68
Under-five mortality rate (per 1,000 live births)	152	94	95
Maternal mortality rate (per 100,000 live births)	n.a.	424	540
Malnourished children, ages 0-3 (%)	n.a.	53	47
Prevalence of HIV (million people)	n.a.	3.5	4.0
Sanitation			
Share of people with access to improved water resources (%)	n.a.	68	78
Share of households with toilet facility (%)	n.a.	30	36

Notes: Poverty estimates are for 1983, 1993/94 and 1999/2000. Demographics and literacy rates are for 1981, 1991, and 2001. Enrolment rates are for 1981, 1991, and 2000. Dropout rates are for 1982, 1993, and 1999. Health and sanitation data for 1992/93 and 1998/99. HIV prevalence is for 1998 and 2001. Improved water resources defined as access to piped drinking water and handpumps

Sources: Poverty-India, Planning Commission based on National Statistical Survey; Deaton 2002. Demographics-India, Office of the Registrar General 1981, 1991, 2001. Education- National Statistical Survey; India, Office of the Registrar General 1981, 1991, 2001; India, Department of Education. Health-India, Office of the Registrar General 1981, 1991, 2001; National Family Health Survey, Sample Registration System. HIV-National AIDS Control Organisation. Sanitation-India, Office of the Registrar General 1981, 1991, 2001; National Family Health Survey.

rates rose, particularly for women. Enrollment rates of primary-age children rose, and the gap in the enrollment ratios of boys and girls narrowed.

Health indicators in the 1990s improved slowly or, in some cases, not at all. Between 1992/93 and 1998/99, the infant mortality rate fell from 79 per 1,000 live births to 68, and population growth slowed. But there has been little progress in reducing India's high maternal mortality and under-five mortality rates and in addressing malnutrition. Many of these outcomes have to do not only with health policy, but with slow progress in improving access to safe water and sanitation.

An estimated four million people in India are now infected with HIV/AIDS, and the rate of infection is increasing. The preference for male children continued to increase in the 1990s.[8] And although polio has disappeared from most countries, India is one of seven where polio is endemic, accounting for 85% of all confirmed polio cases in the world in 2002 (World Heath Organization 2002).

These worrisome trends are somewhat surprising. Worrisome, because they suggest that increased public expenditures alone will be insufficient to improve outcomes. Public expenditures on health and education increased over the 1990s. Surprising, because the 1990s witnessed a large increase in compensation to civil servants, including education and health professionals, which could have contributed to improvements in the delivery of basic education and health services. There is no evidence that it did. To the contrary, households (particularly poor households) are increasingly resorting to the private sector for education and health services.

Economic and Social Outcomes: A Regional Perspective

India's good aggregate performance masks divergence in per capita incomes, poverty, and other indicators of well-being between richer and poorer states.[9]

Poverty declined in both poorer and richer states, but the progress in richer states has been greater. An important part of the explanation is that economic growth has been slower in the states that were poorer to start with (Deaton and Drèze 2002).[10] Faster population growth in states with initially higher incidences of poverty has concentrated poverty in India's northern and eastern states (table 1.5). In 1999/2000, 76% of India's poor lived in states with per capita incomes lower than the all-India average. Indeed, 54% of the poor now live in four states alone: Uttar Pradesh, Bihar, Orissa, and Madhya Pradesh. So making progress in poverty reduction in India requires faster growth in the lagging states.

These are also states with weaker state institutions, and where government finances are most severely stressed (chapters 2 and 3). Recent research by the World Bank and the Confederation of Indian Industry suggests that a weaker investment climate in these lagging states may also be behind this slower growth (chapters 4 and 5).

These diverging trends have translated into large disparities of incomes and other indicators of living standards (figure 1.4). Average per capita incomes in 1997-2000 varied from more than Rs15,000 in Maharastra, Punjab, Haryana, and Gujarat, to below Rs7,500 in Orissa and Uttar Pradesh, and below Rs5,000 in Bihar. Disparities in per capita income

---

[8] The difference is due to female infanticide, the neglect of female children, and the abortion of female fetuses.

[9] See, for instance, Nair (1985), Chaudhury (1966), Majumdar and Kapoor (1980), Rao, Shand, and Kalirajan (1999), Aiyar (2001), and Sachs, Bajpai, and Ramiah (2002). This is similar to the findings for China's provinces.

[10] Recent trends suggest that relative economic performance of India's poorest states is improving, partly because they are growing faster and partly because growth in previously fast growing states is slowing. These trends should be interpreted with caution because recent gross state domestic product estimates are subject to considerable revisions and establishing convergence or divergence rigorously requires a time series longer than just 4-5 years.

Table 1.5. Concentration of Poverty in India, 1983-1999/2000
(% of total number of poor people)

Region	1983	1987/88	1993/94	1999/2000
Poorer states[a]	70	70	71	76
Richer states[b]	27	28	26	22
Others	3	2	3	3
Total	100	100	100	100

a. Includes Andhra Pradesh, Assam, Bihar, Kerala, Madhya Pradesh, Orissa, Rajasthan, Uttar Pradesh, and West Bengal.

b. Includes Gujarat, Haryana, Karnataka, Maharashtra, Punjab, and Tamil Nadu.

Source: World Bank staff calculations, based on India, Planning Commission.

between richer and poorer states are mirrored in indicators of poverty, health, education, safe water, and sanitation. The average person born in Maharastra in the mid-1990s was expected to live 65 years, but a person born the same year in Bihar, Orissa, or Assam would not be expected to live past age 57. The exception is the number of females per 1,000 males, worse and deteriorating faster in richer states, such as Haryana, Maharastra, Delhi, and Punjab.

Accelerating Development in India: Goals and Policy Agenda

Increasing growth to 8% and accelerating progress in a wide range of living standards indicators are the goals set out in the Government's Tenth Plan (box 1.2). But macroeconomic vulnerabilities and structural impediments limit India's ability to accelerate development, as the Plan and the most recent Economic Survey recognize. Meeting these goals will require a radical departure from current policies. Some of the structural weaknesses may already help explain the growth slowdown of the past five years, suggesting that the high growth rates of the mid-1990s were an outlier, not a shift to a higher growth path. They also help explain the mixed performance in improving living standards and the persistence of regional disparities.

The two parts of this report look at the policy agenda to raise growth and achieve the goals of the Tenth

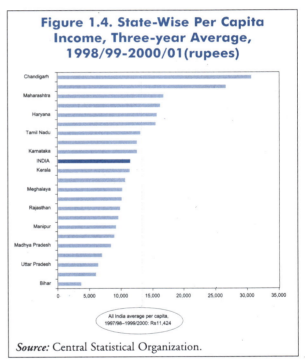

Figure 1.4. State-Wise Per Capita Income, Three-year Average, 1998/99-2000/01(rupees)

All India average per capita, 1997/98-1999/2000: Rs11,424

Source: Central Statistical Organization.

Plan. These reforms can be grouped into two broad areas. The first is improving the management of public resources, by reducing budget deficits, reallocating spending to more productive expenditures, and enhancing the quality of service delivery. The second is improving the investment climate and raising productivity in industry, services and agriculture and rural areas. The concluding chapter looks at the potential impact of these reforms on growth and poverty reduction-and the main risks that may jeopardize their realization.

Box 1.2. Targets for the Tenth Plan and Beyond

Macroeconomic

- Increase annual economic growth to 8% during the Tenth Plan period and to 9.3% during the Eleventh Plan period.
- Double per capita consumption level in 13 years: private consumption expenditure growth at 6.9% a year and per capita consumption growth at 5.3% a year in the Tenth Plan.
- Achieve 12.4% annual growth in exports.
- Restore agricultural growth to 4% a year and increase industrial growth to 8.7% and services growth to 9.3% over the Tenth Plan period.
- Reduce the gross fiscal deficit of the center and states from 10.4% of GDP in 2001/02 to 6.5% of GDP in 2006/07.
- Increase the investment rate to 28% and the savings rate to 27% of GDP.

Poverty

- Reduce the poverty ratio from 26% to 21% by 2007 and to 11% by 2012.

Demographics

- Reduce population growth from 21.3% between 1991 and 2001 to 16.2% between 2001 and 2011.

Employment

- Provide gainful, high-quality employment to at least the new additions to the labor force.
- Reduce unemployment to 5.3% by 2006-07.

Education

- Ensure that all children are in school by 2003 and that all children complete 5 years of schooling by 2007.
- Reduce gender gaps in literacy and wage rates by at least 50% by 2007.
- Increase the literacy rate to 75% during the Plan period.

Health

- Reduce the infant mortality rate from 70 per 1,000 live births to 45 by 2007 and to 28 by 2012.
- Reduce the maternal mortality rate to 2 per 1,000 live births by 2007 and to 1 per 1,000 live births by 2012.
- Reduce the average prevalence of underweight children under three from 47% to 40% by 2007.
- Reduce by half severe undernutrition in children ages 0-6.
- Achieve zero growth of HIV/AIDS infections by 2007.
- Increase the use of public health facilities from 20% at present to 75% by 2010.

Sanitation

- Provide all villages with sustained access to potable drinking water within the Plan period.
- Clean major polluted rivers by 2007 and other notified stretches by 2012.

Environment

- Increase forest and tree cover to 25% by 2007 and 33% by 2012.

Source: India, Planning Commission 2003.

PART I

POLICY AGENDA: MANAGING PUBLIC RESOURCES

The public sector has always played a major role in India's development strategy. Reforms in the 1990s reduced the role of the state and improved the environment for private investment. But developments in the public sector continue to have a major impact on the prospects for economic growth and poverty reduction. That is why the recent deterioration in the fiscal position at the center and in the states is cause for concern. The center and states now spend almost all their revenues on interest payments, subsidies, civil service salaries and pensions, administration, and defense. Of particular concern are power sector losses, placing massive stress on almost all state budgets. This leaves limited resources for public investment, just as large deficits threaten to crowd out private investment. Even when funds are available, the delivery of services to the poor is constrained by weaknesses in public institutions and the regulatory framework for private activities.

Chapter 2 reviews the debate over fiscal sustainability, proposing reforms in fiscal policy and public resource management to steadily reduce the primary deficits at the center and state levels-and to improve the composition of public expenditure. Chapter 3 considers longer term reforms in the civil service to improve the delivery of public services. It looks at the health and education sectors and at social safety nets, suggesting possible reforms to improve the prospects for achieving the targets set by the Tenth Plan and the Millennium Development Goals.

CHAPTER 2

FISCAL POLICY

India's balance-of-payments crisis in 1991 followed an acceleration in economic growth to 5.6% a year in the 1980s from a trend of 3.5% over the previous three decades. Large fiscal deficits fed into current account deficits and depleted foreign exchange reserves, pushing India to the brink of default in 1991. The general government fiscal deficit (center and states consolidated) averaged 9% of GDP before the crisis (figure 2.1). It then fell sharply during the high growth and fiscal restraint of the Eighth Plan period, but resumed growing equally sharply after 1997/98, returning to the 9-10% of GDP range in the Ninth Plan period.

The general government debt-to-GDP ratio rose from about 58% in 1985/86 to 85% of GDP in 2002/03, at which time public sector debt (general government plus central public enterprises) stood at 95% (see figure 2.1). Contingent liabilities from

guarantees in support of loss-making public enterprises, largely in power and irrigation, amounted to 12% of GDP.

In addition to the big rise in the debt burden, the deteriorating quality of the fiscal stance in the 1990s has been another serious concern. Revenues fell considerably during the Ninth Plan period relative to the second half of the 1980s (table 2.1). While 2002/03 shows a large revenue increase, it is based on the budget estimate for states, which tends to be optimistic. Compared with the average for the second half of the 1980s, capital expenditure fell by more than three percentage points of GDP during the Ninth Plan, while the sum of interest, administration, and pensions rose by three percentage points of GDP-and a massive 22 percentage points of revenue. Revenue deficits more than doubled, with spending on interest, administration, and pensions crowding out that on social and physical infrastructure. The fiscal improvement secured in the Eighth Plan period involved a large compression of capital spending.[11]

At the center, revenues declined substantially during the Ninth Plan period relative to the pre-crisis benchmark, while interest payments, subsidies,[12] civil service salaries[13] and pensions, administration, and defense literally consumed 100% of revenues (table 2.2). The primary deficit fell by half, while the revenue deficit increased substantially-as rising interest payments displaced capital spending. The fiscal deficit has been

Figure 2.1. General Government Deficit and Debt Stock, 1985/86-2002/03 (% of GDP)

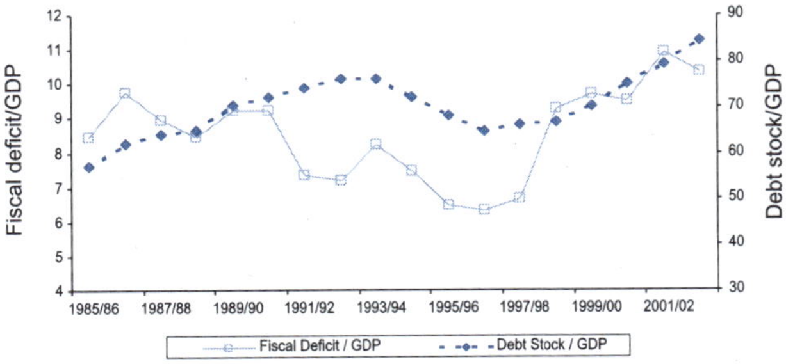

Source: India, Ministry of Finance, budget documents (center); RBI; IMF; World Bank staff estimates.

---

[11] It was hoped the private sector would step into the breach and invest in infrastructure, but this has not happened on the desired scale except for telecommunications. As noted in RBI (2003a), a bigger private role in infrastructure would require institutional reform and "economically efficient user charges to ensure the reasonable return on investment."

[12] Explicit budgetary subsidies.

[13] Excluding railways and posts and telecommunications.

Table 2.1. General Government Fiscal Trends, 1985/86-2002/03 (% of GDP)

	1985/86-1989/90	1992/93-1996/97[a]	1997/98-2001/02[b]	2002/03[c]
Revenues	19.4	17.9	17.0	18.4
Current expenditure [d]	22.1	21.5	23.1	25.3
Social services	5.4	5.0	5.6	5.7
Economic services	6.5	5.8	5.5	6.5
General services	9.5	10.3	11.7	12.8
Capital expenditure[e]	6.4	3.6	3.2	3.5
Gross fiscal deficit	9.0	7.2	9.3	10.4
Memo				
Primary deficit	5.3	2.1	3.5	3.8
Revenue deficit	2.6	3.6	6.1	6.9
Interest	3.8	5.1	5.8	6.5
(Irrigation+power+transport)/GDP	4.7	3.5	3.5	3.8
(Interest+admin.+pensions)/GDP	6.3	8.1	9.2	10.1
(Interest+admin.+pensions)/revenue	32.6	45.1	54.3	54.8

a. Eighth Plan.

b. Ninth Plan.

c. Revised estimates for the center and budget estimates for the states.

d. Refers to revenue expenditure in the budget.

e. Refers to capital outlay and net loans and advances from the center to the states.

Source: India, Ministry of Finance, budget documents (center); Central Statistical Organization; RBI 2001b; World Bank staff estimates.

reduced, but the fiscal stance has worsened. According to the revised estimates for 2002/03, there has been an encouraging increase in revenues, but interest payments, the primary deficit, the revenue deficit, and the gross fiscal deficit have all increased.

Trends in revenues and expenditure at the consolidated state level mirror those at the center, except that the gross fiscal deficit rose significantly after falling during the Eighth Plan period (table 2.3). Revenue deficits have grown alarmingly, while capital expenditures were cut-in part to accommodate growing interest payments. The share

in central taxes plus grants almost fully explains the decline in revenues in the Ninth Plan period relative to the second half of the 1980s. Once again, the signs of a deteriorating fiscal stance are unmistakable. Interest spending has risen, capital expenditure has declined, and developmental spending stagnated, even though the states have primary responsibility under the Constitution for poverty reduction and the people's welfare.

A mechanical comparison of the numbers for the general government, center, and states[14] shows that most of the increase in the general

---

[14] Note that the general government gross fiscal and primary deficits differ from the sum of the respective deficits at the center and states because of the netting out of interest paid by the states to the center and net lending from the center to the states (which is a component of capital expenditure).

Table 2.2. Trends in Central Government Finances, 1985/86-2003/04 (% of GDP)

	1985/86-1989/90	1992/93-1996/97[a]	1997/98-2001/02[b]	2002/03[c]	2003/04[d]
Revenues	10.4	9.2	8.9	9.7	9.3
Tax revenue (net)	7.8	6.8	6.2	6.7	6.8
Nontax revenue	2.5	2.5	2.7	3.0	2.6
Current expenditure	12.9	12.1	12.7	13.9	13.4
Interest payments	3.2	4.3	4.6	4.7	4.5
Subsidies	1.8	1.2	1.3	1.8	1.8
Salaries	0.0	1.1	1.0	1.3	1.2
Pensions	0.4	0.4	0.7	0.6	0.6
Defense	2.5	1.6	1.7	1.7	1.6
Capital expenditure	4.3	2.2	1.8	1.8	2.0
Capital outlay	2.6	1.4	1.1	1.2	1.5
Net lending[e]	1.7	0.8	0.7	0.6	0.4
Gross fiscal deficit[f]	6.9	5.1	5.6	6.1	6.1
Memo					
Primary deficit	3.7	0.8	1.0	1.3	1.6
Revenue deficit	2.5	2.8	3.8	4.3	4.1

a. Eighth Plan.
b. Ninth Plan.
c. Revised estimates.
d. Budget estimates.
e. Excludes state's share of net small savings loans.
f. Divestment receipts are treated as a financing item and not as revenues in computing the deficit.

Source: India, Ministry of Finance, budget documents (center); World Bank staff estimates.

government's revenue deficit between the second half of the 1980s and the Ninth Plan period is traceable to a big deterioration in state finances. But the underlying causes are a complex mix of fiscal developments at the center and states. For example, transfers (tax shares, grants, and loans) from the center to states declined from 7.4% of GDP in 1985/86 to 5% in 2002/03. Similarly, the Fifth Pay Commission has had a big impact for states, which were following the example of the center (Acharya 2001, 2002a). The states have also suffered from rising interest rates over the 1990s in part because of the high, administratively determined interest rates on "small savings" loans (Govinda Rao 2000).

Government Debt Dynamics and External Vulnerability

Despite the growing debt burden and rising revenue deficits, some are of the view that the large fiscal deficit is not a serious problem because the Reserve Bank of India's foreign exchange reserves

Table 2.3. Trends in State Government Finances, 1985/86-2002/03 (% of GDP)

	1985/86-1989/90	1992/93-1996/97[a]	1997/98-2001/02[b]	2002/03[c]
Revenues	12.2	11.8	11.0	12.0
Share in central taxes	2.7	2.6	2.4	2.5
Grants from the center	2.2	2.1	1.7	2.2
Current expenditure	12.3	12.6	13.3	14.5
Education	2.6	2.5	2.7	2.7
Health and family welfare	0.8	0.7	0.7	0.7
Agriculture and allied services	1.1	0.9	0.8	0.7
Rural development	0.8	0.7	0.5	0.5
Interest payments	1.4	1.9	2.4	3.0
Administrative services	1.2	1.2	1.2	1.2
Pensions	0.4	0.7	1.0	0.9
Other	3.9	4.0	4.0	4.6
Capital expenditure	2.7	1.9	1.9	2.2
Capital outlay	1.9	1.5	1.5	1.8
Loans and advances (net)	0.9	0.4	0.4	0.4
Gross fiscal deficit	2.8	2.6	4.2	4.7
Financed by:				
Internal debt (net)	0.5	0.5	0.7	0.6
Loans from center (net)	1.8	1.2	0.9	0.5
Provident and insurance funds (net)	0.4	0.5	0.6	0.5
Memo				
Primary deficit	1.4	0.7	1.8	1.6
Revenue deficit	0.1	0.7	2.3	2.5

a.   Eighth Plan.
b.   Ninth Plan.
c.   Revised estimates.
Source: RBI bulletins; World Bank staff estimates.

are at record levels, as are food stocks.[15] They assert that the high fiscal deficit has countered the slowdown in the private sector and that India will eventually grow out of its debt problem. Developments over the past 18 months appear superficially to support this. Inflation and interest

[15] For a statement of this view and a refutation, see RBI 2003a.

rates have reached their lowest levels ever. Foreign exchange reserves have continued their remarkable growth. And according to banks, the demand for credit from industry remains low, while there is considerable excess capacity in manufacturing.

Arguing in favor of a fiscal consolidation is the worsening trend in debt dynamics (see below). It is one thing to run a 10% deficit when general government debt is less than 60% of GDP, as it was in 1985/86. But it is quite another when that debt is more than 25 percentage points of GDP higher, as it is today, with guarantees amounting to another 12% of GDP. Moreover, the increase in the general government debt-to-GDP ratio has accelerated from less than 2 percentage points of GDP per year over the first three years of the Ninth Plan period (1997/98 to 1999/00) to more than 4.5 percentage points over the last three years (2000/01 to 2002/03), despite the low interest rates. Interest rates on government debt have fallen sharply at the margin. But they will have to persist for several years to improve the debt dynamics, driven by the weighted average yield of all outstanding debt minus the growth rate.

The second issue needing a judgment is how long interest rates will stay low and whether this will be enough to stimulate growth without a fiscal adjustment and faster structural reforms. Interest rates have been driven by a combination of capital flows and weakness in the world economy, which has pushed OECD interest rates to 50-year lows (World Bank 2003c). To the extent that capital flows into India have been driven by one-off events since September 11, 2001-including fears of increased scrutiny of accounts held overseas as part of anti-money laundering drives or by the instability in Iraq-it would be risky to slow fiscal reform on a gamble that such flows will continue indefinitely.[16]

But the increase in IT-related exports and remittances from abroad, which have contributed to unprecedented back-to-back current account surpluses over the past two fiscal years, might well continue-though the bulk of the increase in the Reserve Bank of India's reserves is still explained by the capital account. If capital flows subside and the global economy picks up, interest rates will once again be determined by medium-run inflationary expectations, molded by fiscal and macro fundamentals. As analyzed here, they strengthen the case for a fiscal adjustment.

Government Debt Dynamics

Data on net public debt-defined as general government debt minus net domestic assets and net foreign assets of the Reserve Bank of India plus its nonmonetary liabilities-capture compactly the joint position of public debt dynamics and international liquidity (table 2.4).[17] Except for the primary fiscal deficit and current account balance, there was an across-the-board deterioration during the Ninth Plan relative to the second half of the 1980s and an even more striking deterioration relative to the Eighth Plan. General government debt fell from 71% of GDP at the end of 1989/90 to 65% at the end of the Eighth Plan period. But it then rose an alarming 15 percentage points by the end of the Ninth Plan, and another five percentage points the following year, notwithstanding record low interest rates. Net public debt displays a similar trajectory: the rapid accumulation of reserves is being offset by rising government debt and sterilization.

Interest payments consumed less than 20% of total revenues in the pre-crisis period, compared with over 30% during the Ninth Plan period. Revenue deficits doubled from less than 3% in the second half of the 1980s to 6% during the Ninth Plan period and beyond, capturing a deterioration in

---

[16] Interestingly, a coincident reserve buildup has been observed in all the South Asian countries.

[17] Analyses of public debt sustainability for Turkey, for example, use the notion of net public debt.

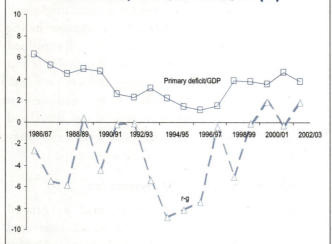

Figure 2.2. Primary Deficits and the Implied Difference between the Real Rate of Interest and Growth, 1986/87-2002/03 (%)

Source: World Bank staff calculations based on India, Ministry of Finance budget documents (center and states); RBI bulletins.

the fiscal stance, with spending on social and physical infrastructure crowded out by rising interest and other current payments (see table 2.1). At the same time, general government debt dynamics took a sharp turn for the worse over the past four years, evident in the implied difference between the real interest rate on the stock of government debt and the real growth rate of GDP (figure 2.2).[18, 19] Primary deficits fell from pre-crisis levels during the Eighth Plan period but have grown steadily since. The implied gap between the real interest rate on the stock of government debt and the growth rates charted a clear upward trend after 1994/95 and has been either close to zero or positive since 1999/00, a trend maintained despite record low interest rates over the last 18 months. The average implied difference between real interest rates and growth rates rose from -6.0 percentage points during the Eighth Plan period to

-0.74 percentage points during the Ninth Plan period, while the primary deficit rose from an average of 2.1% to 3.5% of GDP. Government debt dynamics have accelerated on both counts. Given the large volume of guarantees in support of loss-making public enterprises (especially in the power and irrigation sectors), government debt is on a considerably faster upward trajectory than hitherto observed.

Foreign exchange reserves built up steadily after the 1991 crisis-with a dramatic increase of $22 billion over the past fiscal year, about 40% of it after November 2002. An unknown part of this might have been driven by capital inflows related to fears of the Iraq war, so this pace might not be maintained (RBI 2003b; Kapur and Patel 2003). Furthermore, the reserve accumulation of the past few years has been facilitated by private sector sluggishness, which has prevented fiscal deficits around 10% of GDP from feeding into sizable current account deficits (Ahluwalia 2002a; Acharya 2001; IMF 2002). The current account deficit averaged 2.2% of GDP in the five pre-crisis years, but less than 1% during the Ninth Plan period, even though fiscal deficits were similar (table 2.4). This suggests a crowding out, as well as a relative tightening of monetary policy, discussed later in this chapter.

External Vulnerability

Reserves, $75 billion at the end of 2002/03, and now more than $80 billion, imply a healthy cushion against external vulnerability, using standard measures.[20] An additional factor boosting liquidity has been the shift toward long-term rupee debt in government financing after the 1991 crisis. The average maturity of dated securities issued more than doubled from 6.6 years in 1997/98 to

---

[18] For details of the calculations underlying figure 2.2, see Pinto and Zahir (2003).

[19] A recent analysis of public debt dynamics is contained in Lahiri and Kannan (2002). For related analyses, see Buiter and Patel (1992); Acharya (2001); Ahluwalia (2002a); Srinivasan (2001); Cashin and others (2001).

[20] India (2002) contains a cross-country comparison of external debt indicators that puts India in a favorable light.

Table 2.4. Key Macroeconomic Aggregates, 1985/86-2003/04

Aggregate	1985/86-1989/90 Pre-crisis period	1990/91 Crisis	1992/93-1996/97 Eighth Plan	1997/98-2001/02 Ninth Plan	2002/03[a]	2003/04[b]
Gross fiscal deficit[c]	9.0	9.3	7.2	9.3	10.4	9.8
Revenue deficit[c]	2.6	4.0	3.6	6.1	6.9	6.2
Primary deficit[c]	5.3	4.8	2.1	3.5	3.8	4.1
Debt outstanding[d]	70.6	72.5	65.1	79.8	85.0	n.a.
Net public debt,[e]	60.1	63.8	53.8	70.2	76.3	n.a.
Memo						
Interest/revenue (%)	19.4	24.6	28.5	34.0	35.3	n.a.
Forex reserves (billions of U.S. dollars)[d]	4.0	5.8	26.4	54.0	75.4	n.a.
Current account balance/GDP (%)	-2.2	-3.1	-1.2	-0.7	1.0	n.a.
Real GDP growth (%)	5.9	5.6	7.1	5.5	4.4	n.a.

n.a. Reliable data not available.

a. Revised estimates.

b. Budget estimates.

c. For the general government. The figures for 2002/03 are revised estimates for central government and budget estimates for state governments. For 2003/04, the figures are budget estimates for center and World Bank staff estimates for states.

d For end of last fiscal year in period. External debt is at current exchange rates.

e. General government debt minus net domestic assets and net foreign assets of RBI plus its nonmonetary liabilities.

Source: India, Ministry of Finance, budget documents (center); RBI 2001b; World Bank staff estimates.

14.3 in 2001/02 (RBI 2002a). Moreover, about 90% of central and state government securities are held by nationalized banks, State Bank of India, the Reserve Bank of India, and the Life Insurance Company, with the rest held by Unit Trust of India, National Bank for Agriculture and Rural Development, employee provident funds, and private banks (RBI 2001b).

Since the 1991 balance-of-payments crisis, interest rates have been liberalized, India has become more integrated into the world goods and capital markets, and fiscal fundamentals have deteriorated, even relative to the late 1980s. IMF (2002) notes

that "total public sector debt relative to GDP in India is much greater than in Argentina and Brazil, while the ratio for Turkey recently shot up (during the crisis) to around that of India." And India's primary fiscal deficits are larger-indeed, the other three countries have generally run primary surpluses over the last decade (IMF 2002).

Cross-country comparisons are complicated by such factors as the currency composition of debt, its maturity, whether the real exchange rate is in equilibrium, whether privatization proceeds are included in revenues (thereby artificially boosting the primary surplus, as in Argentina),[21] and the size

---

[21] On this specific point and how it may have put a better complexion on debt dynamics, see Mussa (2002).

of contingent liabilities and potential balance sheet problems in the banking and corporate sectors, a potent factor in the East Asian crisis of 1997/98. Further, countries with unsustainable public debt dynamics that eventually experienced crisis, such as Russia and Argentina, had low international liquidity. This combination proved intractable, even with substantial bailout packages. Indeed, bailout packages could backfire in these circumstances because they provide the means for private portfolio investors to exit, leaving the country burdened with senior loans from international financial institutions denominated in hard currency.

India's public debt dynamics have worsened, with state government finances in crisis, significant nonperforming assets in the financial system, and a large volume of guarantees. But reserves are high, bolstered by limited capital account convertibility, a flexible exchange rate, long-term capital inflows, and a pliant financial system that willingly holds long-term, rupee-denominated government paper. In short, India is not vulnerable to the type of collapse suffered by Russia or Argentina. But without a fiscal adjustment, it is open to substandard growth.

Costs of the Fiscal Stance

The growth target for the Tenth Plan is 8% a year, part of a strategy to double per capita GDP by the end of the Eleventh Plan. Chapter 2 of the plan notes that the investment rate will need to rise by four percentage points to a little over to 28%, with domestic savings contributing an additional 3.5 percentage points and the rise in the current account deficit 0.5 percentage points. The incremental capital-output ratio is expected to fall from 4.5 to 3.6, investments to grow by 14% a year compared with the long-run growth rate of 6.5%, and consumption by

6.9% a year. The chapter notes that private household savings rose over the Eighth and Ninth plans in response to the cut in tax rates and consequent rise in disposable income. This could slow in the Tenth Plan period because of the need to raise the tax-to-GDP ratio, highlighting the need to increase public savings from -1.7% in the base year of the Tenth Plan (2001/02) to +2.1% in its last year (2006/07). Unless this happens, the plan is quite explicit that the growth target is unlikely to be reached. It also cautions that the current account deficit should not be used to slacken the public savings target-and that a safe upper limit is 3% of GDP.

The plan then compares the fiscal deficits projected under the preceding savings-investment scenario (the "desirable deficit" from a growth perspective) with the fiscal deficit that would achieve sustainability, defined as a stable government debt-to-GDP ratio (table 2.5). Comparing columns (2) and (4) shows the sizable fiscal correction for the states to achieve sustainability, even if growth is 8%. Comparing columns (3) and (4) shows that an even bigger fiscal correction is needed to generate the needed public savings for investment and growth. So, achieving sustainable debt is "easier" than generating the public savings consistent with 8%

Table 2.5. Sustainable and Desirable Deficits in the Tenth Plan Context

	Sustainable deficit[a]		Desirable deficit[b]	Base year
	Growth target 6.5	Growth target 8.0		
	(1)	(2)	(3)	(4)
Combined	7.4	8.6	6.8	9.3
Center	4.4	5.2	3.6	4.9
States	3.0	3.4	3.2	4.5

a.   Table 2.21 of Tenth Plan.
b.   Table 2.22 of Tenth Plan.
Source: India, Planning Commission 2003.

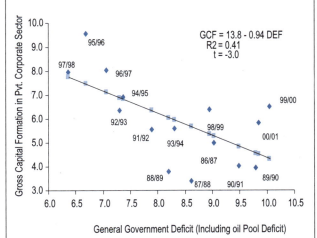

Figure 2.3. Gross Capital Formation in Private Corporate Sector and the General Government Deficit, 1986/87-2000/01 (% of GDP)

GCF = 13.8 - 0.94 DEF
R2 = 0.41
t = -3.0

Source: National Accounts Statistics; India, Ministry of Finance; World Bank staff estimates.

the cyclical slowdown of the private sector. But real interest rates for borrowers remained high after 1996/97 and through 2001/02, averaging more than 12% a year (figure 2.4).

There may be several reasons behind the high real interest rates, including the interest rate liberalization of 1993/94, a sharp worsening in public debt dynamics, and a pronounced shift toward long-term rupee debt in deficit financing. What has emerged is a mix of a "loose fiscal-tight money" policy[23] that has helped to keep inflation low and prevent worsening public debt dynamics from spilling over into the current account and depleting reserves, as happened in the late 1980s, leading to the 1991 crisis. But this has been at the expense of growth and welfare, as rising interest payments crowded out spending on social and physical infrastructure. Even though interest rates

growth. In other words, growth could continue to be substandard even if a crisis does not erupt-and avoiding crisis is not enough.

India has a relatively closed capital account and substantial government ownership of financial institutions. The incentives would favor government financing needs, with a residual claim for the private sector. And the higher the deficit, the higher the real interest rate-and therefore the fewer the private sector investment projects likely to be profitable, increasing the severity of crowding out. Not surprisingly, there is a well-documented negative association between fiscal deficits and private investment (figure 2.3).[22] One could argue that a rise in fiscal deficits was needed to counteract

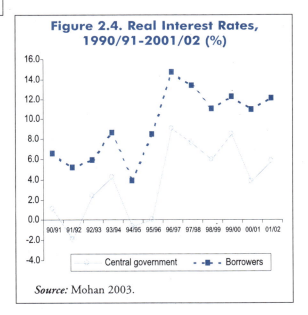

Figure 2.4. Real Interest Rates, 1990/91-2001/02 (%)

Central government   - ■ - Borrowers

Source: Mohan 2003.

---

[22] See World Bank (2000a) and Reynolds (2001).

[23] The term "loose fiscal-tight money" refers to the additional burden on monetary policy to achieve stabilization goals and foreign exchange reserve targets given the deterioration in public finance fundamentals after 1996/97, meaning higher real interest rates for the private sector. As RBI (2003a) paragraph 4.67 notes, "The growing reliance on market borrowing for financing the fiscal deficit has been accompanied by restraint on reserve money growth and moderation of inflationary pressure. This has also had the effect of raising interest payments." And paragraph 4.85: "Continuing foreign exchange inflows and the recessionary conditions enabled the Reserve Bank to move to a softer interest rate regime in spite of a rising fiscal deficit." But the continuance of inflows suggests that interest rates are still "too high" in a relative sense.

have declined sharply over the past 18 months or so (for a variety of reasons in the external environment), public debt dynamics have continued to worsen.

In addition, significant micro barriers to financing the private sector could prevent the decline in marginal interest rates on government debt from translating into low lending rates to the real sector, except for the best credits. The Indian financial system is segmented and must conform to various minimum lending and portfolio composition requirements. For example, the prime lending rate tends to be kept high because it cannot be exceeded when lending to the priority small-scale sector.

Insurance companies must hold at least 50% of their assets in government debt and provident funds, at least 50% in central government debt and 25% in state government debt. Annual inflows into small (postal) savings, which compete with banks for deposits, are invested wholly in government debt. These flows have grown from an average of 7.9% of GDP in the Eighth Plan to nearly 10% currently, consuming nearly the whole increase in net household financial saving. The administratively determined interest rates for these instruments were set artificially high, at 10.5-13% until 2000 and are still at 7.5-9%, with tax concessions. This worsens the public debt dynamics while raising the cost of funds for banks and hence lending rates to the private sector. Moreover, banks are under pressure to reduce their nonperforming assets, which attracts them even more to government debt. And nonbank financial corporations, which held little government debt and funded riskier firms, represented an average of 7.7% of GDP in the Eighth Plan but only 1.1% in the Ninth. Their decline probably contributed to the rapid growth in bank deposits after 1996. So, dominant government ownership of the financial sector, the portfolio problems of banks, the investment rules for insurance companies and provident funds, and the interest rates on small savings all create a natural proclivity toward

lending to government. This is reinforced by the incentive structure in banks: managers complain of being subject to criminal investigation if a loan to a private enterprise goes sour.

A last point is that the substantial shift in the composition of government spending away from capital expenditure directly inhibits private investment and reinforces the macro and micro crowding out. An empirical investigation concludes that a rise in government consumption crowds out private consumption, a rise in public investment in manufacturing crowds out private investment, and public investment in infrastructure has strong positive complementarities with private investment (RBI 2002c). So, the rise of revenue deficits, accompanied by an offsetting decline in government social and infrastructure spending, has also contributed to crowding out the private sector.

Fiscal Reform Priorities

In addition to the Tenth Plan document, concerns about the fiscal situation have been expressed in key government reports and pronouncements. According to the *Economic Survey, 2002-03*, "Higher fiscal deficits, besides constraining growth have resulted in higher government borrowings.... The revenue deficit which constituted 49.4% of the fiscal deficit in 1990/91 accounted for 70.2% of fiscal deficit in 2001/02....While the expenditure composition both for the center and states continues to reflect a preponderance of wages, salaries, interest payments and subsidies, there has been some welcome relief on the interest rates in recent months. The high fiscal deficit continues to complicate the task of conducting counter-cyclical fiscal policies and augmenting outlays on the much needed social and physical infrastructure, and poverty alleviation programs" (page 22). During the 2003/04 Union Budget discussions, the Finance Minister informed the Rajya Sabha on March 14, 2003 that "Of our revenue, 50% is swallowed by payment of just interest on (government) debt. Another 20% goes on subsidies and 25% on defense. What am I left with?"[24] And RBI (2003a) notes that "…fiscal performance during the reform period, however, was characterized by a clear divide in the mid-1990s in the attainment of fiscal targets. There was evidence of the successful fiscal correction during 1991/92 to 1996/97 (except for 1993/94) in terms of a significant fall in the fiscal deficit and in public debt as a proportion of GDP. Since then there has been a significant reversal of trend. Indeed, many deficit indicators presently are even higher than the levels prevailing at the time of the crisis in 1991. The revenue deficit has not only persisted, but has grown in size during this period… Several pointers indicate a reversal of the fiscal consolidation process in the recent years. These include decline in tax-to-GDP ratio, downward rigidity in current expenditure, steady deterioration in public investment in productive sectors, slow progress of PSUs (public sector undertakings) restructuring and faster accumulation of public debt" (chapter IV, page 1).

In view of the preceding analysis, fiscal reforms are needed to ensure a phased reduction in the primary and revenue deficits of the center and state governments, and to reallocate expenditure toward more productive uses. The discussion turns to proposals for policy reforms in four key areas:

- ✦ Tax reform.
- ✦ Subsidy reduction.
- ✦ Financial policy.
- ✦ Fiscal management.

Tax Reform

The gross tax revenue of the central government fell from 10.3% of GDP in 1991/92 to 8.6% in 2001/02 (India, Planning Commission 2003). The goal is to raise taxes back to 10.3% of GDP by the end of the Tenth Plan. Plan projections assume a big increase in tax buoyancy-from 0.8 in the Ninth Plan to 1.26 in the Tenth. Most of this increased buoyancy is expected to come from indirect taxes, particularly customs duties. Achieving this goal rests on several key assumptions: complete withdrawal of import tariff exemptions (except on strategic imports), a strong resumption of growth in manufacturing, the sector with the highest tax buoyancy, and extending the tax net to include the booming services sector. The states' own tax collection is projected to be raised from 5.9% of GDP in the base year to 6.6% by the end of the Tenth Plan. This increase rests crucially on the implementation of a unified VAT covering all goods and services.

The decline in the tax-to-GDP ratio in the 1990s is due partly to the "costs of reform," reflecting the reduction in customs and excise duties to increase competition and enhance efficiency. But it also reflects the costs of incomplete reform. The shift toward direct taxes has failed to compensate fully for the reduction in indirect taxes implemented as part of the reforms during the 1990s. As the Kelkar Committee reports emphasize, the lowering of tax rates needs to be complemented by eliminating exemptions, bringing services and agriculture into the tax net, and improving technology-based tax administration (Kelkar 2002). These reforms deserve the highest priority in view of the decline in the tax-to-GDP ratio in the 1990s and the direct positive effect this will have on reducing primary and revenue deficits. In this respect, while tax administration has been given due prominence in the Union Budget for 2003/04, there has been a tendency to increase exemptions and special rates, even for excise taxes, despite the rationalization of main rates. And there has been no move to tax agricultural income, which will perpetuate incentives to disguise nonagricultural income as agricultural income.

---

[24] Times News Network, *Times of India,* March 14, 2003.

Table 2.6. Government Subsidies, 1997/98–2003/04

Item	1997/98	1998/99	1999/2000	2000/01	2001/02	2002/03[a]	2003/04[b]
Billions of rupees at current prices							
Food (including sugar)	79.2	92.1	94.8	121.0	175.1	242.0	278.0
Fertilizer	99.2	116.0	132.4	138.0	126.0	110.1	127.2
Petroleum	n.a.	n.a.	n.a.	n.a.	n.a.	62.7	81.2
Interest subsidies	0.8	14.3	13.7	1.1	2.1	7.7	1.8
Others	6.2	13.6	3.9	8.3	8.9	23.8	10.9
Total subsidies	185.4	235.9	244.9	268.4	312.1	446.2	499.1
Percent of GDP							
Food (including sugar)	0.5	0.5	0.5	0.6	0.8	1.0	1.0
Fertilizer	0.7	0.7	0.7	0.7	0.5	0.4	0.5
Total subsidies	1.2	1.4	1.3	1.3	1.4	1.8	1.8
Memo (%)							
Food (including sugar)/gross fiscal deficit	10.7	9.5	8.9	10.0	12.1	16.3	16.7
Food /revenue	5.9	6.2	5.2	6.3	8.7	10.2	10.9
SEB losses/GDP	0.9	1.2	1.4	1.2	1.4	n.a.	n.a.

n.a.   Reliable data not available.

a.   Revised estimates.

b.   Budget estimates.

Source: India, Ministry of Finance, budget documents (center); India, Planning Commission 2002a.

Subsidy Reduction

Subsidies. The central food subsidy amounted to Rs242 billion with fertilizer subsidies adding another Rs110 billion, a total of 1.4% of GDP in 2002/03 (table 2.6). Foodgrain and input subsidies have distorted farmer cropping and investment decisions, contributing to natural resource degradation (soil nutrient imbalances, water logging, salinity). At the same time, public investments in agriculture have declined over the last decade, in large part due to the pressing need to meet subsidy requirements in the foodgrain, fertilizer, irrigation, and power sectors. The main reform goal therefore would not be to achieve fiscal savings. It would be to achieve faster growth in agriculture by shifting central expenditures from food (subject to the maintenance of a minimum social safety net) and fertilizer subsidies toward productivity-enhancing investments, including irrigation, rural infrastructure, and research and extension (see chapter 5). The petroleum subsidy, about 0.4% of GDP, is to be phased out over the medium term.

Power reform. This is a key reform both for fiscal sustainability and for spurring growth through more efficient provision of power services to industrial and commercial users and more reliable provision to the rural areas. Estimated State Electricity Board (SEB) losses in 2001/02 were

Rs332 billion, about three times those in 1996/97.[25] To put this in perspective, the gross fiscal deficit of the states was 4.4% of GDP in 2001/02, or about Rs1,183 billion. Subtracting from this the actual subsidy paid by the states to SEBs of Rs83 billion gives a fiscal deficit net of the subsidy of Rs1,100 billion. This means that if the total losses of SEBs were consolidated with the fiscal deficits of the states, these would rise on average by 30%. Given the low actual subsidy received, SEBs have been defaulting on their payments to central government agencies (suppliers and lenders) to finance a part of these losses. Bond issues by SEBs guaranteed by the state governments, rapidly adding to the contingent fiscal liabilities of the states, are another source of financing (CRISIL 2002). SEBs have also been "borrowing" from their employees by running arrears on related pension and provident fund obligations. They have thus been unable to maintain their assets.

SEB operations also entail significant transmission and distribution losses (technical and commercial losses as well as theft), in some states as high as 40-50%. Owing to poor collections, outstanding receivables of various state utilities grew from Rs145 billion in 1996/97 to Rs248 billion in 1999/2000. Tariffs covered only 68% of the cost of supply in 2001/02. There is also high dispersion in tariffs, with commercial and industrial users cross-subsidizing agricultural and domestic consumers and being charged rates far in excess of the cost of supply. Given the poor quality of supply, many manufacturing companies install their own generators. Moreover, recent studies show that subsidies are regressive. The poor benefit little from subsidized electricity, both in urban and rural areas, providing little justification for continued subsidies to consumers (World Bank 2001b, 2002j).

The financial and social case for reform is clear, as are the essential elements. Average tariffs need to be raised to reflect cost of supply. Universal metering of consumption is required, especially for agricultural and domestic consumers. Payments discipline needs to be enforced. And a targeted subsidy scheme needs to be introduced for poor households and farmers so that the cross-subsidy burden on industrial and commercial users can be eliminated. It is also accepted that there will be greater incentive to sustain reform with the privatization of the distribution business.

But political will has often been found wanting, especially for raising tariffs for farmers, or for implementing better governance. The fundamental problems affecting the sector stem from the apparent unwillingness of the state and central governments to allow the sector to function along commercial and economic lines. The Government of India has recently initiated a few potentially decisive steps to give stronger incentives to states for reforming their power sectors. For these to work, privatization of distribution, stronger action on tariffs, better governance, and financial restructuring are needed.

Parliament has passed a new Electricity Act, and the Ministry of Finance has instituted the Accelerated Power Development and Reform Program (APDRP) in support of power reforms. Other measures include the work of the Deepak Parekh Committee on state-specific reforms and decisions to have independent agencies rate SEBs. The Ahluwalia Committee had recommended that the past-due arrears of SEBs to central government agencies-Rs415 billion at the end of February 2001-be compensated by bonds issued by the respective state governments, guaranteed by the Government of India and carrying a tax-free interest rate of 8.5% a year.[26] For this, a tripartite agreement involving the Reserve Bank of India, state governments, and

---

[25] India, Planning Commission (2002a). The actual financial loss is even greater because of collection problems.

[26] Report of the Expert Group, Settlement of SEB Dues, May 2001.

the Ministry of Power was signed in March 2003. Under the agreement, state governments have also agreed that in case of SEB default on payments of bills to central agencies, the Reserve Bank of India would deduct at source a corresponding amount due to the states. While initial signs are encouraging, the effectiveness of this agreement in imposing a hard budget constraint on states, and thereby providing a stronger incentive for reform, will depend on its continued enforcement by the Government of India. The APDRP could be another effective step. But if the scheme is to provide incentives to states for reform, it needs to clearly link assistance strictly to tangible and irreversible measures for reversing SEB losses and improving governance. Without such a link, the APDRP may weaken the resolve to reform.

Financial Policy

Since 1992/93 varying but relatively small sums have been spent to assist nationalized banks, regional rural banks, Unit Trust of India, Industrial Development Bank of India, and Industrial Financial Corporation of India-with another 0.8% of 2002/03 GDP identified to help the latter three. The banks' reported gross nonperforming loans were 10.4% of all loans in March 2002. Net of provisions the figure was 5.5%. And net nonperforming loans as a percent of assets were 2.3% or about 1.5% of GDP. Some financial analysts have suggested that nonperforming loans are substantially understated by various "evergreening" methods, but a doubling of the gross figure would put net nonperforming loans at less than 7% of bank assets, or about 4.5% of GDP. Another indicator of risk-lending for stocks, real estate, and commodities-is less than 4% of lending.

Off-balance sheet operations are equal to nearly 60% of the balance sheet, but three-fourths of them are forward exchange contracts (half by the foreign banks) mostly related to exports and imports and often with, the Reserve Bank of India as the counterparty.[27] These numbers are low in comparison with East Asia and China. But this has to be looked at in the context of public sector debt above 90% of GDP in an environment of worsening government debt dynamics.

There are two key reform issues. The first is enhancing the role of the financial system in efficient resource allocation. The second is minimizing risks. The first is closely related to the fiscal stance. As long as deficits are high, a high proportion of bank assets will be invested in government debt. As of March 2002, about 28% of bank assets were invested in government debt and another 5.6% was with the Reserve Bank of India. Indian banks have one of the highest ratios of government debt to deposits in the world, similar to Latin American countries and much higher than most East Asian comparators, even after the crisis. A fiscal adjustment would clearly help-it would also relieve crowding out.

Measures are also needed to contain risk and manage nonperforming assets. In this connection, the new Securitisation and Reconstruction of Financial Assets and Enforcement of Security Interest Act (2002), which allows banks to take over collateral more easily, could push debtors to pay up. Similarly, establishment of credit information bureaus should help in sharing information on credit risk, which would lower transaction costs while helping to control nonperforming loans. It would particularly help small and medium-scale enterprises, which suffer from very high real lending rates owing to the perception of high risk (Mohan 2003).

One relevant topic is interest rate risk. Financial institutions that have invested in long-term government paper made large trading profits as

---

[27] While not a serious issue today, this could potentially encumber Reserve Bank of India reserves, so it bears monitoring.

interest rates fell, but these financial institutions now face the possibility of rising interest rates. To counter this, the Reserve Bank of India has issued a directive on creating an investment fluctuation reserve.

Insurance and provident funds, heavily invested in government debt, will face losses as interest rates rise. Moreover, state provident funds have also invested in special purpose vehicles guaranteed by the state. Many of these assets are now no longer earning interest, making the performance of the state provident funds even more dependent on debt servicing by cash-starved states, now that the guarantees are beginning to be called. The ability of these provident funds to meet their obligations is likely to affect public confidence in government debt issues more broadly. The administratively set returns on the provident funds are significantly above market rates-encouraging management to engage in risky investments in the nonregulated part of their portfolio. This policy also generates potential contingent liabilities for the central and state governments along the lines of Unit Trust of India. Linking rates on the provident fund more closely to the market, and reducing the role of administratively fixed rates, would help control the continuing buildup of these problems. A similar link to rates on small savings would reduce interest costs for states.

Guarantees. The contingent liabilities stemming from borrowings of parastatals guaranteed by state governments are a critical issue. According to a recent study, such guarantees have risen sharply since 1996, mostly in connection with borrowings by SEBs and special purpose vehicles established in connection with large irrigation projects. It is estimated that of the market borrowings by state entities guaranteed between 1995 and 2002, Rs440 billion will be called over the next five years (CRISIL 2002). This may not seem much, but the estimate excludes guaranteed loans from the National Bank for Agriculture and Rural Development, the Housing and Urban Development Corporation, the Life Insurance Corporation, the National Cooperative Development Council, the Rural Electrification Corporation, public sector banks, and regional rural banks. Moreover, the guarantors-the state governments-are already heavily indebted. Not surprisingly, the spread on state guaranteed bonds relative to central government securities widened from 2-2.5% in 2000 to more than 4% in 2002.

Another problem is that even when state-guaranteed bonds are not being serviced, creditors do not treat them as nonperforming assets unless the guarantee is invoked and payment is not received for two quarters. There is reluctance to invoke guarantees, so defaults remain hidden, adding to the uncertainty and instability. Given the extensive list of creditors, a default would hurt the integrity and credibility of public institutions. Containing the problem requires a need for a clear and transparent framework for guarantees. One idea is to create a guarantee redemption fund (RBI 2003e). But given the fiscal constraints, finding resources for the fund would not be easy. And the fund would work only if fundamental problems in power and irrigation are corrected.

Fiscal Management

There is growing recognition that fiscal institutions need to be strengthened. This will require changes at the center, in the states, and in center-state fiscal relations. The central government needs to lead by example, getting its own house in order and providing the right incentives for fiscal adjustment at the state level. And it needs to give states enough flexibility to use their limited resources efficiently.

Legislating for fiscal prudence. The Fiscal Responsibility and Budget Management Bill, passed by the Lok Sabha (lower house of parliament) in early 2003, mandates the elimination of the center's revenue deficit by March 2008. The bill pertains only to the central government, but three states-Karnataka, Punjab, and Tamil Nadu-have so far passed similar acts to limit their own deficits. And others are following suit. The proof of the usefulness of these pieces of legislation will be progress toward their fiscal goals. A useful feature of the acts is the requirement that the central and concerned state governments annually publish multiyear fiscal strategies-developing time-bound road maps for restoring fiscal sustainability and publicly monitoring progress. If carefully implemented, this could enhance the credibility of India's fiscal policy.

State borrowing. While states ultimately have to be responsible for their own fiscal adjustment, reforming the borrowing regime they operate in ("hardening their budget constraints") will also help induce fiscal reform. Global borrowing caps should be introduced and enforced by the Government of India, using powers under Article 293 of the Constitution. The caps should cover both on-budget borrowing and off-budget borrowing through state-level public enterprises and special purpose vehicles, whose debt-servicing becomes a contingent liability in the budget. In return for much tighter control by the Government of India over the annual quantum of borrowing, states could be given much greater freedom over how they arrange that borrowing. States should be allowed to borrow responsibly from the markets within their global cap. And borrowing from captive sources-small savings, negotiated loans, and Government of India loans-should be phased out. If necessary, a safety net can be provided for uncreditworthy borrowers.

Performance and reform-based transfers. The volume of center-to-state transfers linked to reform and performance needs to be expanded. The creation of the Fiscal Reforms Facility, recommended by the Eleventh Finance Commission, and the APDRP for the power sector are steps in the right direction. The Fiscal Reform Facility provides grant funding for states that reduce their revenue deficit as a ratio of revenue receipts.

Although the funding attached to the Fiscal Reform Facility is small given its universal coverage (only 2% of all transfers to the states), it has had a significant impact. First, it has required states to draw up "Medium Term Fiscal Restructuring Plans" which, for the first time, have placed fiscal policy at the state-level in a medium-term strategic framework. Second, the borrowing levels agreed under the plans have started to take on the nature of global borrowing caps. They have thus helped the Government of India to start to discipline state borrowing in an environment characterized by multiple borrowing windows. (Less progress has been made in preventing states from circumventing central controls on budget borrowing through use of off-budget special purpose vehicles. Orders issued by the Government of India and the Reserve Bank of India seem to have had little impact on this.) In 2002/03, the Fiscal Reform Facility also started to provide authorization for qualifying states to borrow additional funds from the market.

Multilateral agencies also provide financing to reforming states through the Government of India. It would be useful for assistance to fiscal reformers to be passed on not as loans but as grants, both to increase the incentives for reform and to help such states reduce their debt burden. Public reporting of access by various states to reform facilities-and of reasons for both access and denial to access-will help ensure transparency and consistency.

Measures to simplify expenditure management. India's five-year plans help provide a strategic framework for development efforts, but the division of budgetary resources into "plan" and "nonplan" is counterproductive. It adds complexity to the budgeting-and perpetuates a perception that plan spending is always better than nonplan and should always be increased. Militating against fiscal correction, this leads to chronic underfunding of maintenance (nonplan) relative to capital spending (plan). Unfortunately, substantial government assistance is provided for state plan spending, making elimination of the plan-nonplan distinction at the state level a complex and unpopular proposition. But the Government of India could take the lead by abolishing the distinction at the central level. It could also propose to states that its financial support to them be delinked from their annual plans. Funding currently provided as plan support would be provided on the basis of an agreed and explicit set of criteria-which initially could be based on those currently in place-but could be termed "development support" rather than "plan support." Any such move would require consensus among states to succeed. The government could help build this support by announcing that the move would enable funding for nonplan areas, such as maintenance.

Centrally sponsored schemes are provided by the Government of India to the states, largely (though not entirely) as grants, for achieving such national goals as poverty alleviation and universal enrollment. But the schemes have tended to proliferate, and there are now more than 300, leading to budgetary rigidity and poor implementation at the state level. A practical solution would be to consolidate the schemes into a smaller number of programs, with a minimum size, and to give the states flexibility to run them in accord with their needs and priorities. Some central ministries have already moved in this direction by adopting a cafeteria approach: a cluster of schemes is clubbed together under one umbrella, and the selection of individual schemes from this cluster is left to the states.

Government Debt Projections: Why Fiscal Adjustment?

The case for fiscal adjustment is illustrated by general government debt projections to the end of the Tenth Plan period, 2006/07, under a base case scenario of "no reform" versus a "reform" scenario. In both scenarios, the debt trajectory is driven mainly by the primary (noninterest) fiscal deficit-because based on actual developments in recent years, interest rates are unlikely to be substantially below growth rates without an undesirable reversion to financial repression. But given the extraordinarily low interest rates in today's weak global economy, it is assumed that real interest rates remain below the growth rate for a year or two, depending on the scenario (even though, as noted above, the average interest rate on government debt has been close to or above the growth rate for the past four years).

Two other factors deserve emphasis. Extrapolating from current trends, the pressure to fully absorb SEB losses into state fiscal deficits will grow, effectively raising the general government primary deficit by this amount. And it would be prudent to assume that guarantees-12% of GDP in 2002/03, generally in support of loss-making enterprises-will devolve at the rate of 1% of GDP per year over the projection horizon.[28]

If the goal is to stabilize or reduce the debt-to-GDP ratio, generating primary fiscal surpluses is a must. So the focus of reform will have to be on cutting the primary deficit and raising growth. Moreover, it is envisaged that the cut in the primary deficit will be achieved without reducing capital expenditure. Cuts in the primary deficit will thus automatically mean cuts in the revenue deficit, improving the quality of public spending. But the net impact on the revenue deficit will also depend on the path of interest payments.[29] For fiscal measures, revenue mobilization needs to be given

---

[28] Note that this assumption pertains only to the existing stock of guarantees, and does not take account of any new guarantees which may be issued after 2002/03.

[29] The Government of India has initiated debt swaps and prepayment of external debt in order to reduce interest payments. However, these measures are unlikely to be a substitute for a fundamental fiscal adjustment.

Box 2.1. Assumptions Underlying the Debt/Deficit Projections

✦ The initial level of general government debt is 85.6% of GDP, its level at the end of 2002/03 (including about 0.8% of GDP proposed for bailouts in connection with Unit Trust of India, the Industrial Development Bank of India, and the Industrial Financing Corporation of India).

✦ The primary deficit of the general government stays at 3.5% of GDP in the base case, a little below its average level over the past six years.[30] In the reform scenario, the primary deficit goes down linearly from 3.5% of GDP to 0.7% by the last year. This comes from raising central government revenue by 1.7 percentage points and state revenues by 0.7 percentage points by the terminal year, as envisaged in the Tenth Plan document, and from eliminating the petroleum subsidy of 0.4% of GDP. It is assumed that taxes rise as a result of eliminating exemptions, widening the tax net to include services, and implementing the state value-added tax.

✦ Food and fertilizer subsidies amount to about 1.4% of GDP. Under reforms, 0.5% of GDP is maintained as a minimum social safety net; the balance of 0.9% is phased out while productivity-enhancing investments in agriculture, such as rural infrastructure and research and extension, increase by the same amount. There is no change in the base case.

✦ SEB losses in the base case remain 1.5% of GDP and in the reform scenario go linearly to zero by the terminal year as a result of aggressive power sector reforms.

✦ Divestment receipts remain 0.5% of GDP in both scenarios.

✦ Guarantees (contingent liabilities) accumulated by the end of 2002/03 devolve at the rate of 1% of GDP per year in both scenarios.

✦ Growth, real interest rates, and inflation (%) are as follows:[31]

	2003/04	2004/05	2005/06	2006/07
Growth (base)	5.5	5.0	5.0	5.0
Real interest rate (base)	4.0	5.0	5.5	5.5
Inflation (base)	5.5	5.0	5.0	5.0
Growth (reform)	5.5	7.0	7.5	8.0
Real interest rate (reform)	4.0	6.5	7.5	8.0
Inflation (reform)	5.0	3.5	3.5	3.5

Source: World Bank staff estimates.

top priority, because revenues are low and debt is high while spending is roughly in line with other countries (IMF 2002).

The major policy levers flowing out of the preceding analysis are raising tax revenues, reducing SEB losses, and eliminating the

---

[30] The primary deficit incorporates a portion of seigniorage in the form of Reserve Bank of India profits and dividends, which enter nontax revenue.

[31] The 8% Tenth Plan target would imply a growth rate of 8.9% per year over the remaining years of the Tenth Plan period, which seems unattainable at this point. The base case assumes a compound average growth rate of 5% during the Tenth Plan period-the reform scenario, 6.5%, reaching 8% in the terminal year.

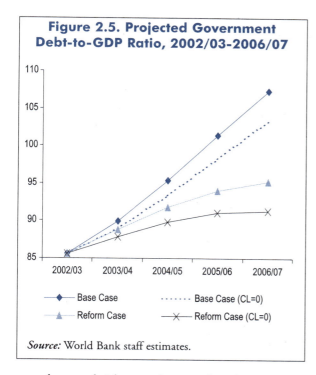

Figure 2.5. Projected Government Debt-to-GDP Ratio, 2002/03–2006/07

Source: World Bank staff estimates.

In the base case, general government fiscal deficits rise steadily to 13% of GDP, as one would expect with primary deficits at 3.5% of GDP, debt exceeding 100% of GDP, and nominal interest rates of some 10% (figure 2.6). With reforms, deficits remain in the 10% of GDP range because of the drag from the high debt stock and the impact of rising interest rates as growth picks up; deficits will decline slowly as debt levels are brought under control.[32] The only sure way to bring about a faster decline is to achieve primary fiscal surpluses. In these scenarios, the calling of guarantees is ignored in projecting debt levels and hence interest payments. While SEB losses are factored into the projection of debt levels and interest payments, they are not included in the deficits shown for comparability with present deficit reporting practices. So the "true" picture especially under the base case is likely to be worse

petroleum subsidy, supplemented with structural reforms to spur growth. The base case assumes that fiscal and structural reforms will proceed slowly or not at all. The reform scenario assumes a systematic plan to implement the needed fiscal and structural reforms over the Tenth Plan period (box 2.1).

In the base case, the general government debt-to-GDP ratio reaches 107% by the end of the Tenth Plan period (figure 2.5). In the reform scenario, it reaches 95%. These results are being driven by the general government primary deficit, SEB losses, and the calling of guarantees-underlining the need for implementing fiscal and structural reforms. The broken lines are debt-to-GDP excluding contingent liabilities, which would lower the debt-to-GDP ratio to 103% by 2006/07 in the base case and 91% in the reform scenario.

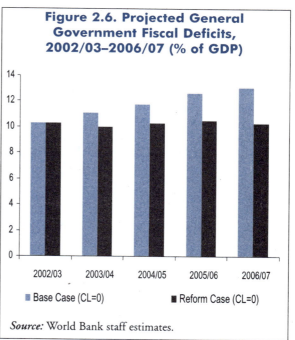

Figure 2.6. Projected General Government Fiscal Deficits, 2002/03–2006/07 (% of GDP)

Source: World Bank staff estimates.

---

[32] The deficit projections here, which are repeated in table 2.7, are substantially higher than those reported in table 2.5 based on the macroeconomic framework for the Tenth Plan. The reason is that table 2.5 is formulated on the basis on either achieving debt sustainability (at a minimum) or the growth target of 8% a year (much more difficult); in this sense, it embodies an ideal outcome. By contrast, the projections in figure 2.5 and table 2.7 are more in the spirit of a probable outcome given conditions at the end of 2002/03 and the scenarios specified in box 2.1.

than depicted unless power sector losses are aggressively eliminated.

What is the potential for a more efficient composition of public spending under reform? There is not much difference in interest payments between the two scenarios-because of the high level of initial debt, the absence of primary fiscal surpluses even in the reform scenario, and similar levels of nominal interest rates. But the reform scenario permits significantly higher "other spending" (defined as total spending minus subsidies and interest) by the end of the Tenth Plan period (table 2.7). The increase in revenues (2.4 percentage points of GDP), the elimination of petroleum subsidy (0.4 percentage points), and the reduction in food and fertilizer subsidies (0.9 percentage points) will reduce the general government revenue deficit by close to 4 percentage points of GDP. But interest payments are projected to rise by about 3 percentage points-from 6.5% of GDP in the first year of the Tenth Plan to about 9.5% of GDP by the terminal year, 2006/07. So the net reduction in the revenue deficit will only be about 1 percentage point of GDP. But

the quality of spending will have vastly improved.

Three points emerge. First, it is not going to be easy to eliminate revenue deficits by 2007/08. Further, the focus must be on raising revenues, cutting subsidies, and controlling salaries-that is, on the noninterest component of the revenue deficit, because there is little or no control over interest payments. In the same vein, it may be necessary to lay down intermediate targets by specific budgetary category in the medium-term fiscal frameworks required by the central and state-level Fiscal Responsibility Acts. Second, even under a reform scenario, the government debt burden will continue to be heavy in the medium term. And third, without reform, the debt burden and ratio of interest payments to revenues will increase quickly, fueling inflationary expectations and eventually higher inflation. Private investment will be dampened if the private sector feels it is going to be taxed to service the debt, leading to anemic growth.

To conclude, a program of progressive and phased fiscal adjustment must be a cornerstone of the

Table 2.7. Fiscal Projections, Base Case and Reform Case, 2003/04-2006/07 (% of GDP)

Item	2003/04	2004/05	2005/06	2006/07	2003/04	2004/05	2005/06	2006/07
		Base	case			Reform	case	
Primary deficit	3.5	3.5	3.5	3.5	2.8	2.1	1.4	0.7
Interest payments	7.6	8.3	9.1	9.6	7.2	8.1	9.1	9.6
Fiscal deficit	11.1	11.8	12.6	13.1	10.0	10.2	10.5	10.3
Revenues	17.5	17.5	17.5	17.5	18.1	18.7	19.3	19.9
Total spending	28.6	29.3	30.1	30.6	28.1	28.9	29.8	30.2
Subsidies	1.8	1.8	1.8	1.8	1.5	1.2	0.9	0.5
Other spending	19.2	19.2	19.2	19.2	19.4	19.6	19.8	20.1
Interest/revenue (%)	43.3	47.2	51.9	54.7	39.8	43.6	47.1	48.2

Source: World Bank staff estimates.

Government of India's attempts to spur poverty-reducing growth and avoid an unsustainable path for public debt. Even in a reform scenario, the general government fiscal deficit is likely to remain in the 10% range over the next few years. But with primary deficits more or less eliminated by the end of the Tenth Plan period, the deficit should later decline as debt levels and interest payments are brought under control. The focus needs to be on tax reform and eliminating SEB losses. The reallocation of food and fertilizer subsidies-amounting to about 1% of GDP towards rural infrastructure and agricultural R&E, while maintaining 0.5% of GDP as a minimum food social safety net-will raise development spending without a negative fiscal effect.

Fortunately, India is not facing an imminent macroeconomic crisis of the type in Argentina or Russia. But it is paying a heavy price in growth and welfare for its current fiscal stance. On the positive side, India has the time to put in place an orderly fiscal adjustment over the Tenth Plan period. And in the absence of an impending crisis, it is hard to develop the political momentum for reform. Indeed, in some key areas, such as the power sector, there are strong political and vested interests against reform. India has recognized the need for fiscal adjustment in the Tenth Plan and in recent legislation. The challenge now is for the Government of India and the states to translate this commitment into an overall road map and into specific policies for fiscal consolidation. The payoff in freeing up resources for priority public programs and improving the climate for private investment will be well worth the effort.

CHAPTER 3

DELIVERY OF PUBLIC SERVICES

Sustained growth may be the most powerful driver of poverty reduction, but investments in human development are also essential. Health and education are the most important assets of the poor, allowing them to both contribute to and benefit from growth through higher-paying employment. And, when incomes fall below minimum standards, the poor and vulnerable need access to effective safety nets.

Delivering adequate social services requires increasing their level, but more important it requires improving the quality of expenditures-by improving the governance and productivity of India's civil service at the center, state, and local levels. In many of India's poorest states, such as Bihar and Uttar Pradesh, the private sector delivers health and education services to a large share of the population, including the poor. So improving service delivery also requires an appropriate regulatory framework for private contributions in health and education.

How, then, to improve the performance of the civil service and the quality of public service delivery? Critically important are reforms to improve the transparency, accountability, and independence of the civil service. Several states are already implementing innovative reforms in delivery of public services, often with the aid of information technology. The challenge is to broaden these initiatives and apply them across the country, including the poorer states, where the governance environment is weak. To achieve the targets in the Tenth Plan and the Millennium Development Goals, both the public and private sectors will have to be harnessed, with careful monitoring of progress along the way.

Civil Service Reform

Size and Structure of the Civil Service

In aggregate numbers, India's civil service is not particularly overstaffed when compared with other countries. Central government civilian employment is around 3.4 million, state employment is around six million, and another four million or so teachers and health workers work in government and grant-in-aid institutions. That puts India's civil service employment at around 1.4% of the population. Although international comparisons can be tricky, the average for Asia in the 1990s was around 2.6%, and for OECD countries 7.7%.

Even though India's civil service is not unduly large by global standards, there is a pronounced imbalance in the skills mix. Around 93% of the civil service comprises Class III and IV employees for both the Government of India and various state governments. Class III encompasses frontline delivery workers, but also includes a large number of office staff (clerks and typists) whose functions are rapidly being made redundant by advances in information technology. Class IV employees function entirely in a support role (peons, sweepers, messengers, watchmen), and most could be let go without any discernible impact on the functioning of the Government. This overabundance of support and logistical personnel often exists alongside chronic shortages of skilled staff in rural schools and health clinics.

Changes in the skills mix need to be accompanied by measures to reduce administrative fragmentation. Within the Government and in many states, the number of ministers, ministries, and departments has proliferated far beyond any rational assignment of functions. The number of cabinet ministers for OECD countries has come down in recent years to an average of 14. The Government of India has 31 cabinet ministers and another 45 ministers of state. Most Indian states have between 35-40 cabinet departments, and some states (Uttar Pradesh) have more than 70.

Compounding the problem are relatively weak mechanisms for policy coordination in many states, since most departments report directly through their minister. Nor does fragmentation end with administrative structures. Budget heads are not always closely aligned with departments. The civil service is divided into dozens of cadres, each with its own service, terms, and conditions, with controlling authorities widely disbursed throughout the various departments. Rigid terms and conditions make it difficult to transfer staff to cadres where they could be better used. Institutional reforms are thus needed to reduce the administrative fragmentation and align the structure of the civil service more closely with modern day functions.

Costs of the Civil Service

The Fifth Pay Commission has been called "the single largest adverse shock to India's strained public finances in the last decade" and an act of "fiscal profligacy" without parallel (Godbole 1997; Acharya 2001). The compensation paid to civil servants (here defined as salaries and dearness allowance) rose by around 40% between 1996/97 and 1997/98. Over the 1990s, the Government of India's wage bill rose by an average nominal rate of 14.3% a year, substantially higher than the 9.5% average increase in the Consumer Price Index.

The situation in the states is even more dire (table 3.1). In a sample of states, a mixture of the richer southern states and poorer northern ones, the wage bill increased on average by nearly 1% of state GDP between 1996/97 and 1998/99. Orissa is extreme but not atypical. In the 1990s, its salary and pension obligations increased 4.7 times, while revenues increased approximately threefold. By 1999/2000 more than 180% of Orissa's own source revenues were going to cover salary and pension expenses.

Wages for selected categories of staff are consistently higher than they could expect to make in the private sector, with premiums ranging from 27% for engineering technicians to 145% for low-end service workers (table 3.2). For teachers, the premium is around 100%.[33] So, even before the recent salary increases, the vast majority of Indian civil servants were already better compensated than other employees-explaining the low attrition rates

Table 3.1. Ratio of Civil Service Salary and Dearness Allowance to GDP, Government of India and Selected States, 1995/96-2000/01 (%)

Region	1995/96	1996/97	1997/98	1998/99	1999/2000	2000/01
Government of India	1.3	1.2	1.6	1.5	1.5	1.4
Andhra Pradesh	4.8	4.3	5.0	4.7	5.4	5.5
Karnataka	n.a.	n.a.	4.9	4.5	4.8	4.4
Orissa	7.0	8.3	7.6	9.1	9.2	8.6
Rajasthan	n.a.	6.8	7.0	8.6	8.2	7.9
Uttar Pradesh	5.6	5.4	6.2	6.1	5.9	6.0

Note: Government of India data on salaries is based on salaries for sanctioned strength of central government employees.

Sources: India, Ministry of Finance budget documents; Central Statistical Organization.

---

[33] International comparisons of average primary school teacher salaries to per capita GDP indicate a ratio of around 5 to 1 in India, compared with 1.7 to 1 in a sample of 39 Asian countries between 1970 and 1990. See Nelson (1994) pp. 111-127.

Table 3.2. Ratio of Average Wages in the Public and Private Sector, Selected Categories of Employment, 1993/94 and 1999/2000

Occupation[a]	1993/94	1999/2000
Professional, technicians, and related workers	1.52	1.72
Engineers	1.07	1.34
Engineering technicians	1.30	1.27
Physicians and surgeons	1.65	2.00
Nurses	2.00	2.00
Teachers	1.75	2.02
Administrative, executive, and managerial workers	1.26	1.42
Clerical and related workers	1.60	1.74
Stenographers and typists	1.69	2.14
General clerks (receptionists, office attendants)	1.54	1.72
Service workers	2.25	2.45
Sweepers, cleaners, and building caretakers	1.79	1.93
All	1.92	2.33

a.   ILO 1968, based on National Classification of Occupations.

Source: World Bank forthcoming, "Wage Differentials Between the Public and Private Sectors in India."

throughout the public sector even for highly skilled positions.

Recent experience suggests that it may be wise to hold off on holding periodic pay commissions, which provide impetus for substantial wage increases. Instead, the central and state governments could opt for limited annual wage increases, or even pursue a freeze for 2-3 years, followed by a limited relaxation for skilled positions. Or, as recommended by the Fifth Pay Commission, the process of constituting commissions every ten years could be abandoned in favor of a permanent pay commission, which could continually analyze and make recommendations for appropriate compensation in consultation with the states. Whatever the system adopted, more emphasis needs to go to local market comparators (particularly those involving the private sector) in determining salary levels. Efforts to rationalize the number of cadres and review the classification of posts would also improve managerial flexibility and consistency between various categories of employees.

The costs of the civil service are raised further by burgeoning pension liabilities. At the center, pension spending for civil servants increased dramatically in the 1990s, with average yearly growth surpassing 20%, to reach 1% of GDP. And in Uttar Pradesh the ratio of pension spending to state GDP increased from 0.4% to 1.2% in the 1990s. Pension expenditures for the center and the states are likely to keep on growing at a fast pace, especially for states, where employment more than doubled over the past 30 years. Preliminary estimates conducted in 2001 using the World Bank Pension Reform Options Toolkit actuarial model suggest that the present value of central and state pension liabilities could amount to 25% of GDP.

In the light of rising pension liabilities, the Government announced in February 2003 a plan to establish a fully funded defined contribution scheme for new civil servants. Individuals will be able to choose from a limited number of prequalified private asset managers and one public asset manager. The system will be centrally administered to reduce costs. A new specialized pension regulatory agency will be created to supervise the new scheme.[34] The shift to a fully funded defined contribution scheme will force the payment of pension liabilities as they accrue-more transparent and more financially viable.

Critical design issues are still to be defined, including the contribution rate, the criteria for selecting private asset managers, and the structure of the public asset manager to minimize governance problems. The implementation plan will also have to be carefully devised to minimize risks, and a strong and effective regulatory agency will have to be established. Since this reform will apply to new civil servants, primarily younger workers, it will contain pension costs only over the longer term. Indeed, in the short to medium term, fiscal outlays may rise, as the Government has to meet the combined costs of the old and new schemes. Better measurement of the pension liabilities of current civil servants would likely point to unsustainability and the need for further reforms, including changes in eligibility criteria and a possible shift of younger civil servants (on a voluntary or mandatory basis) to the new defined contribution plan.

The proposed defined contribution scheme for civil servants constitutes the first attempt to address the problems besetting the pension system in India. The reform faces the dual challenges of establishing a sound, well-regulated funded pension system for new federal civil servants and, more importantly, motivating further and deeper reforms within the rest of India's pension system. The new scheme should serve as a model for the states to reform their own pension plans. Some states (such as Tamil Nadu) are already contemplating similar changes for new entrants.

Once implemented at the central level, the Government also intends to expand the new scheme to the unorganized private sector, which remains uncovered by formal pension plans. While laudable, it is likely that coverage of the unorganized sector will expand only gradually based on other international experiences.[35] This raises questions about the viability of the new scheme unless it is able to attract a wider group of workers, including private sector employees participating in the Employee Provident Fund (EPF) and the Employee Pension Scheme (EPS). At a minimum, the reform could allow new workers in the private sector to join the new scheme and allow others to opt out of the EPF and EPS.[36] The success of this reform could well set a benchmark for deeper changes in the EPF and EPS over the medium term.

The Return on Civil Service Expenditures

While the odd success story may be found, the recent wage gains generally were not compensated by any commensurate increase in the overall quantity or quality of government services. Indeed, the mandate of India's public

---

[34] Its regulatory authority will not cover existing pension plans. The Employee Provident Fund, the Employee Pension Scheme, and occupational plans will remain unsupervised despite performance concerns.

[35] Inadequate coverage of the formal pension schemes also threatens to increase poverty among the elderly as informal arrangements become more strained. This raises the need to better target social assistance for the elderly poor.

[36] There are also concerns about poor investment practices of occupational pension schemes (in particular, self-lending to the sponsoring enterprises and related parties). Asset management under occupational pension plans could now be transferred to asset managers under the new scheme.

service has been shrinking, as governments withdraw from direct involvement in economic production and focus more on a regulatory and facilitative role for private sector growth.

Qualitative improvements have often relied heavily on the application of information technology to streamline and re-engineer business processes, such as the Bhoomi program for registering property records in Karnataka or the e-Seva "one stop shops" for more than 40 government services in Andhra Pradesh. Even when information technology has made many functions redundant, civil servants and powerful unions have extracted pledges of "no job losses" as the price for allowing the innovations to go forward, thus limiting the economies and efficiency gains to be reaped. One southern Indian state, for example, computerized part of its stamps and registration function. The result: faster client service and a reduction in turnaround times by nearly half. By some estimates, as many as 48% of the department's staff of approximately 3,200 were made redundant by this decision, yet they are retained on the state payroll at an estimated cost of more than $3 million a year.

Experience varies, but both the center and the states have on average resisted pressure for new recruitment in much of the 1990s and beyond. But even the best performers have yet to embark on a significant program of staff reduction. As a result, many line departments find themselves in a more precarious position, with a growing proportion of their nonplan resources taken up by salaries, over which they have very limited control. For example, in the Andhra Pradesh Department of Stamps and Registration, only about 16% of nonplan resources went to nonwage funding from 1995/96 to 1999/2000. Other critical departments in Andhra Pradesh, such as those looking after primary education, spent 93% of their noncapital budget on salaries

in this period-to the detriment of spending on training and learning materials, maintenance, and scholarships. Because it is difficult to shed labor or adjust personnel inputs, the burden of any shocks falls disproportionately on nonwage expenditures, making rational planning almost impossible.

Another fundamental problem haunting India's civil service is the failure to use staff productively. In Uttar Pradesh, for example, the Public Works Department has a total strength of 77,000, including roughly 9,000 technical staff, 12,000 administrative staff, and 56,000 gang laborers. With 51 laborers for every 100 kilometers of road, it has one of the highest manual staffing ratios in India, and market manual wage rates are about a third of Public Works Department rates. As a result, the cost of keeping this gang labor force is substantial-in 1998/99, the actual expenditure on maintenance was Rs2.8 billion, while establishment costs were Rs3.4 billion. As discussed below, absenteeism among frontline workers is often appalling, with few sanctioned or dismissed from service despite chronic violations.

The burden of weak administration falls particularly on the poor, who suffer from skewed government spending, limited access to services, and employee indifference. One assessment of spending for health and nutrition in northern India revealed that of every Rs100 of expenditure, the poorest 20% of households received about Rs10, whereas the richest 20% received Rs41 (World Bank 2002a). In rural areas, only 4% of the poorest households had access to electricity and 25% had access to drinking water, compared with 28% and 66% for the richest. Innovative survey research by the Public Affairs Center in Delhi and Bangalore reveals that the average slum dweller needed to make six trips to a government agency to resolve a problem, while the number of trips among general households was four

(Paul and Shekhar 1999; Shekhar and Balakrishnan 1999). The rate of success was more than four times higher for general households-averaging 27%, compared with only about 6% for slum dwellers.

Improving Public Service Delivery

There are many reasons for the poor quality of public service delivery in India. Internally, administrative structures and responsibilities are highly fragmented, while human resource management places more weight on seniority than merit. It will obviously take time to reform these long-standing structures and systems. But experience throughout India shows that civil servants do respond to external pressure for delivery of better services. Three key elements for success:

+ Better public access to information.

+ Stronger accountability.

+ More independence from political interference.

Better access to information. To demand better public services, citizens need to be better informed about service standards, norms, and procedures-and have ready access to forms and other such material. Opening access to information short-circuits the rent-seeking opportunities that secrecy provides. Citizens' charters are one vehicle to empower the public in their dealings with service providers. It is important, however, that such charters be developed in consultation with major stakeholders and widely disseminated. One model is the charter developed by the Greater Mumbai Municipal Corporation in June 1999, with assistance from Praja, an NGO.

NGOs can also do much in collecting raw data, transforming it into usable information, creating databanks that other organizations can tap, and disseminating relevant information to a wider audience through report cards, surveys, and public hearings. In Bangalore, for example, the Public

Affairs Committee conducted a user survey of maternity wards that led to a major restructuring of the service by the Bangalore City Corporation. Other NGOs have concentrated on public interest litigation to prod governments into action to improve the performance in laggard services.

Several states are using information technology to improve access to information. Tamil Nadu has placed all major government orders of public interest on its website. Andhra Pradesh's portal contains extensive information about Government departments, schemes, and policies. It also allows citizens to contact Government officials directly, from the Chief Minister's office on down. And it provides (initially) for limited online transaction processing as well. Computerization is also being used to re-engineer business processes and speed up decision making.

Finally, the center and several states are promoting greater transparency by adopting right to information legislation. Maharashtra provides access to cabinet-level documents (with some narrow exceptions), a public records commission to improve record keeping and cataloguing, an independent appeals process, penalties for noncompliance, and a high-level council to monitor implementation. These initiatives will be followed closely, to see whether they can counter well-entrenched practices and interests within the civil service to limit public access to information.

Stronger accountability. The vast majority of staff at the center and in the state governments are promoted on the basis of seniority and merit. In practice they will be promoted as a matter of course regardless of their performance as long as no adverse remarks are entered against them. Performance evaluation is weak and poorly linked to the system of rewards and promotions. Even more problematic is the failure to punish or weed out corrupt or incompetent officers. The process of sanctioning malfeasance or maladministration is fraught with multiple review and appeals stages, resulting in years of delay. In only a minority of cases are criminal or administrative sanctions imposed.[37] As a result, Indian civil servants have little to motivate them to better performance beyond their innate professional ethic.

The Indian administrative structure was designed in colonial times to facilitate the collection of revenue and preserve law and order. Government reporting relationships are inwardly focused and strongly hierarchical, with the pivotal role played by the district collector and magistrate. At the subdistrict level, all lines of authority flowed upwards to the district collector and magistrates, who in turn reported to superiors in the state capital. While a host of developmental functions have been added since independence, these basic reporting relationships have survived largely unchanged. Recently, reforms have attempted to enhance their "external" accountability and customer orientation. Some states, such as Madhya Pradesh, have sought to empower local communities by allowing them to recruit their own teachers through an Education Guarantee Scheme. Others, such as Janmabhoomi in Andhra Pradesh, regularly bring bureaucrats in contact with local villagers to listen to their concerns.

Independent audits by the Comptroller and Auditor General (CAG) are one of the primary institutional mechanisms for executive accountability. But the CAG mainly focuses on financial irregularities. Some performance appraisals are carried out, but they rarely indicate how management can be strengthened. Discussion of CAG reports by the Public Account

Box 3.1. Karnataka's Ombudsman

The Karnataka Lok Ayukta is probably the strongest of all ombudsman offices in the country. As in Madhya Pradesh, Karnataka has placed the Vigilance Department under the full control of the independent Lok Ayukta, to strengthen his capacity for autonomous action. In addition, the Karnataka Lok Ayukta Act vests the Lok Ayukta with wide statutory powers-from investigating corruption to addressing citizen grievances against any public servant, including the Chief Minister. He also has the right to initiate prosecution directly. Karnataka's Lok Ayukta is appointed for a fixed five-year term by the Chief Minister in consultation with the Speaker of the House, the Leader of the Opposition, and the Chief Justice. Once appointed, he can be removed only for "proven misbehavior" or "incapacity" by the Governor, after a two-thirds majority vote in both chambers of the legislature.

The Lok Ayukta in Karnataka has been very active in investigating corruption in health and education facilities around the state, regularly visiting districts to hear complaints, unearthing large financial scams in Karnataka's city municipal corporations, and raiding regional transport and stamps and registration offices to catch people red-handed. The growing activism of the Lok Ayukta has forced many departments to furnish effective redress to citizens to avoid further investigation and adverse media attention. The growing credibility of the Lok Ayukta as a channel for redressing grievances is reflected in the dramatic increase in complaints in just one year-from 303 in January 2002 to 1,026 in December 2002.

---

[37] In this regard, the comparison of Uttar Pradesh with Hong Kong's Independent Commission Against Corruption (ICAC), arguably the most effective anticorruption agency in Asia, is instructive. The average Hong Kong citizen is 39 times more likely to institute a complaint; the ICAC is more than 240 times more likely to investigate a case during the year in which the complaint is made; and a Hong Kong civil servant is 24 times more likely to be charged with a crime than his or her counterpart in Uttar Pradesh. Furthermore, disciplinary cases in Uttar Pradesh can wind through the courts for as long as 20 years, and a large majority ultimately end in acquittal. (Source: World Bank staff calculations based on annual reports for the Uttar Pradesh Vigilance Department, the Uttar Pradesh Lok Ayukta's Office, and the Hong Kong ICAC, 1997-99.)

Committees of parliament and state assemblies are not open to the public and often come with a long delay, which reduces the prospects for effective follow up. Clearly, audit procedures should be improved. But there should also be wider use of other accountability mechanisms. The Lok Ayukta (Ombudsman) in Karnataka seems to be generating good results and may hold valuable lessons for other states (box 3.1). The success of vigilance and ombudsman functions depends on having enough independence, budget, and staff resources to investigate and prosecute corruption. In addition, a comprehensive anticorruption strategy should include: a radical overhaul and simplification of the procedures for imposing major and minor penalties, expanded "whistleblower" protection, and publication of the property and tax returns of senior officials. Each state should be asked to pass the Corrupt Public Servants (Forfeiture of Property) Act, already drafted by the Law Commission.

More independence from political interference. This topic is sensitive, for the right to transfer civil servants is clearly vested within the political leadership under Article 310 of the Indian Constitution, which maintains that civil servants serve at the "pleasure" of the ruling authorities. Yet few would disagree that both civil servants and politicians often abuse this power-the former in seeking prime postings, the latter for a variety of legitimate and occasionally illegitimate reasons. The result in such states as Uttar Pradesh has been a reduction of average tenure for key senior civil service positions to less than a year. Chronic political instability in Uttar Pradesh and Manipur has led to the frequent collapse of government, leading to new rounds of transfers as the next group of political leaders rewards supporters and puts its "own" staff into place. Compounding this problem: the absence of effective transition mechanisms. Since most reforms in large public organizations require several years to produce results, it is impossible for even the most capable

and well-intentioned manager to implement lasting improvements.

Several approaches have been tried to curb the excess transfers. Karnataka, for example, has a new system of cadre management authorities to approve transfers, posting the number of transfers on a public website. This system has reduced transfers below the 5% norm in most departments. The success of these initiatives should be followed closely and extended to other states as appropriate.

Health, Education, and Social Safety Nets

Official estimates of poverty, literacy, and net enrollment rates have been improving dramatically since the 1980s, but not enough to achieve the targets set in the Tenth Plan or even the less ambitious Millennium Development Goals. Indeed, progress in health indicators has been slowing precipitously. Infant mortality rates of 115 per 1,000 live births in the 1980s fell to 79 in 1992 but only to 68 in 2001. And mortality of children under five appears not to have improved in the 1990s-even worsening (from 94 per 1,000 live births in 1992 to 95 in 2001). Education indicators have continued to improve, but there are still wide disparities across states, gender, and caste in completion of primary education. For example, illiteracy rates for men ages 15-24 have declined from 27% to 20% and for women from 46% to 35%-showing substantial progress in levels and gender differences, but still with some way to go.

The gaps in both mortality and educational status between the poor and nonpoor are striking: the 1998-99 National Family Health Survey indicates differences in child mortality between the poorest and richest deciles of wealth of 100% to 400% across states, with enrollment rates varying by multiples as well (World Bank 1998b, 2002l). For example, the range of under-two mortality rates from the poorest 5% to the richest 5% is from 19% to 4% in Tamil Nadu and from 12% to 6%

in Maharashtra. Similarly, in education, the range of completion rates from the poorest 20% to the richest 20% is from 17% to 78% in Bihar and 44% to 95% in Karnataka. Since mortality rates are quite low and enrollment rates near universal for the better-off, improvements in the average rates needed to reach the Tenth Plan goals cannot be achieved without directly improving the health and education of the poor.

Plausible rates of economic growth alone will be insufficient to reach the Tenth Plan goals. If real GDP were to grow at 6% a year, India and the majority of states would not reduce infant mortality to half of the 1990 rate or achieve full primary enrollment by 2015. Nor can the goals be achieved by simply increasing public expenditures-without complementary measures to improve the effectiveness of public service delivery. This conclusion is corroborated by analyses of the National Family Health Survey: the presence of public health care facilities in a village has no effect on mortality, controlling for income, education, access to good roads, and water supply (World Bank 1998b, 2002l). While the effectiveness of public expenditure in education is better, higher spending alone is still not enough to achieve universal enrollment, let alone universal completion of lower primary education.

Public expenditures on health and education have increased over the past decade. But, because both health and education are labor-intensive, the bulk of this increase has been due to sharp increases in the wages of public service providers, following the Fifth Pay Commission recommendations in 1997. The impact of the Commission's recommendations on spending was somewhat higher in education and health than in other sectors. In some states the wage bill tops 90% of the total costs (figures 3.1 and 3.2). The increase in the wage bill following the Commission decision led to increases in pay rates and not in the numbers of teachers, doctors, or nurses. This widened the gap in pay between public and private doctors and

teachers (though not nurses), with all three professions now receiving twice the private pay while in public service. This spending increase was not likely to improve health or education outcomes-and it didn't.

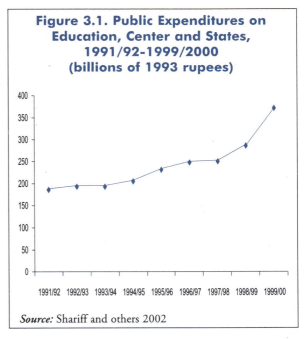

Figure 3.1. Public Expenditures on Education, Center and States, 1991/92-1999/2000 (billions of 1993 rupees)

Source: Shariff and others 2002

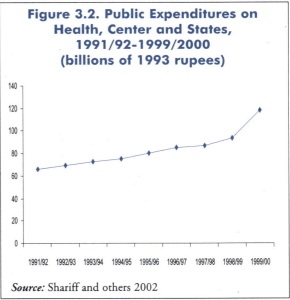

Figure 3.2. Public Expenditures on Health, Center and States, 1991/92-1999/2000 (billions of 1993 rupees)

Source: Shariff and others 2002

The main weakness in the social sectors is in the implementation of good policies. The quality of services needs to improve. As one indication, recent estimates of absentee rates for teachers and medical providers are high, and the problem is generally much worse in poorer states (table 3.3). In Bihar surprise visits to schools indicated that as many as 26% of the teachers were not present-and for medical practitioners, the rates are more than twice that. Since these people are on the payroll, it is not surprising that public money does not translate directly into better outcomes. If vacancy rates (positions unfilled) are included, the bias against poor people is even more pronounced.

These and other indicators of low quality are not lost on the public. Bypassing free public services to use the private sector is common, even among the poor. Data from the National Sample Survey of 1995 indicates that more than half of visits to medical providers by people in the poorest quintile in rural areas are to the private sector. Similarly, the use of private schools is increasing rapidly in general and to some extent among the poor. English-medium schools are seen as a means of upward mobility.

The cause of the implementation problem is that politicians and bureaucrats are not accountable for social outcomes-the health status of the people, the learning by students-and that they do not hold personnel providing the service accountable. Incentives to public providers make no one feel responsible for better or worse outcomes.

+ For systemic reasons the interests of the poor are not reflected in policy decisions for health and education. Influential urban and wealthier constituencies, for example, don't consider reaching remote areas or handling disease problems that mostly affect the poor to be high priorities. Building facilities carries the

Table 3.3. Absentee Rates from Primary Facilities in Selected States, 2003 (%)

State	Primary school teachers	Primary health care workers
Andhra Pradesh	31	n.a.
Assam	31	58
Bihar	26	58
Gujarat	21	52
Haryana	19	35
Karnataka	23	43
Kerala	18	n.a.
Orissa	14	35
Punjab	18	n.a.
Rajasthan	23	39
Tamil Nadu	17	n.a.
Uttar Pradesh	26	42
Uttaranchal	25	45
West Bengal	21	43

n.a.   Reliable data not available.
Source: World Bank forthcoming, World Development Report 2004.

political benefits of being very visible and having opening ceremonies. But basic public health activities-such as hygiene, education, and mosquito control-are not as beneficial to politicians.

+ Policymakers have too few means of influencing the incentives facing service providers. As in civil service reform, the weakness of administration-in this case illustrated by the lack of control over staff behavior-hurts the poor and denies them basic services.

+ The influence of parents and patients on public providers (as in monitoring and sanctioning) is not effective enough to compensate.

+ The intrinsic motivation of providers, while strong, is not sufficient to meet social objectives.

One way to make outcomes more of a motivating factor in service delivery is to generate and disseminate information on progress. Parents and patients should know what they are entitled to and have a place to lodge complaints when they do not receive services. Public officials should know whether the public is satisfied or not. Providers and policymakers should know (and be constantly learning) about what works. This requires outcomes to be more regularly measured and their determinants analyzed.

One critical role of the central government, when states have the primary responsibility for the delivery of publicly funded services, is to be an independent source for this measurement. Initially, measurement of outcomes may just be for information and the sake of openness. Over time, such measures could be used to hold states accountable for improvements-perhaps conditioning fiscal transfers on progress. The increase in expenditures in figures 3.1 and 3.2 did not translate into better social indicators-primarily because the spending was simply an increase in payments for inputs rather than outcomes.

Centrally sponsored schemes could also be made more flexible, and in many cases, as for preventative health care, their functions and funding should be at least partially passed on to the states, for what works in Kerala may not work in the north. Measures to ensure ownership, political independence, and conscientious behavior of civil service staff may be unnecessary in states with a track record of good governance. Solutions to the problem of implementation can be found in the experimentation that such flexibility allows. The centrally sponsored schemes should also be evaluated rigorously, based on survey data. The lessons will help all states improve their programs, thus warranting central involvement.

Creating institutions and establishing measurement and evaluation procedures that will yield more effective policies and better social outcomes will take time. The solutions will also vary by sector.

Health Strategy and Policy Priorities

There are two deep problems in the health sector: a lack of realism for the public sector's role in the

Table 3.4. Health Spending in India and Comparator Countries, 2001

	GDP per capita	Total health spending (% of GDP)	Public health spending (% of GDP)	Private health spending (% of GDP)
Pakistan	420	4.1	0.9	3.2
India	460	4.9	0.9	4.0
Indonesia	690	2.7	0.6	2.1
China	890	5.3	1.9	3.4
Russia	1,750	5.3	3.8	1.5
Thailand	1,940	3.7	2.1	1.6
South Africa	2,820	8.8	3.7	5.1
Brazil	3,070	8.3	3.4	4.9
Malaysia	3,330	2.5	1.5	1.0
Mexico	5,530	5.4	2.5	2.9

Source: World Bank 2002s.

health system and a lack of priorities for the public sector's possible contributions. There is a strong tendency in the public sector (and in much public discussion) to believe that provision in government facilities is the whole of the health sector. In fact, government expenditures on health are only about 20% of the total. The share is even less for the number of visits to providers, since the public sector is more prominent in expensive hospital care than it is in primary care. There is also a strong tendency in the public sector to believe that its clientele is predominantly poor. In fact, the use of the public sector is much greater for those better off. Most public inpatient services (more than 65%) are used by the richest 40% of the population (compared with 19% for the poorest 40%), as are most outpatient services (48% for the richest 40% and 31% for the poorest 40%) (Mahal and others 2001).

International comparisons support the observation that the private sector dominates India's health system (table 3.4). India's public expenditure on health reflects its low income. For a large range of countries public health expenditures are highly correlated with income-with shares of public health spending increasing with income. Unusually, India's private spending on health care is higher as a share of income than that of such significantly richer countries as Thailand and Malaysia. This indicates a substantial demand and willingness to pay for health care, to be kept in mind when considering financing options.

Many factors, most outside the health sector, contribute to health status. Clean water, sanitation, and efforts to reduce indoor air pollution are all essential for a healthy environment (box 3.2). Education (probably for women more than men) and income also have a strong impact, particularly through nutritional status. Government programs to improve health outcomes need to reflect the priority for clean water, sanitation, and clean air- and for simple medical care. Improvements in both sanitation and simple medical care are essential to

achieve substantial reductions in child mortality. Although the situation is improving, 64% of households still have no toilet facilities.

Most medical care is now in the private sector- and for the poor, mostly by very poorly trained or untrained practitioners. There is no way to expand free publicly supplied medical care to replace these practitioners. With limited funds, and more important with the difficulties of managing a dispersed network of primary health centers with personnel who do not want to live in rural areas, replacing a private market is a low return activity. It should thus be a low priority. So, while there is room for expanding health expenditures as India grows, the extra spending must complement private expenditure rather than displace it. Improving the private market- through training, public information, and accreditation-is a far better option. And over time, public financing of private provision could be increased, subject to evaluation to make sure it works.

Attracting private investment to hospitals is also a way to expand services-a complex solution since it depends on payment mechanisms, such as insurance, that will allow payment to private facilities. Some reform proposals are being pursued, but there is likely to be substantial learning from social insurance funds and their subsequent revisions of policies. It may take a long time to establish such mechanisms. Progress will be faster in states where financial accountability is easier to establish. In the meantime, a clearer regulatory structure for the hospitals themselves would help. Even with insurance or other payment systems, explicit subsidies for poor patients will be necessary. And before such systems take effect, ensuring better access to catastrophic medical care is a priority for the poor-and may be more a matter of improving roads, communications, and administrative procedures for admission than increasing facilities.

Box 3.2. Building a Healthy Environment

Water, sanitation, and hygiene. Adequate water and sanitation are central to improving health outcomes. Contaminated water can lead to water-borne illnesses, such as viral hepatitis, typhoid, cholera, dysentery, and many other diseases that cause diarrhea. Indians lose 22 million disability-adjusted life years annually to diarrheal diseases, the second-largest contributor to the country's disease burden (WHO 1999). Diarrhea and other diseases caused by poor water quality are estimated to be responsible for approximately 1.5 million deaths a year among children each year in India (Parikh and others 1999). Inadequate quantities of water make personal hygiene difficult, facilitating the spread of many diseases and infections. Although water quality is important, multicountry studies have shown that improved hygiene through hand washing and improved sanitation through latrine usage have a greater impact on health outcomes. Hygiene and sanitation improvements reduce diarrhea, parasitic infections, morbidity, and mortality more than water quality (Esrey and others 1991; Hutley and others 1997).

India has been increasing water supplies, but sanitation coverage has lagged behind. Providing adequate clean water and promoting sanitation and hygiene would reduce the burden of water-borne diseases. But infrastructure alone will not necessarily decrease child mortality in poor families, which tend to be most vulnerable to disease. Piped water leads to improved child health outcomes in India, but the gains tend to be lower for children with less educated mothers and in less wealthy families (Jalan and Ravallion 2001). This points to combining education and poverty reduction strategies with infrastructure investment to protect the health of children in India.

Indoor air pollution. Indoor air pollution is a larger problem in India than in most parts of the world. Smoke emissions from the use of biomass fuel (wood, dung, and straw) are estimated to be responsible for about 500,000 premature deaths and about half a billion illnesses each year (World Bank 2002l). Young children, who spend much of their time at home, are particularly vulnerable to the health consequences of exposure to smoke from solid fuel.

A recent assessment concluded that the deaths of as many as 444,000 children under five years old may be attributable to solid fuel use (Smith 2000; Smith and Mehta 2000). Another study estimated that child mortality is about one-third lower in households using clean fuels than in comparable households using biomass (Hughes and others 2000). Converting to clean fuels would eliminate this health risk.

But for the majority of rural households, biomass will continue to be the main cooking fuel, largely due to its relatively low cost (World Bank 2003a). So there is a need to find and promote cleaner ways of using biomass. International experience shows that highly successful programs typically include financial assistance for technical development, stove design, marketing, and public awareness campaigns. The national government can contribute by evaluating programs, providing training and seminars, and sharing information among programs. The dissemination of information about health risks of biomass fuel and mitigation options can lead to a greater willingness to switch to safer fuel or at least modify behavior and cooking areas. Community interventions are needed to assure that solutions are cost-effective, sustainable, and tailored to local conditions.

Within the health sector, combating communicable diseases should continue to be the highest priority for public funds. Why? Because there are clear and considerable externalities of control, including such true public goods as swamp drainage and large-scale pest control. Because the benefits are heavily skewed to the poor-with the difference in incidence of communicable disease for the rich and the poor many times that for noncommunicable disease (figure 3.3). And because relative to medical care, most of these activities are much easier to administer. For example, pulse polio campaigns require professionals to be in rural areas only periodically, without forcing them to move their families.

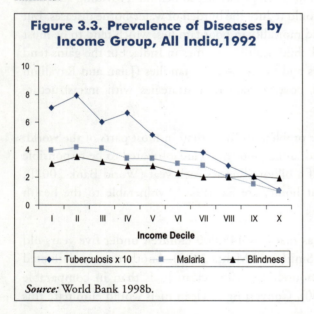

Figure 3.3. Prevalence of Diseases by Income Group, All India,1992

Income Decile

◆ Tuberculosis x 10   ■ Malaria   ▲ Blindness

Source: World Bank 1998b.

The largest emerging problem in communicable disease control is the increase in Human Immunodeficiency Virus (HIV) infections and Acquired Immuno-Deficiency Syndrome (AIDS) cases. Estimates of the spread of HIV infections, ranging from 4-8 million in 2002, are subject to much dispute. But there is no dispute that the infection is spreading rapidly. Some predict that as many as 20-25 million cases will occur as soon as 2010 (a more than doubling of current, estimates of prevalence). The HIV/AIDS crisis presents a unique challenge for India's leadership. There are many competing needs for the public health infrastructure, and it is important to ensure that HIV/AIDS programs neither undercut resources to deal with other killers like tuberculosis, malaria, and diarrhea-nor get marginalized.

The main focus of HIV/AIDS policy should be prevention. Treatment is expensive and has the possibility (as demonstrated in the United States, Europe, and Australia) of undermining prevention activities by making contracting the disease less of a catastrophe. Instead, treatment should be used only if it can complement prevention efforts-say, as an inducement for testing. Surveillance of the disease should not be limited to public antenatal clinics and other standard locations. Much more attention is needed for accurate measurement of the incidence as well as for research to understand the sexual (and drug use) behavior of people if effective prevention strategies are to be designed. While the political obstacles are severe, the epidemic can begin to be controlled only if there is a candid public discussion of sex. People must be able to know the extent of their risk and how to reduce this risk through safe sex. If this is not done, the country will face a genuine disaster.

Education Strategy and Policy Priorities

Progress in education has been much greater than in health. Enrollments have responded to higher expenditures. Political support has been more reliable in many states. And there are several notable success stories. But there are large variations across states, and the current rate of aggregate progress in education indicators is insufficient to attain the goals in the Tenth Plan. Of 200 million children ages 6-14, 42 million do not attend school. There are problems of high dropout rates, low levels of learning achievement, and low participation of girls. There are also systemic issues of widespread teacher vacancies, high teacher absenteeism, and inadequate teaching and learning materials.

Table 3.5. Education Spending in India and Comparator Countries

	GDP per capita (dollars)	Public expenditure per student		
		Primary education	Secondary education	Tertiary education
Pakistan	420	n.a.	n.a.	n.a.
India	460	7.2	23.1	92.5
Indonesia	690	3.2	8.7	12.2
China	890	6.1	12.1	85.8
Russia	1,750	n.a.	20.5	15.8
Thailand	1,940	12.5	12.8	38.2
South Africa	2,820	14	17.9	61.3
Brazil	3,070	12.5	12.6	72.8
Malaysia	3,330	11.2	19.9	86.1
Mexico	5,530	11.7	13.8	45.2

n.a.   Reliable data not available.
Source: World Bank 2002s.

India's overall spending on education is not much different from that of other countries with similar incomes (table 3.5). But the composition is skewed somewhat toward the secondary level and considerably toward higher education. Given the very sophisticated academic tradition coexisting with mass poverty, it is perhaps not surprising that higher education is expensive in relation to GDP. But this does not mean that higher education is a high priority use of public money-the main source of funding can be private.

To accelerate progress in elementary education, the Government of India launched the Sarva Siksha Abhiyan (Education for All) program in 2000/01, aiming to provide eight years of schooling for children ages 6-14 by 2010. It has also enacted a Constitutional amendment (86th) that makes free and compulsory education a fundamental right for children ages 6-14. Universalizing the completion of schooling through the fifth standard and then through the eighth, across all Indian states will require additional public resources for these levels of education and improvements in the effectiveness of using public resources. The central issues:

◆ How to ensure that all children, particularly poor children, become enrolled in primary school and are able and willing to complete an elementary education of reasonable quality?

◆ What can be done to improve community-school relationships and make the education system, including the teachers, more accountable to the communities they are intended to serve?

◆ How, and how much, can the experiences of educationally stronger states be replicated in weaker performing states to improve completion rates and learning achievements?

Education differs from health in that it is more possible to rely on communities and parents to monitor and evaluate performance. Parents are in the best position to monitor what goes on in schools. They may not know the best pedagogical techniques, but they do know whether the teacher comes to work. And even illiterate parents can tell if their children are learning anything. So effective reform will almost certainly put more power into their hands. In urban settings where there is the possibility of choosing schools, increasing market power with vouchers might be experimented with (maybe for the poor, maybe for everyone, with limits on topping up). The essential feature is to allow money to follow the student-and to allow schools enough autonomy to be able to compete for it.

In rural areas, where little or no real choice is practical, increasing parent voice and influence over school operations is a good option. Making schools more accountable to the community is critical, possibly as far as giving parents the right to hire and fire teachers through local school committees. The most promising developments in primary education have been in Madhya Pradesh, where communities have been allowed to hire informal, less qualified teachers at much lower wages than possible in the civil service-with much better attendance and educational outcomes. Other states, such as Rajasthan and Uttar Pradesh, have also experimented with para-teachers, who appear to provide better services, despite their lower qualifications and salaries.[38]

States will differ in the degree and form of relying on parents and communities-depending on their ability to monitor and ensure good performance from their teachers. While parents in the community schools in Madhya Pradesh can dismiss and hire teachers, other states might find that ordinary complaint procedures through panchayats can work as well. In all cases the active participation of parents is likely to be a major factor in all successful education reforms for a long time to come.

There may also be more scope for competition in education than is ordinarily considered.

Competition can be for concessions to establish a school in a village even if there will be only one. And competition can be enhanced by making it easier for children to reach another school. Kerala, for example, gives substantial subsidies for transportation. Parents can shop around for better schools, and the revenue of the school depends on enrollments.

Schools need enough autonomy to attract teachers and students. Circumstances across India differ enormously, and reaching the poorest and most remote children requires flexibility and experimentation. Once again, localities must be allowed the freedom to find their best solutions. Higher levels of government can help by establishing more regular measurement of attendance and learning outcomes and providing other information needed to evaluate progress. This helps individual districts adjust their strategies and learn from each other.

Experience is accumulating on making contracts with government contingent on better performance on tests. NGOs and possibly for-profit institutions can be given operating budgets contingent on independent measures of teaching improvements. While overreliance on test scores carries risks (such as "teaching to the test" and ignoring less quantifiable aspects of education) many parents would be happy if enough teaching was taking place for test scores to improve. One way or another, schools should be more accountable for better outcomes. This can be done in many ways-contracts with local governments, contracts with state departments of education, giving parents a greater say in school governance, or a greater choice between schools. The common feature is separating the funder of the school and the provider, with the latter beholden to the former.

---

[38] For example, a recent evaluation of a remedial education program run by Pratham (an NGO) concluded: "Hiring remedial education teachers from the community appears to be 10 times more cost-effective than hiring new teachers." See Duflo (2003).

There is substantial demand for upper primary and secondary education, partly a result of the success in increasing primary enrollments. In many states, secondary schools are grant-in-aid institutions (private schools paid for by public funds) and there is concern over the quality of education in such facilities. In many states, there are also concerns about leakages from grant-in-aid expenditures. Again, more regular evaluation of outcomes can improve oversight of such contracts and increase public accountability for the use of funds.

Providing Effective Social Safety Nets

Antipoverty programs, or social safety nets, suffer from the same lack of focus on outcomes. The poverty problem has changed dramatically since India established the major antipoverty programs in the early post-independence era, such as the Public Distribution System (PDS). Then, mass poverty-at rates of 60% or more-meant that universal programs were bound to help poor people. Now, with poverty rates below 30% and falling, there is more need to avoid waste of public resources by making sure that program funds actually reach poor people. This requires more careful monitoring of programs to determine how much it costs to transfer a rupee to a poor person.

The costs vary widely. One study compared five programs and found that it cost from Rs1.8 for each rupee ultimately received by someone below the poverty line through the Integrated Child Development Service, a nutrition and pre-school education program, to more than Rs6.3 through the "two rupee per kilo" food distribution scheme in Andhra Pradesh (Radhakrishna and Subbarao 1997). The PDS cost more than Rs5.3 per rupee transferred. Included were the administrative costs of determining eligibility and implementation and the "leakage" costs of benefits to people above the poverty line. Since many state programs are tied to PDS eligibility conditions, its inability to discriminate between poor and nonpoor (there were 2.8 nonpoor for each poor beneficiary) is a matter of great concern.

One general rule is that self-targeted programs, such as the Maharashtra Employment Guarantee Scheme, tend to reach the poorest better than those that rely on administrative discretion for eligibility. Self-targeted programs allow people to choose to participate but are designed to attract the neediest. For example, if wages in an Employment Guarantee Scheme are below prevailing wages, only the neediest will volunteer. These programs are cheaper in administration, since there is no eligibility to check, and leakages, since only the poor will volunteer (Ravallion and Datt 1995). The lesson, though, is that one existing program is not better or worse than another. It is, once again, that all programs should be continually re-examined for their effectiveness. Regular monitoring, measuring actual outcomes, and refocusing of programs is essential.

Toward the Future

Many internal and external observers of Indian administration have argued that decentralization and local empowerment will ultimately be essential in improving the quality of service delivery at the village level. Faced with slow and uneven progress on decentralization, the 73rd and 74th amendments to the Constitution, ratified in 1992, obligated states to decentralize to lower levels. The amendments created distinct rural and urban governments, mandated periodic elections, and established an important accountability mechanism, the Gram Sabha (village assembly). But they left other matters of implementation to the states. The most visible achievement of these reforms has been the high degree of political decentralization. With the election of more than three million local politicians-a third of them women and around a fifth from scheduled castes and tribals-India's decentralization has, at least nominally, opened the state to democratic participation.

But progress on the fiscal and administrative aspects of decentralization has been much more modest and hesitant. Administrative evolution has often failed to take account of the limited capacity of local governments, the economies of scale in delivering services, or the potential role of the private sector. And a serious overlap of responsibilities among state, district, block, and village governments obscures the lines of accountability to voters. For the most part, local governments still raise little revenue of their own (though the potential is much higher) and deliver few services. Instead, they are usually treated by state and central bureaucracies as service agents for higher level governments.

India now needs to move from its decentralized patchwork toward an intergovernmental framework that improves service delivery without increasing fiscal pressures. Good fiscal management would suggest re-allocating public funds from central and state schemes to a well-designed fiscal framework for local governments-guaranteeing their autonomy and accountability while helping them to match resource allocations with local preferences. It would also suggest creating incentives for local governments to collect a share of their revenues from local taxpayers (as through land taxes). Flows of funds from the center and state governments should depend on good local performance and resource mobilization. Performance should be monitored not only by the local audit fund, but also by local journalists, civil society groups, and panchayat leaders from neighboring districts. This would help strengthen accountability and ensure greater participation and empowerment of local communities-one of the primary objectives of the decentralization process.

The federal structure, the common institutions and practices across states, and the ongoing program of decentralization make India a fertile laboratory for reform. A variety of changes at the center, state, and local levels, implemented with varying degrees of success, can be quickly scaled up and disseminated across the country. India is a leader in the information technology revolution, and states such as Andhra Pradesh and Karnataka are making impressive gains in applying information technology solutions to a variety of public sector problems. For all their weaknesses, cadres such as the Indian Administrative Service remain a tremendous reservoir of talent and capacity. Perhaps most important, some broader dynamics-such as the rise of the Indian middle class and the growth of NGOs dedicated to governance-are fostering social demand for good governance. So, while the Indian public sector reform agenda has remained fairly fixed for a decade or more, India itself is changing in ways that make reform more feasible.

PART II

POLICY AGENDA: IMPROVING THE INVESTMENT CLIMATE

India's economic performance has been aided by the structural reforms introduced over the past decade. On that, there is little doubt. But higher levels of private investment and productivity will be needed to raise the growth rate to 8% a year, as targeted in the Tenth Plan. Compared with many other countries in Asia, India's private sector faces a relatively unfavorable investment climate. This constrains productivity and job creation in industry and services. It also reduces India's ability to compete in world markets. Constraining agriculture are the imbalances in public expenditure-that favor subsidies over productivity-enhancing investments-and the remaining restrictions on trade and competition-both of which need to be remedied. And developing the nonfarm sector will be essential for providing employment opportunities in rural areas and supporting agriculture.

CHAPTER 4

INDUSTRY AND SERVICES

Structural reforms stimulated industrial and services growth and investment in the early 1990s (box 4.1). The industrial sector grew 7.6% a year, and manufacturing 9.8% a year, in real terms from 1992/93-1996/97 (table 4.1). Private investment in industry grew 20.1% a year in real terms over the same period (figure 4.1). But the momentum slowed in the second half of the decade, with industrial growth averaging only 4.5% a year and manufacturing growth only 3.8% during 1997/98-2001/02. Growth in private investment in industry actually fell -3.4% a

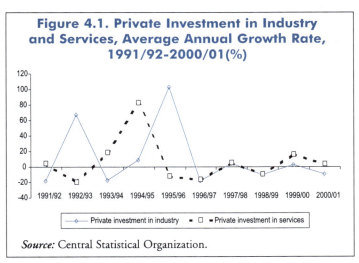

Figure 4.1. Private Investment in Industry and Services, Average Annual Growth Rate, 1991/92-2000/01(%)

Source: Central Statistical Organization.

Table 4.1. GDP, Industry, and Services Growth Rates, 1992/93-2002/03 (compound annual growth rate %)

	1992/93-1996/97	1997/98-2001/02	2001/02	2002/03
GDP at factor cost	6.7	5.5	5.6	4.4
Industry	7.6	4.5	3.3	6.1
Mining and quarrying	3.6	3.8	1.0	4.8
Manufacturing	9.8	3.8	3.4	6.1
Electricity, gas, and water	5.5	5.9	4.3	5.2
Construction	3.6	7.0	3.7	7.1
Services	7.5	8.1	6.8	7.1
Trade, hotels, transport, and communication	8.8	7.9	8.7	7.8
Trade, hotels, and restaurants	9.1	7.1	8.8	n.a.
Transport, storage, and communication	8.1	9.6	8.5	n.a.
Financing, insurance, real estate, and business services	8.0	7.5	4.5	6.5
Community, social, and personal services	5.1	9.1	5.6	6.4

n.a.   Reliable data not available.

Source: Central Statistical Organization.

year during 1997/98-2000/01. The manufacturing sector in India accounts for only 16.8% of GDP, compared with 35% in China and 25-35% in the South East Asian economies.

The services sector, by contrast, has recorded strong growth throughout the past decade. Domestic reforms to allow private participation and more competition, coupled with more liberal foreign direct investment (FDI) policies and access to global markets, played a key role in raising the growth of business services (primarily information technology), telecommunications, and hotels and restaurants. But such services as retail trade, potentially an engine of job creation and growth, have not been liberalized-and thus have grown much less rapidly.

FDI in India stood at about 1.3% of GDP in 2001/02, declining to 0.9% in 2002/03, compared with 4% in China and 2-3% in many emerging market countries.[39] FDI in India has been oriented to the domestic market, not to exports, unlike that in China and South East Asia. No significant increase in India's penetration of world markets in industrial products has been observed over the past decade, with the share of nonagricultural exports in world exports of the same commodities increasing only marginally from 0.5% in 1990/91 to 0.55% in 2000/01. Even so, India has achieved a prominent position in global services, today accounting for 1.4% of global exports in services. But this growth took place on the back of a narrow set of subsectors-primarily software exports, which grew at an annual average rate of 49% during the second half of the 1990s. India's performance in travel and transportation services, where the underlying growth is linked to trade in goods, has been mediocre.

The organized industry and services sectors now account for 27 million jobs, of which just 7 million jobs are in manufacturing and 17 million are in the services sector (70% of the organized sector jobs are in public sector units). By comparison, the total labor force in India is around 406 million, with just under 1 million workers moving out of agriculture every year. Organized services generated 760,000 new jobs over the past decade, while employment in organized manufacturing has remained almost unchanged, with only 350,000 new jobs created between 1993/94 and 1999/2000. Growth in total manufacturing employment (organized and unorganized) in India averaged only about 2% a year during 1994-2000, with the unorganized sector accounting for the bulk.[40]

Over the past 12 months, industry has begun to show signs of recovery, fueled mainly by better use of existing capacity rather than by new investments-and by lower interest rates, giving huge windfall gains for industry. Industrial growth for 2002/03 is estimated to be 6.1%, compared with 3.1% for the previous year. But, as emphasized in the Tenth Plan, much higher industrial sector growth will be required to create the targeted 100 million or so new jobs over the next decade. This will need faster growth in labor-intensive services, such as retail trade. The plan notes that sustained growth and employment will require a step up in domestic investment, particularly private investment, and in productivity.

The investment climate varies considerably across the states. In general, there is a clear link between the investment climate and industrial performance

---

[39] In accordance with the new and expanded definition of FDI released by the Government on July 2, 2003, FDI is defined to include, besides equity capital (which comprises the equity capital of unincorporated entities, now also including the equity capital of foreign banks' branches in India, control premium and noncompetition fees), reinvested earnings of incorporated and unincorporated entities and other capital (including short-term and long-term borrowing, trade and suppliers' credit of more than 180 days, and financial leasing).

[40] Based on the National Sample Survey figures in India, Planning Commission 2001b.

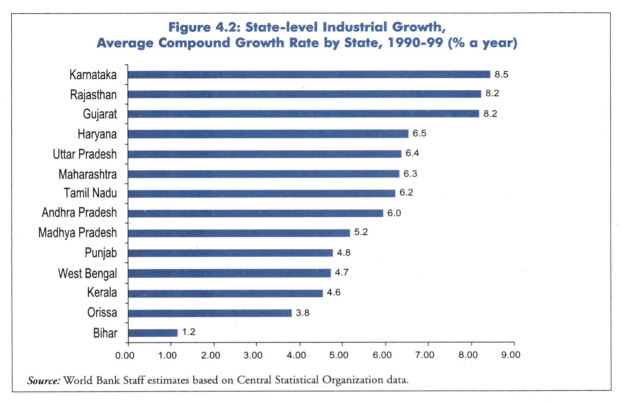

**Figure 4.2: State-level Industrial Growth,
Average Compound Growth Rate by State, 1990-99 (% a year)**

State	Growth Rate
Karnataka	8.5
Rajasthan	8.2
Gujarat	8.2
Haryana	6.5
Uttar Pradesh	6.4
Maharashtra	6.3
Tamil Nadu	6.2
Andhra Pradesh	6.0
Madhya Pradesh	5.2
Punjab	4.8
West Bengal	4.7
Kerala	4.6
Orissa	3.8
Bihar	1.2

Source: World Bank Staff estimates based on Central Statistical Organization data.

(figure 4.2). Indeed, Karnataka and Gujarat, rated as the better investment climate states by the World Bank-CII study (2002), recorded high industrial growth rates (in excess of 8% in the 1990s). Karnataka is also the leader by far in exports of information technology services and inflows of FDI.

But even the better investment climate states are still way behind the curve compared to India's South East Asian and East Asian competitors. Kerala and West Bengal, ranked among the poorer investment climate states, had much lower industrial growth during the 1990s. The only real outlier was Uttar Pradesh, where, despite a rather poor investment climate, industry grew at 6.4% a year during the 1990s. But Uttar Pradesh's industry grew from a very low base, and the growth in the late 1990s may be attributed largely to central government (rather than state) reforms.

India has intrinsic advantages that should allow it to emerge as a major hub for manufacturing and labor-intensive service industries. The advantages include relative macroeconomic stability (if fiscal issues are addressed), a local market among the largest in the world, a large and low-cost labor force, a critical mass of well-educated workers in engineering and science, and an abundance of raw materials. But more than five decades of protectionism, state-ownership, and selective interventions have created deep distortions, stifling India's private sector development, competitiveness, and growth.

It is now widely accepted within India that the Government would do far better by focusing on creating a conducive environment and level playing field for the private sector. More specifically, improving industry and services requires tackling three key sets of issues simultaneously: removing product market distortions, improving the efficiency of factor markets, and alleviating infrastructure bottlenecks. Success in achieving the ambitious targets in the Tenth Plan will depend on progress in all three areas.

Investment Climate: Key Constraints and Policy Priorities

Product Market Distortions

Small businesses. A key area where industrial policy reforms need to move faster is in the small-scale industry reservations. At the start of the reform program of the 1990s, about 800 items were reserved for exclusive production in the small-scale industry sector, which meant that investment in plant and machinery in any individual small-scale industry unit could not exceed a specified monetary ceiling. Over the years, this list has been only slightly pruned, so that, in June 2003, 674 items remained reserved exclusively for the sector, although larger-sized industrial firms can now obtain a license to produce products reserved for the small-scale industry sector, if they are exported.

For 610 of the reserved categories, total investment in plant and machinery for any single firm is capped at Rs10 million (a little over $200,000), while for 64 reserved items, the cap has been raised to Rs50 million (about $1 million). This policy of product reservation and investment ceilings has held back the small-scale industry sector from achieving economies of scale and greater efficiencies-by inhibiting small firms from investing beyond the stipulated limits, expanding their operations in the domestic market, and then moving into exports. Now is the time to eliminate this reservation policy-to unleash India's businesses, encouraging them to grow and compete on world markets.

Trade policy. Import licensing has been abolished. For tariff reductions progress was rapid until the mid-1990s, but the process has since slowed (box 4.1). And high import tariffs remain a key constraint to better industrial performance and competitiveness, driving up the prices of manufactured products, suppressing demand, and providing opportunities for inefficient firms to survive and for efficient firms to capture rents. Many tariffs-mostly on agricultural products and processed foods, but also on some industrial products (such as automobiles)-are far above the new "peak" customs duty rate of 25% introduced in the 2003/04 budget. In March 2003, the unweighted average protective tariff, including the protective effect of the special additional duty, was about 32.7% overall-30.7% for industrial goods and 46.8% for agricultural products including processed foods. Far lower than pre-reform levels in the 1980s, this is still very high by world standards.

Comparing the unweighted average customs duty rates of 105 developing countries between 1996 and 2000, India's average tariff was the second highest (next to Morocco). Even without allowing for the special additional duty, India's tariffs are much higher than average tariffs in other large developing countries-more than twice China's and Brazil's, four times Indonesia's, and two and a half times the average of developing countries (table 4.2). Reducing import tariffs is critical to improving industrial performance. India should aim to reduce import tariffs on all imports to a single rate (say, 10%) over the next three to four years. Comparable to the rate of tariff reduction in China and Brazil over the past decade (China's import duties are expected to average 9% by 2005), this schedule would give domestic manufacturers the time to restructure and become competitive.

Various tariff exemptions that increase effective protection, create other distortions, and complicate tax administration should be eliminated, preferably by bringing down the general level of tariffs and reducing the demand for special treatment. A "jumbo exemption" notification was introduced in 1996 to consolidate and bring greater clarity to the previous impenetrable maze of exemption notifications. But since then the jumbo has grown, and the total number of exemptions now appears to be about double the number in 1996. In 2002/03 the jumbo exemption customs notification listed 415

Box 4.1. Key Structural Reforms since 1991

The structural reform program started in 1991 envisaged a decisive shift in industrial and trade policy, in private and foreign investment in industry and services, and in financial policy. There have been major changes, but slow progress in liberalizing trade and industry remains a serious concern.

Industrial policy reforms. Central government industrial controls were mostly dismantled in the early 1990s. The earlier reservation of 18 industries for the public sector, which prevented the private sector from investing in these areas, has been reduced to three (defense aircrafts and warships, atomic energy generation, and railway transport). Central government industrial licensing has been almost completely abolished, except for a few hazardous and environmentally sensitive industries (a pervasive regime of government inspection and clearances remains). The requirement that investments by large industrial houses be cleared separately under the Monopolies and Restrictive Trade Practices Act to discourage the concentration of economic power has been abolished, with the act replaced by a competition law that will attempt to regulate anticompetitive behavior.

These reforms notwithstanding, three key areas need immediate attention: removing small-scale industry reservations, reducing government interference and bureaucratic hassles in the entry and operation of firms, and improving the bankruptcy framework to facilitate the exit of troubled firms.

Trade policy reforms. Import licensing was abolished for most capital and intermediate goods in 1991. But for manufactured consumer goods and agricultural products it was removed only in stages between 1997 and 2001, following pressures from the United States, the EU, and other developed countries under the WTO dispute settlement mechanism. Unweighted average tariffs declined sharply-from 128% in 1990/91 to 34.4% in 1997/98. But the trend was reversed in 1998/99 when average tariffs increased by about 5 percentage points, remaining above the 1997/98 levels until a new reduction program began in 2002/03. The increase during 1998/99-2001/02 was due to protective import taxes on top of customs duties, initially a "special duty," then a "surcharge" (both now abolished), and now the Special Additional Duty.

Industrial tariffs were reduced again in the 2003/04 budget, but agricultural tariffs, omitted from the reduction program, are now much higher than nonagricultural tariffs. India used the Uruguay round negotiations to support its industrial tariff reductions in the 1990s. But about a third of its industrial tariffs remain unbound, and most of the rest are bound at a high 40%. With a few exceptions, agricultural tariffs are bound very high-mostly at prohibitive rates of 100%, 150%, or 300%.

Policies toward private sector participation and competition. India has advanced considerably in reducing the state's role in industry and services, and in opening them to domestic and foreign competition. Public sector units in aluminum, car manufacturing, telecommunications, and information technology have been privatized. In telecommunications, banking, insurance, and health-previously under the exclusive control of public sector monopolies-private companies, both domestic and foreign, have been allowed to operate. Foreign direct investment (FDI) was substantially liberalized at an early stage of the reforms and extended at regular intervals.

Limits on the share of foreign equity allowed have been liberalized by allowing 100% foreign ownership in a large number of industries and majority ownership in almost all the others. Procedures for obtaining permission were also greatly simplified by notifying lists of industries eligible for automatic approval up to the specified levels of foreign equity (100%, 74%, and 51%) and by requiring potential investors to register only with the Reserve Bank of India. In 1993 qualified institutional investors were allowed to invest in Indian companies by purchasing shares in the stock market, subject to a maximum percentage, progressively liberalized.

Financial sector reform. Reforms in banking have included:

+ Dismantling the complex system of interest rate controls.

+ Introducing prudential norms and capital adequacy requirements in line with international standards.

+ Strengthening banking supervision.

+ Creating a more competitive environment in banking through more liberal licensing of private banks and expansion by foreign banks.

+ Strengthening the framework for bad debt recovery through the Securitization, Reconstruction of Financial Assets and Enforcement of Security Interest Act (2002).

+ Improving the bankruptcy framework through amendments to the Companies Act (2002).

A number of reforms have also been introduced to strengthen stock market regulation. Even so, concerns remain about the integrity of the markets.

items for which some kind of exemption is allowed, each item corresponding to a harmonized system code (two digit, four digit, or six digit). And many are supplemented by one or more of 43 detailed product lists, which contain over 1,100 detailed product descriptions.

The vast majority of these exemptions are for intermediate material inputs or for machinery and equipment items and may involve one, two, or all three of the basic customs duties, the additional duty, and the special additional duty. Other complications come from exemptions and partial exemptions that give excise tax advantage to small Indian firms over larger Indian firms and help the small firms in competing with imports. Although the benefit to small firms has been reduced by value-added tax (VAT) principles, the small firm exemption increases the opportunities for tax evasion and the costs of tax administration.

Other forms of protection are undermining other efforts to liberalize the trade regime, the most serious being antidumping. Starting in 1993, antidumping has become a major activity in India, with more than 300 cases completed, nearly all resulting in specific duties on imports from particular firms and countries, added on top of normal import duties. The ad valorem equivalents of the antidumping duties range from around 10% of normal international prices to more than 100% of international prices, with the total resulting import tariffs often prohibitive. The effects of antidumping duties go beyond the products actually subject to antidumping duties, since domestic firms can use the threat of bringing actions to prevent or limit competition from imports. India's antidumping activity (especially following recent antidumping duties imposed on imports from firms in Nepal and Bangladesh) is influencing other South Asian countries to also

Table 4.2. Unweighted Average Customs Duty Rates in India and Other Developing Countries, Various Years (%)

	All goods	Agriculture	Manufacturing
India 2001/02 (Customs duty only)	32.3	41.7	30.8
India 2002/03 (Customs duty only)	29.0	40.6	27.4
India 2002/03 (Customs duty and special additional duty)[a]	35.0	47.1	33.3
India 2003/04 (Customs duty and special additional duty)[a]	32.7	46.8	30.7
Pakistan 2001/02	20.4	21.8	20.2
Pakistan 2002/03[a]	18.2	13.9	18.3
Brazil 2000	14.1	12.9	14.3
China 2000	16.3	16.5	16.2
Indonesia 2000	8.4	6.3	8.9
Thailand 2000	16.6	39.9	14.6
South Korea 2000	12.7	47.9	6.6
105 developing countries (1996-2000)	13.4	17.4	12.7

Notes: The India 2001/02 tariffs are customs duties from the World Trade Organization (WTO) Trade Policy Review, January 2002. They do not include the special additional duty. The India 2002/03 and 2003/04 averages are from Arun Goyal, Easy Reference Customs Tariff 2003-2004, plus additional information supplied by the author. The protective effect of the special additional duty was estimated from the average customs duty by assuming an average 16% additional duty rate. The 2001/02 average tariffs for Pakistan are from the January 2002 WTO Trade Policy Review on Pakistan. The 2002/03 average tariffs for Pakistan are estimated from the 2001/02 averages by assuming that all 30% tariffs were reduced to 25% following the cut in the general maximum rate from 30% to 25% in the 2002/03 budget. There are no other explicitly protective import taxes than customs duties in Pakistan. The average tariffs for other developing countries were compiled by Francis Ng (DECRG-TR) from WTO, IDB CD ROM 2000, and Trade Policy Review, various issues, 1993-2001; World Bank.

a. Estimate.

Source: Sattar and Pursell 2003.

embark on antidumping, thus complicating efforts to reduce barriers to regional trade.

Other methods are also used to provide extra protection. Specific tariffs mostly protect textile fabric and garment producers against low-priced import competition, the ad valorem equivalents of which (based on export prices from China and Korea) can be prohibitive, ranging from 50% to more than 100%. Government mandated import monopolies (state trading enterprises) control imports of foodgrains and fertilizers. Applying maximum retail price rules to imported consumer goods raises the effective excise tax rate

as a proportion of the CIF prices of some imports, above the equivalent rate on domestically produced products. Sanitary and phytosanitary rules and technical regulations are applied in ways that discriminate against imports. And a new customs ordinance gives discretionary power to the Ministry of Finance to quickly increase customs duties without obtaining the parliamentary clearance previously required.

The Government has been streamlining its export policies, especially the large number of schemes used to exempt, offset, or refund import duties on imported inputs used by exporters.[41] But many long-standing problems in the administration of these schemes have continued, including delays and high negotiation and transactions costs for exporters. The underlying reason for the difficulties is the still very high levels of tariffs and indirect taxes. They mean that fast and complete rebates or exemptions are essential for profitable exporting. But they create large potential economic rents from the misuse of the schemes. That leads to different schemes to meet different circumstances and to complex layers of control.

India has many well-justified concerns about the policies of other countries that restrict exports of goods and services where it has a clear comparative advantage. And it is one of the most active developing countries combating these policies in various international fora, especially at the World Trade Organization (WTO). Of particular concern:

- Agricultural protectionism in the EU, United States, and other developed countries.

- Escalated tariff structures in developed countries.

- The multifiber arrangement restricting textile and garments exports.

- Developed-country regional preferential policies, such as the North American Free Trade Agreement, which divert imports from India and other excluded suppliers.

- The misuse of antidumping, sanitary and phytosanitary regulations, and technical regulations as protective instruments.

- The reluctance of developed countries to allow Indians and people from other developing countries to provide services by temporarily moving within their borders.

India's negotiating stance on developed country restrictions has been combined with defensive positions for its own commitments, as indicated by prohibitively high agricultural tariff bindings, many unbound industrial tariffs, and conservative bindings under the General Agreement on Trade in Services. Because of the current and future size of its economy, India has some bargaining leverage in offering to trade some of these restrictions for concessions by other countries (Mattoo and Subramanian 2003). But these potential economic benefits should be weighed against the current and ongoing economic costs of not taking advantage of the opportunity offered by the WTO process to help lock in liberalizing reforms-by making them more difficult to reverse under the pressure of domestic protectionist forces.

The WTO bargaining process can also help overcome domestic interests resisting trade liberalization by balancing greater import competition in the domestic market with better and more secure access to export markets. From this perspective, some of the recent directions of Indian trade policies-especially the routine use of antidumping, sanitary and phytosanitary regulations, and technical regulations for protection, and the subsidized exports of rice and wheat-are emulating developed country practices about which India complains. They are likely to undermine its credibility in negotiating for multilateral rules to limit their future use.

Domestic taxes. The business environment in India has greatly benefited from VAT principles and the gradual broadening and simplification of the previously extremely complex central government indirect (excise) tax system, now known as CENVAT. Under way since the mid-1980s, this has continued with major improvements in recent years (especially for

---

[41] Current export policies are outlined in the Ministry of Commerce "Report of the High Level Committee for the EXIM Policy, 2002-07" (India, Ministry of Commerce 2002b).

textiles), despite a recent move to a basic three-tier structure (8%, 16%, and 24%) rather than a system with a single basic rate. But in sharp contrast to an overwhelming majority of developing countries-by 1998, 116 countries around the world had a VAT or VAT-like tax-India has not yet introduced a VAT. It announced that sales taxes would be replaced by a VAT regime on April 1, 2003, but that has been delayed. If fully and uniformly implemented across all states, the VAT should help eliminate distortions caused by the cascading effect of sales taxes applied at each stage of the value chain.

Meanwhile, the prevailing indirect tax regime in India creates significant distortions and transactions costs, and the indirect tax rates remain high relative to other developing countries (see table 4.2). A recent calculation suggests that lowering domestic sales taxes in India would significantly reduce costs in the value chain, lower consumer prices, and result in rapid growth in domestic sales volumes (McKinsey and CII 2002). It would do this without having an adverse impact on government revenues (given the elasticity of demand for manufactured goods and that a reduction in rates would encourage firms to move from the unorganized to the organized sector, bringing them into the tax net). Another tax-related distortion worth mentioning relates to various states in India granting discretionary tax holidays. While this problem has been reduced since the abolition of sales tax concessions after 1999, it does continue to fragment manufacturing capacities, resulting in high costs.

Foreign direct investment. While FDI policies have been significantly liberalized, FDI is still allowed only in selected sectors (such as telecoms

Table 4.3 Indirect Tax Rates in Selected Developing Countries[a] (%)

	Standard rate	Significant other VAT rates[b]
Asia		
China	17	n.a.
India	8, 16, 24	n.a.
Indonesia	10	5, 20, 35
Korea	10	2, 3.5
Pakistan	10	n.a.
Philippines	10	n.a.
Singapore	3	n.a.
Sri Lanka	12.5	n.a.
Thailand	10	n.a.
Africa		
Kenya	16	12
Mauritius	10	n.a.
South Africa	14	n.a.
Latin America		
Chile	18	n.a.
Mexico	15	10

n.a.   Reliable data not available.

a.   With the exception of India, all of the countries in the table have introduced VAT (or a VAT-like) tax.

b.   Excludes the zero-rate on exports. While such multiple VAT rates are likely to complicate VAT administration, they are politically attractive by ostensibly serving-though not necessarily effectively-an equity objective. In fact, most OECD countries have multiple VAT rates. Still, the administrative price for addressing equity concerns through multiple VAT rates is likely to be higher in developing, than in developed countries.

Source: Tanzi and Zee 2000.

and insurance). And it is still subject to limits, particularly on full ownership by foreign players. For example, FDI currently is not permitted in pure retailing (global retailers can participate in India's retail sector only through wholesale trade or by operating retail outlets through local franchises). In apparel, another important sector for job creation, FDI is limited to 24% of equity.

In housing construction, restrictions on foreign ownership of land limit the entry of foreign builders and developers into the construction market, so that foreign players face higher risks when operating in India-because they cannot take land ownership as collateral for the capital they have invested.

Phasing out these FDI limits would bring the necessary capital into these sectors (the local capital markets and the pockets of the Indian players are not deep enough to provide the necessary equity commitment). It would also generate growth and employment. And as several studies show, the entry of multinationals would likely lead to technology and skills transfers to domestic firms. If foreign firms introduce new products and processes, domestic firms would benefit from the accelerated diffusion of technology. Diffusion could also occur from labor turnover as domestic employees move from foreign firms (which typically focus more on job training programs) to domestic firms.

Business entry. While the "License Raj" has been substantially reduced at the center, it survives at the state level, along with a pervasive "Inspector Raj."[42] Private investors require many permissions from state governments to start a business. They also have to interact with the state bureaucracy in day-to-day operations because of laws governing pollution, sanitation, worker welfare, and safety.[43] Starting a business in India requires 10 permits, compared with 6 in China. And the median time in India is 90 days, three times the 30 days in China (World Bank 2003b). Complaints of delays, corruption, and harassment in these interactions are common.

A recent survey found that managers in India spend 16% of their time dealing with the bureaucracy, compared with 9% in China, 11% in Latin America, and 12% in transitional Europe (World Bank 2000c). The opportunity cost of managers' time is considerable. The persistence of controls also opens the door to possibilities for corruption. The same survey found that the share of firms making irregular payments in India is about 90%, almost twice that in Malaysia. To reduce the costs of investment related to delays and rent-seeking, all procedures for entry of firms need to be simplified and expedited. This requires re-engineering the gamut of regulatory processes, especially at the state and local levels. Needed are clear principles of transparency, an absence of discretion, and strong accountability. Introducing "single window" clearances would help greatly.

Factor Market Distortions

Inefficiencies in factor markets-for labor, capital, and land-coupled with a weak bankruptcy framework further constrain the business environment. There is less agreement on the way forward in these areas, and there are strong political and vested interests against change.

Labor market restrictions on hiring and firing workers are one of the greatest challenges of doing business in India, according to the Global Competitiveness Report-India ranks 73rd of 75 countries (China ranks 23rd). Employment in India's registered firms (those with more than 100 employees) is highly protected. Any registered firm wishing to retrench labor can do so only with the permission of the state government, and permission is rarely granted. These provisions, especially onerous for labor-intensive sectors, make labor rationalization very difficult and discourage the hiring of labor in the organized sector. They are obviously especially burdensome for exporters

---

[42] It may be noted that the License Raj still exists in some traditional areas, notably tariff and other protection policies, and the rebate and tariff exemption schemes for exporters.

[43] India, Ministry of Commerce (2002a) provides a good review of some existing procedural complexities with public and private investment.

competing with producers in other exporting countries. And they explain the tendency of FDI to focus on the domestic market rather than to use India as a base for exports. A recent survey found that the typical Indian firm reported having 17% more workers than it desired and that the labor laws and regulations were the main reason it could not adjust to the preferred level (World Bank-CII 2002e).

The Government recently announced its intention to raise the limit for seeking permission from 100 to 300 workers. But this requires legislative changes by Parliament (repealing section 5B of the Industrial Disputes Act), and the political sensitivity of such changes is likely to make them very difficult to implement. Contract labor is not subject to these retrenchment laws, but flexibility in hiring contract workers is limited by the Contract Labor Act, which allows the use of contract labor only for activities of a temporary nature. Amendments to the Contract Labor Act, now being considered, would allow the use of contract labor for all activities-not just temporary activities.

Various expert committees appointed by the Government and the Reserve Bank of India emphasize that the lack of adequate, timely financing on competitive terms is the single most important constraint to small and medium-scale enterprise (SME) growth and development.[44] With the shrinkage of the nonbank financial sector, credit to small units has declined since 1997.[45] Small players in India typically cannot get any startup financing from commercial sources. Even after they have reached a break-even point in their operations, profitable small businesses face shortages of working capital, investment funds, and other types of financing, undermining their ability to grow. Interest rate caps on small loans lead to the rationing of credit from formal financial institutions, so that even the better-performing SMEs are often forced to resort to informal sources of finance-at interest rates significantly above the prime lending rate. High interest costs for Indian small businesses affect their international competitiveness: the interest costs over sales were a quarter higher for Indian firms than firms in South East Asia (World Bank-CII 2002e).

In large part, the problem of SME financing may be attributed to market inefficiency. Transaction costs for SME lending are high because most banks use the same lending technologies for small business financing as they do for large corporations, but they do not have the credit information on SMEs to assess credit risk. And lenders perceive the default risks of lending to small business as high, because small firms often lack collateral that would secure loans. Problems in using land as collateral (lack of updated land and property records and the uncertainty surrounding ownership), the nonrecognition by lenders of other types of collateral, difficulty in collateral enforcement and loan recovery, and a bankruptcy framework that does not allow for the easy exit of troubled firms further drive up the risk of default.

To improve the efficiency of financial markets for SMEs, the Government needs to:

◆ Remove interest rate caps on small loans.

◆ Facilitate the establishment of well-functioning credit information bureaus and credit rating agencies for small borrowers.

---

[44] See, for example, India, Planning Commission (1997), the "The Interim Report of the S.P. Gupta Study Group on Development of Small Enterprises" (India 2000) and the "Report of the S.L. Capoor High Level Credit Committee on SMEs" (India 1999).

[45] Public sector banks' lending to small firms has declined from 2.5% of GDP in 1997/98 to 2.2% in 2001/02, with total lending rising only 30% over the period. But private banks' lending to the sector has grown 50% over the period, and foreign banks' lending has more than doubled (from a small base), perhaps reflecting their ability to evaluate borrowers and earn reasonable returns in the sector.

◆ Introduce legislative changes in mortgage registration to make the process more customer-friendly.

◆ Update land and property records for small loans.

◆ Simplify the legal framework for collateral enforcement and loan recovery by introducing alternative (out-of-court) methods of dispute resolution between creditors and debtors. The recently enacted Law on Securitization, Reconstruction of Financial Assets and Enforcement of Security Interest, which allows for the out-of-court settlement of bad loans, should be extended to small loans.

◆ Promote collateral substitutes and peer group security in providing and pricing loans to SMEs.

◆ Strengthen the bankruptcy framework to facilitate the easy exit of small firms, given their higher mortality rate. And banks should introduce new technologies (such as credit scoring) for SME credit and motivate branch managers to provide loans to commercially viable SMEs.

Problems with the use and transfer of land affect larger firms. Indeed, some 90% of land parcels in India are reportedly subject to disputes over ownership, which take decades to settle in court. And obsolete tenancy and rent control laws keep a large part of urban real estate off the market. Freezing rents at unrealistically low levels in Mumbai, for instance, has raised rents for new properties to phenomenal levels while keeping rents for old properties very low. This hampers the growth of domestic retail trade and construction by making it very difficult for new players to enter. A report on "India's Growth Imperative" by the McKinsey Global Institute argues that land market distortions account for about 1.3 percentage points of lost growth per year (McKinsey Global Institute 2001). The central government has already abolished the Urban Land Ceiling Act, which made changes in land use very difficult. But only a few states have repealed their corresponding Urban Land Ceiling Acts, which they should now do.

Outdated bankruptcy procedures and ineffective laws have led to inefficiencies in the system, making industrial restructuring almost impossible. Recent estimates show that it is common for proceedings to take more than two years, and more than 60% of liquidation cases before the High Courts have been in process for more than 10 years. Not surprisingly, when looking at the share of firms that go bankrupt, India has a much lower share (0.04%) than other emerging markets (figure 4.3).

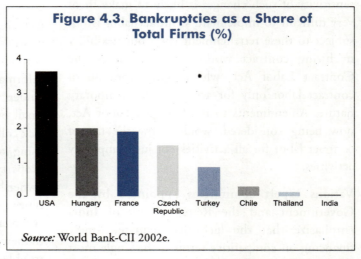

Figure 4.3. Bankruptcies as a Share of Total Firms (%)

Source: World Bank-CII 2002e.

The recent Amendments to the Companies Act (2002) should improve the bankruptcy framework. They stipulate the abolition of the Bureau of Industrial and Financial Restructuring and the creation of a new umbrella body-the National Company Law Tribunal-that will restructure, amalgamate, and wind down companies (previously performed by the high courts and district courts) and revive and rehabilitate sick companies (previously assigned to the restructuring bureau). Under the new framework, courts will no longer have any powers in mergers and liquidations, and this should help expedite the restructuring and liquidation of sick companies.

For this new bankruptcy framework to be effective, repealing the Sick Industries Companies Act is essential. The new framework will also depend to some extent on the pace of labor market reforms, since the successful winding down of companies may be hampered by problems in retrenching workers. The recent law on the enforcement of creditors' rights should help industrial restructuring, unlocking the resources tied up in nonperforming enterprises for more productive use. But to help the restructuring of small firms, the law needs to be extended to cover them.

Infrastructure Bottlenecks

Severe capacity shortfalls, poor quality, and high costs of key infrastructure continue to constrain Indian businesses.[46] The most important and difficult area for reform is power.

Power. Access to reliable power at reasonable cost is a prime concern for most Indian businesses. Industry surveys have found that acute power shortfalls, unscheduled power cuts, erratic power quality (low voltage coupled with fluctuations), delays and informal payments required to obtain new connections, and very high industrial energy costs, hurt industry performance and competitiveness. Nationwide, the shortfall in 2001/02 was estimated at 7.5% for energy and 13% for peak demand, with substantial variation across states in availability and reliability. Firms in Karnataka are reported to face, on average, daily power cuts of 2.4 hours, compared with 6.6 hours (mostly unscheduled cuts) for their counterparts in Haryana (TERI 2000).

Unscheduled power cuts impose substantial costs on firms. Average industrial production losses per outage unit are reported at Rs5 for firms in Karnataka and Rs22 in Haryana (TERI 2000).[47] Production losses due to outages are estimated at 7.6-7.9% of the production costs for industries in Haryana and 12.4-15.3% in Karnataka. Some 40% of the industries surveyed in Andhra Pradesh report damage to equipment due to the poor quality of power-with damage much more costly for industries with sensitive equipment, and process and quality heavily dependent on motor speed.

Industry is charged tariffs much above the cost of supply, due to the cross-subsidization of power tariffs by state governments and the widespread power theft euphemistically referred to as "transmission and distribution losses." In most states, political factors dictate that agricultural consumers pay little or nothing for the power they consume. Households also pay relatively little-often conniving with the electricity departments to draw much more power than is billed. Industry ends up paying an average tariff of Rs3.81/kWh (as against an average tariff of Rs2.39/kWh for all categories) and an average cost of public power supply of Rs3.50/kWh. Industrial tariffs for larger firms in India are 8-9 cents/kWh, among the highest in the world, higher than 8 cents in Argentina, 7 in Bolivia, 6 in Brazil and Thailand, and 3-4 in China. Typical rates in Western Europe are 6-7 cents/kWh.

A great proportion of Indian firms have been forced to operate their own (captive) generators,

---

[46] This section focuses on infrastructure bottlenecks that are in most critical need of being addressed in order to improve the business environment. One sector that is not covered is telecommunications, mainly because considerable progress has been made with reforms, and most business surveys report that Indian firms are reasonably satisfied with the country's telecommunications infrastructure. The challenge now is to improve rural telephone density and further improve overall access rates to communication services.

[47] The wide difference between the two states is because the average production cost for industries is higher in Karnataka than in Haryana, and firms in Haryana rely more heavily on self-generation.

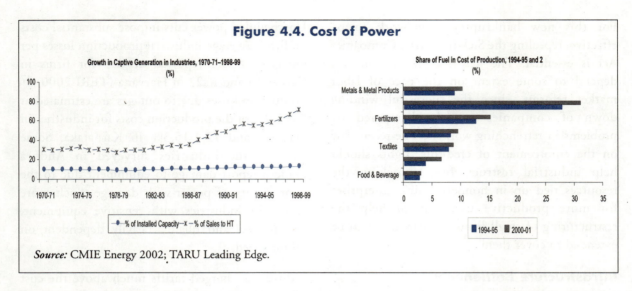

Figure 4.4. Cost of Power

Growth in Captive Generation in Industries, 1970-71–1998-99 (%)

Share of Fuel in Cost of Production, 1994-95 and 2 (%)

Legend: % of Installed Capacity — % of Sales to HT

Metals & Metal Products, Fertilizers, Textiles, Food & Beverage

Legend: 1994-95, 2000-01

Source: CMIE Energy 2002; TARU Leading Edge.

further increasing the cost of power for industry, further reducing firm competitiveness. The share of fuel costs in the overall production costs of Indian firms in all the major industrial sectors was higher in 2000/01 than in 1994/95 (figure 4.4). Captive power generation capacity is about 22,000 megawatts, one-fifth of the total capacity of the power utilities. Some 69% of the manufacturing firms surveyed across India had their own power generator, far more than the 30% in China (World Bank-CII 2002e).[48] For garments and electronics, energy costs in Indian firms were found to be twice those in Indonesia, the Philippines, and Thailand (figure 4.5). While large firms can bear such costs, SMEs suffer severely. They either have to go without power, or else install their own generator: the typical Indian SME has its own generator, tying up one-sixth of its capital, stunting its growth.

Urgent priorities are rationalizing power tariffs, depoliticizing tariff-setting, and implementing a phased reduction in cross-

subsidies that operate against industrial consumers. Several states have begun to depoliticize tariff-fixing by establishing statutory regulatory authorities-and others should follow suit. Andhra Pradesh and Karnataka have introduced price incentive schemes to encourage industry to shift to the grid. The initial results for Andhra Pradesh are encouraging, with a 22% increase in demand in 2003. Time-of-day tariffs need to be introduced

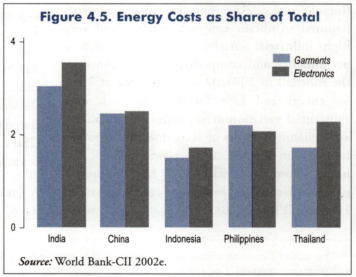

Figure 4.5. Energy Costs as Share of Total

Legend: Garments, Electronics

India, China, Indonesia, Philippines, Thailand

Source: World Bank-CII 2002e.

---

[48] In states that have made more progress with power sector reforms (Maharashtra) a smaller proportion of firms (45%) had captive generators. In contrast, more than 85% of firms surveyed in Delhi and Punjab, and more than 97% of firms surveyed in West Bengal, reported having captive generators.

for industries with peak and off-peak rates. To minimize financial losses to the power utilities, cost recovery needs to be enhanced by charging higher tariffs to agriculture and residential consumers.

These measures must be accompanied by steps to encourage greater private investment in power. Key reform measures include improving the financial and operational performance of the SEBs and increasing distributional efficiency through commercialization and privatization. The strategy for privatizing distribution should focus on the commercially viable segments of the network and develop alternatives for improving services and targeting subsidies in rural areas. Going after a broader range of investors and mitigating the perceived risks will be keys to privatizing the distribution business. Trading by industries with self-generation, along with other power suppliers, should be encouraged by providing open access to the transmission and distribution networks and eliminating cross-subsidies over an agreed time frame.

Since power reform is primarily the responsibility of the states, alleviating bottlenecks requires the full commitment of state governments. The central government can support them by introducing legislation to foster reforms to encourage private involvement. The new Electricity Act (2003) should help through its provisions for moving to open access, removing entry barriers to new generation, delicensing off-grid supply in rural areas, trading distribution licenses, stopping theft, and deepening regulatory reforms.

The new legislation effectively empowers Indian states to accelerate power sector reforms in the direction of greater competition, better governance, and private sector investment. But many implementation details remain to be decided, and the act's success will depend on state action. The central government has also introduced a scheme to provide financial assistance to states willing to adopt power reforms. More critical, however, are continuing government efforts to maintain a hard budget constraint for state utilities, including rigorous policies on payments to central generation and transmission utilities.

Transport. Ensuring speedy, reliable, door-to-door transport services is also critical to industrial performance. India has one of the most extensive transport systems in the world, but there are severe capacity and quality constraints. While notable progress has been made with the implementation of the National Highways Development Project, India currently has no interstate expressways linking the major economic centers, and only 3,000 kilometers of four-lane highways (China has built 25,000 kilometers of four- to six-lane, access-controlled expressways in the last 10 years). Poor riding quality and congestion result in truck and bus speeds on Indian highways that average 30-40 kilometers an hour, about half the expected average.

The Government and some states are implementing major highway upgrading programs, with the four-laning of 13,000 kilometers of national highways most notable. In addition, the Tenth Plan proposes road upgrading projects totaling 10,000 kilometers, and recognizes the need to start investing soon in a program of access-controlled expressways to provide faster and safer transport in high-volume corridors. Meeting the Tenth Plan targets will a big increase in private funding, previously limited. Although private financing of transport infrastructure has increased considerably in recent years, it can realistically be expected to fund only a small fraction of sector investment.

In the short to medium term, much can be gained through greater efforts to strengthen the policy, regulatory, and legal framework, to reduce uncertainties about political interference and weak contract enforcement. Better cost recovery from users would also help. India introduced a national fuel tax in 1999, but resource mobilization through such charges remains low. Reform should also focus on strengthening the public works departments by improving their financial performance and accountability. And users and other stakeholders must have a strong voice in overseeing the planning and implementation of transport infrastructure.

India's high-density rail corridors also face severe capacity constraints, compounded by poor maintenance. The average rail speed is only 24 kilometers an hour. Capacity expansion, an urgent priority, must be accompanied by efforts to improve efficiency in the use and maintenance of existing capacity. Indian Railways continues to be a patient resisting bitter medicines, despite the many prescriptions available. It recently slid into operating deficits and now depends on the central budget for its large investment program.

Reforming railways will require large-scale financial restructuring, involving the shedding (or even ring-fencing) of noncore assets or businesses. The Government also needs to address price distortions from the long practice of cross-subsidization from freight to passenger services, causing excessive freight tariffs, discouraging the use of railways, and preventing Indian Railways from serving the nonbulk high-margin transport market. (The freight traffic of Indian Railways as a percentage of traffic units is a mere 5% compared with 79% in China; Indian roads account for 60% of land transport freight and 80% of passenger traffic).

For the ports, berth capacity is no longer a serious constraint. The corporatization of major ports and the establishment of an independent tariff regulatory authority have helped bring in the private sector to develop new ports. But the efficiency of existing capacity, particularly in the older ports, needs improvement. In these ports, the low productivity of port equipment and labor

delays turnarounds and increases handling costs for cargo and containers.

The average turnaround for vessels has come down from 8.1 days in 1990/91 to 3.7 days in 2001/02 (and in some of the newer ports, such as the Jawaharlal Nehru Port Trust, to 1.04 days). But India still has to catch up with international standards, where the turnaround time is in hours. This will require strong efforts to modernize equipment and improve labor productivity, together with measures to reform customs administration. The time taken to get goods cleared through customs is 50% longer in India than in Korea or Thailand, and triple what many OECD countries report (World Bank-CII 2002e). Costs associated with shipping a container of textiles to the United States are more than 20% higher from India than from Thailand, and 35% higher than from China (figure 4.6).

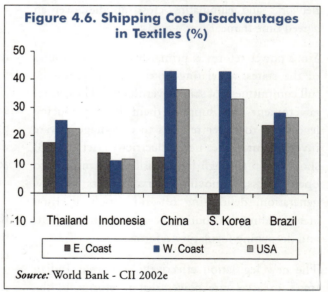

Figure 4.6. Shipping Cost Disadvantages in Textiles (%)

Source: World Bank - CII 2002e

Promoting greater private sector participation in the provision and financing of infrastructure is a key concern. In the long run, the Government cannot attract and sustain private investment in infrastructure unless it addresses the policy problems that underlie investor concerns-by raising prices to cost covering levels and establishing a sound legal and regulatory framework.

In the short run, various public-private partnerships-involving subsidies, risk-bearing, and other forms of financial support from government-may help attract private investment and close financing gaps. Such arrangements allow government to bear risks that the private sector feels it cannot mitigate through other means-for example, risks related to the demand for services or the cost of financing.[49] Frequently used instruments for government support to infrastructure projects include cash subsidies, in-kind grants, tax breaks, capital contributions, and guarantees of risks. In general, instruments such as cash subsidies and tax breaks are not desirable, particularly for countries facing fiscal constraints. Tax breaks may improve the bottom line but not target particular consumer groups-and they can cause serious distortions and create opportunities for graft. Where there are imperfections or gaps in the financial markets, capital contributions and the guarantee of risks not under the Government's control may be the best instrument to use. If the concerns relate to political and regulatory risks, some form of government guarantee offering compensation may be the most appropriate.

While public-private partnerships may help attract some private financing for infrastructure, they can also risk postponing the day of reckoning and impose serious costs on taxpayers (in forgone taxes or revenues from public assets, higher expenditures, or contingent liabilities on the Government's budget).[50] Given India's huge unmet investment needs in infrastructure, selective use of various public support arrangements could help private sector innovators pilot transactions that have good underlying cash flow, but where they cannot carry the full costs of the policy,

regulatory, and legal risks. In short: icebreaking services. Beyond that, the success of scaling up investment in infrastructure will depend less on clever financing and more on the framework underpinning private participation in infrastructure. In the long run, government cannot attract and sustain private investment in infrastructure unless the policy, regulatory, and legal problems that underlie investors' concerns are addressed. So public-private partnerships should be seen, at best, as temporary measures and should be entered into with caution.

Estimated Impact of a Better Investment Climate on Overall Economic Performance

The potential gains from removing key investment climate bottlenecks have been estimated in the range of 2-4 percentage points of annual economic growth. A 2001 study estimated that addressing the inefficiencies generated by the multiplicity of investment regulations, distortions in the land markets, and widespread government ownership of business would free India's economy to grow as fast as China's-at 10% a year-and to create some 75 million new jobs (McKinsey Global Institute 2001). That would ward off the looming crisis in employment to reabsorb the majority of workers displaced by productivity improvements. A 2002 study estimated that, if each Indian state could attain the best practice in India in terms of investment climate, the economy should grow about 2 percentage points faster (World Bank-CII 2002). The survey also indicated that, if India could achieve Chinese or Thai levels in areas of the investment climate where it lags behind those countries, its growth acceleration would be even faster.

---

[49] For a more detailed discussion on the available instruments for public-private partnerships in the infrastructure sector, based on international experience, and the factors that government should take into consideration when selecting an appropriate instrument, see Basu and others (2003).

[50] For a discussion on the ways to measure costs associated with various types of government support and methods to value guarantees, see Irwin (2002) and Irwin, Klein, Perry, and Thobani (1997).

CHAPTER 5

AGRICULTURE AND RURAL DEVELOPMENT

About 75% of India's poor are in rural areas, and a large proportion of them depend on agriculture for employment and as a major source of livelihood. Analysis of the 55th National Sample Survey (1999/2000) shows that agricultural households[51] make up 54% of poor rural households[52] — and in some states, such as Rajasthan and Uttar Pradesh, more than 70%. The large number of poor agricultural households and their income vulnerability are major concerns for policymakers, driving agricultural policies (trade protection and marketing controls) and public spending (investments and subsidies). Improving agriculture's performance, especially increasing foodgrain output to achieve self-sufficiency to meet its food security goals, has also been a major government priority.

According to the latest census, about 235 million people (58% of the labor force) were employed in the agricultural sector in India in 2001,[53] most of them in low productivity activities.[54] Their prospects are not bright. Large numbers of workers are tied to agriculture in almost all states. Agricultural growth is slowing down. The share of agriculture in GDP is shrinking from about 35% in 1980/81 to 23% in 2001/02. And the opportunities for employment in the rural nonfarm sector are limited.

Given the conditions for agricultural households, the Government's National Agricultural Policy and Tenth Plan place high priority on raising agricultural productivity to promote faster agricultural growth-and on promoting the faster growth of the rural nonfarm sector. Promoting both is vital because of their strong backward and forward linkages.[55] Opening greater employment opportunities in the rural nonfarm sectors would create demand for agricultural labor, contributing to higher agricultural wages and incomes. This will require improving access to basic infrastructure (roads, markets, electricity, water) and services (market information, credit, education).

Agricultural growth rates are slowing, with dire consequences if appropriate actions are not taken. The slowdown can be partly traced to the continuing decline in productivity-enhancing investment by the Government. Although most domestic trade restrictions were lifted in 2002, the possibility of their re-imposition at any time reduces private incentives to invest in agriculture. Improving agricultural performance requires progress in two key policy areas. First is rebalancing government expenditures from subsidies toward more productivity-enhancing public investments, including irrigation, rural infrastructure, research, and extension. Second is permanently removing restrictions on domestic trade to improve

---

[51] These include households involved in cultivation and agricultural wage labor.

[52] Based on the Planning Commission rural poverty line.

[53] These include 128 million cultivators and 107 million agricultural laborers. In rural areas, dependence on the agricultural sector is even greater. About 228 million workers, or nearly three-quarters of the rural population, were employed in the agricultural sector.

[54] Average labor productivity is measured by the sector gross state domestic product divided by the number of workers employed in the sector. In major states, excluding Punjab and Kerala, agricultural labor productivity on average amounts to about one quarter of labor productivity in the nonagricultural sector.

[55] Forward linkages take the form of the agricultural sector supplying products for downstream processing or direct consumption, agricultural surplus providing investment funds to the nonfarm economy, and consumption by agricultural household of goods and services from the nonfarm sector. Backward linkages take the form of the nonfarm sector stimulating growth in the agricultural sector by supplying inputs and investing in the agricultural sector (Lanjouw and Feder 2001; Haggblade and others 2001).

the investment climate for farmers while supporting a regulatory framework to ensure fair competition.

Agricultural performance. The recent slowdown in agricultural GDP growth-to 1.8% a year from 1997/98 to 2001/02) can be largely attributed to extensive droughts in many states and to flooding in some northern states (table 5.1). Several recent studies find that total factor productivity (TFP) in agriculture has been declining between the 1980s

and 1990s (Kumar 2002; Sharma 2002). In the Indo-Gangetic Plains, the seat of the green revolution, Kumar finds TFP growth of 2% a year between 1981 and 1990, but negative growth between 1990 and 1996. These and other studies attribute the deceleration in TFP growth to the slowdown in productivity gains from the earlier adoption of high-yielding varieties, the decline in public investments in the agricultural sector, and the rise in natural resource degradation (box 5.1).

Table 5.1. GDP, Agriculture Sector Growth Rates[a], 1980/81–2001/02 (%)

	1980/81-1989/90	1990/91-1999/00	1992/93-1996/97	1997/98-2001/02
GDP at factor cost	5.6	5.8	6.7	5.5
Agriculture, forestry, and fishing	3.4	3.0	4.7	1.8
Agriculture	3.5	3.0	4.8	1.7
Forestry and logging	0.0	0.6	0.1	2.4
Fishing	5.9	5.2	7.7	2.9

a.   Compound annual growth rate.
Source: Central Statistical Organization, National Accounts Statistics.

Box 5.1. Damaging the Land

As recently as 1999, the Government estimated that nearly half of the country's 329 million hectares of soil could be categorized as degraded (India, Ministry of Finance 1999).

✦ One study asserts that the majority of Indian soil has been harmed, concluding that only 36% of land area suffers no serious damage. It found that 5% faced low-level degradation (less than 15% yield loss), 11% was moderately degraded (15-33% yield loss), 43% was highly degraded (33-67% yield loss), and 5% was so damaged that the land became unusable.

✦ A study in Uttar Pradesh showed that waterlogging and salinization led to significant declines in paddy and wheat yields over a 10-year period (Joshi and Jha 1991).

The productivity losses leads to significant economic losses.

✦ A study from the mid-1990s estimated that agricultural output loss due to soil degradation amounts to about $1.9 billion a year (Brandon and Hommann 1995).

✦ One researcher estimated that waterlogging and salinization caused annual cereal production loss amounting to about 5% of agricultural GDP (Young 1993).

Dregne and Chou (1992) found that human-induced water erosion led to irreversible soil productivity losses of 20% or more in some parts of India.

Public investments in agriculture. Total investments in agriculture and its allied sectors (fishing and forestry) have been increasing. But since the mid-1980s they were driven largely by private investments, mainly in farm equipment, minor irrigation, and land improvements (figure 5.1). Public investment systematically declined.[56] Its share of annual agricultural gross capital formation fell from 44% in 1985/86 to 23% in 2000/01, a major cause for concern because of the potential negative impact on agricultural growth over the longer term. Gulati and Bathla (2002) estimate that a 10% decrease in public investments (including irrigation and power) leads to a 2.4% annual reduction in agricultural GDP growth. Because of the complementarities, lower public investment would also worsen the environment for private investment in agriculture. Gulati and Bathla estimate the elasticity of private gross capital formation in agriculture to cumulative financial public investment to be 0.16 in irrigation and 0.15 in power.[57]

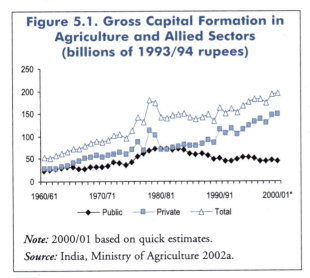

Figure 5.1. Gross Capital Formation in Agriculture and Allied Sectors (billions of 1993/94 rupees)

Note: 2000/01 based on quick estimates.
Source: India, Ministry of Agriculture 2002a.

Public investment in the agriculture sector over the last decade declined in large part because of growing subsidy requirements, major contributors to the rising fiscal deficit in the central and state governments. For example, central government food subsidies reached Rs242 billion ($5 billion) in 2002/03, 1.0% of GDP. Fertilizer subsidies, while declining, amounted to Rs110 billion ($2.3 billion), 0.4% of GDP. Foodgrain and input subsidies have distorted farmer cropping and investment decisions, which are both economically inefficient and contributing to widespread soil and land degradation. The bias toward subsidies also reduces resources for much-needed social investments and for appropriate operations and maintenance of critical rural infrastructure.

Policymakers question why India should reduce its agricultural subsidies, in view of the large agricultural subsidies provided by the EU and United States. These issues clearly need to be raised and addressed through bilateral and multilateral negotiations. But India's reduction of agricultural subsidies is no longer purely an issue of its fiscal costs and of using its fiscal resources more efficiently. The extent to which these subsidies are eroding the core foundation for sustained agricultural growth over the longer term, due to inadvertent natural resource degradation, is just as critical, perhaps even more.

Foodgrain (Rice and Wheat) Policy

Foodgrain policy rests on two major pillars. One is to ensure farmers a reasonable income through government procurement at a minimum support price for rice and wheat. The other is to ensure

---

[56] According to the Indian System of National Accounts, the public capital formation statistics primarily comprise investments in major and medium irrigation schemes. Gulati and Bathla (2002) re-estimate public gross capital formation to include investments in power (Concept II) and power plus investments made in agriculture and allied activities as defined under budgetary heads of the government accounts (Concept III). Under both concepts, public capital investments declined.

[57] Gulati and Bathla (2002) also find that availability of institutional credit and terms of trade between agriculture and nonagriculture also has a positive and significant influence on private gross capital formation.

adequate availability of foodgrains for consumers at reasonable prices through the distribution of subsidized foodgrains and the stabilization of prices through buffer stocking operations.

The Targeted Public Distribution System (TPDS), introduced in June 1997, aims to ensure access by the poor and other vulnerable groups to essential food commodities. The program supplies rice, wheat, and sugar nationally, and other commodities such as edible oils and coarse grains in some states, at subsided prices. The shift to the TPDS was a significant milestone in the Government's food security strategy, targeting a larger share of the foodgrain subsidy to the poor relative to the nonpoor.[58] To support the TPDS and price stabilization activities, trade restrictions on the private sector were enforced by the central and state governments.

The Essential Commodities Act (1955) empowers the central and state governments to enforce controls on movement, storage, exports and imports, and access to trade credit. Controls were enforced or lifted depending on the severity of supply shortfalls and price rises, thus eliminating private sector incentives for spatial and temporal arbitrage. In 2002 the Government finally lifted the licensing requirements and movement and storage restrictions on private dealers. But the potential for re-imposition continues to discourage private investments in the foodgrain sector. Recognizing this, the Government is considering the amendment of the Essential Commodities Act to permanently remove these trade restrictions, with provisions for their enforcement only in emergency conditions. In 2003 restrictions on the use of risk-management instruments, specifically futures contracts, were also removed.

Steady increases in the minimum support price for rice and wheat encouraged increased production, necessitating greater government procurement. But strong political pressure from states where the largest procurement take place-Punjab, Haryana, and Andhra Pradesh-stalled efforts to contain the increases. With the reduction in foodgrain off-take, with the shift to TPDS, and with the downward trend in world market prices, limiting export possibilities, buffer stocks rose to more than 60 million metric tons in July 2002, more than three times the norm of 18 million tons (India, Ministry of Finance 2003b). The buffer stock component of the food subsidy thus rose from 12.5% in 1997/98 to about 41.6% in 2001/02. The overhang of burgeoning buffer stocks put downward pressure on market prices, and combined with high minimum support price necessitated even greater government procurement.

To reduce surplus stocks, the central government instituted several measures-increasing the monthly allocations under the TPDS for all households, lowering the issue price for families above the poverty line, increasing the use of foodgrains for welfare schemes and drought relief, selling at prices below economic costs, and subsidizing exports. These measures raised the food subsidy bill even more.

Recent analysis of the impact of the shift to the TPDS indicates higher participation of persons below the poverty line at the all-India level and in most states (Deininger and Umali-Deininger, forthcoming). Despite this improvement, many of the poorest are still unserved. The most frequently cited reasons that households cite for not purchasing foodgrains from the TPDS are: "the item was not available in the ration shop," "not having a ration card," and "unsatisfactory quality."

Recognizing the crisis of mounting buffer stocks and food subsidies, the central government

---

[58] Its predecessor, the Public Distribution System, by contrast was a general entitlement scheme, which was widely criticized for its failure to serve the population below the poverty line. It was also criticized because it provided meager income, suffered from urban bias, leakage, and diversion and supplied deteriorating quality of grain, and lacked transparent procurement and delivery systems.

established a high-level committee to develop proposals for a long-term foodgrain policy, with the report released in 2002. The committee proposals to remove the rice levy and all restrictions on foodgrain trade, and reactivating them only in emergency conditions, will improve incentives for the private sector. But some of the other proposals raise concerns. The proposed policy toward maintaining self-sufficiency-it also ties farmers to low-value rice and wheat production-will come at the cost of efficiency. The continuing large public sector role envisioned in foodgrain markets will crowd out private sector participation.

The proposal to set the minimum support price to cover the cash costs plus the returns to family labor, land, and capital is a positive step. But in the longer term, fostering competitive markets would better ensure remunerative returns to farmers. So, the minimum support price should be reduced to cover the cash cost only, which complemented by others schemes (employment schemes, TPDS) would serve as a safety net for farmers. Otherwise the Government would be determining farm prices rather than the market.

The proposed reversion to an untargeted public distribution scheme is likely to bring back the earlier problems food subsidies being captured by nonpoor households, escalating the subsidies. Effectively targeted safety nets would help protect the poor from price and income shocks, while drastic supply shocks would be mitigated by a cost-effective and well-managed price stabilization mechanism.

There is broad agreement in India that the current foodgrain policy is not sustainable-but only limited agreement on the way forward. Significant political economy constraints, necessitating complex negotiations between the center and the states, compound the complexity of managing the reform process. Future progress will require a strong government commitment.

Input Policies

The Government's agricultural policy of the last three decades has relied on subsidizing key inputs to promote growth and ensure food security-subsidies that are fiscally unsustainable. Fertilizer subsidies, that are largely concentrated on urea, have distorted input use. Power and irrigation subsidies are causing fiscal crises in many states and, with deteriorating state finances, crowding out productivity-enhancing public investments. They are also leading to salinity, water logging, and declining groundwater tables in many areas.

Fertilizer Policy

Fertilizer subsidies were introduced in the 1970s in response to the sharp rise in the prices of oil and have since remained. Domestic producers of urea are given a designated plant specific retention price, essentially from a cost-plus formula. The fertilizer subsidy to the firm is the difference between the retention price and the farmgate price of fertilizer. Di-ammonium phosphate production and muriate of potash, generally imported, receive a flat-rate subsidy under a concession scheme. The fertilizer subsidy, now equivalent to 0.4% of GDP, is wholly borne by the central government.

Who are benefiting from the fertilizer subsidies: farmers or domestic fertilizer manufacturers? Gulati and Narayanan (2002) estimate the distribution of the subsidy based on the difference between farmgate prices of domestically produced fertilizer relative to imports. While the actual farmer share varies yearly due to the fluctuation in world prices, the average subsidy share of farmers was about 67% from 1981/82 to 1999/2000, and that of industry was about 33%.

Concerned with rising subsidy costs, the Government established a High Powered Fertilizer Pricing Policy Review Committee in 1997. Its report, completed in 1998, recommended:

◆ Deregulating the fertilizer industry.

+ Discontinuing the unit-wise retention price.

+ Basing prices on the long-run marginal cost.

+ Abolishing allocations under the Essential Commodities Act.

+ Giving new units a guaranteed price for 15 years.

+ Setting up a Fertilizer Policy Planning Board.

In 2001/02 the Government announced its policy to rationalize fertilizer pricing and implement the recommendations of the Expenditure Reforms Commission for a phased program of price increases (7% a year) and complete decontrol of urea by April 2006. Since then, the Government has implemented a number of reform actions (table 5.2). Continuing the commitment to the proposed timetable would lead to a significant reduction in fertilizer subsidies over the next few years.

Water Resources and Irrigation

Surface irrigation has been a pillar of the Government's agricultural strategy for increasing agricultural productivity and incomes, fostering agricultural growth and rural poverty reduction, and reducing volatile production fluctuations, thus improving food security. Public investments in surface irrigation accounted for a major share of expenditures in agriculture. Owing to increasing costs of expanding irrigation projects to more difficult areas, and higher costs of borrowing, capital expenditures at the national level increased from about Rs53.5 billion in 1985/86 to Rs63.1 billion in 2001/02 (constant 1993/94 rupees),

Table 5.2. Recent Fertilizer Policy Reforms

Budget period	Reform announcement	Reform actions taken
2001/02	First phase of decontrol to commence on April 1, 2001. Unit specific RPS will be replaced by a Group Concession Scheme. Current maximum retail price (MRP) arrangement will be continued and the concession for each group calibrated to enable units to sell urea at stipulated MRP.	Proposal for replacement of the Retention Price Scheme by a Group Concession Scheme being prepared by the Ministry of Fertilizers
	Concession rate for urea units based on naptha/furnace oil/low sulfur heavy stock be linked to international prices of feedstock.	Implemented in 2001. Maximum retail prices of urea, DAP, MOP and complex fertilizers increased and rate of subsidy on SSP reduced by Rs50/mt.
2002/03	Urea, di-ammonium phosphate (DAP), and muriate of potash (MOP) prices increased by 5% and reduce the subsidy on single phosphate (SSP) by 50/mt. Prices of complex fertilizers will be suitably modified	[Urea price increase reversed in March 2003]
2003/04	Issue price of urea will be raised by Rs12 and DAP and MOP by Rs10 per bag Implementation of Group Concession Scheme beginning April 1, 2003	

Source: India, Ministry of Finance budget speeches and implementation of budget announcements from 2001-03.

about 24% of the total central and state capital expenditures.[59] These investments contributed to an all-India increase in net surface irrigated area from 15.7 million hectares in 1981/82 to 17.7 million hectares in 1998/99.

Water resource management is a state subject. A major challenge for all states is intersectoral competition-between agriculture, the largest consumer, and other sectors such as industry, drinking water, and other users. In some areas, drinking water supplies have fallen to crisis levels due to overextraction of groundwater. Surface irrigation is suffering from a vicious circle: deteriorating infrastructure hurts agricultural productivity, contributing to poor cost recovery and the fiscal crisis in many states.

Who benefits from surface irrigation and its associated subsidies? In general, small and marginal farmers account for the major proportion using canal irrigation. The distribution of canal-irrigated land according to farm size varies considerably by state, however. In 10 of the 15 major states examined, small and marginal farmers accounted for half the total of canal-irrigated area (World Bank 2003b). Household analysis of the incidence of canal irrigation subsidies in Rajasthan finds, however, that its distribution is regressive, with a marginal farmer receiving about a tenth of the subsidies received by a large farmer (Sur and Umali-Deininger 2003.

The Government's national water policy (2002) aims to address the constraints, by ensuring the long-term sustainable allocation and efficient use through a comprehensive and integrated approach to planning and management of water resources, river basin by river basin. It puts priority on rebalancing expenditures from the creation of new assets to demand-driven investments in rehabilitation and maintenance. It also promotes cost recovery of at least operations and maintenance costs to ensure longer-term financial and fiscal sustainability of operations. And it seeks to re-orient water agencies toward greater attention to clients and the delivery of good quality water services. Several states have begun to adopt these measures in varying degrees, including Andhra Pradesh, Karnataka, Maharashtra, Rajasthan, Tamil Nadu, and Uttar Pradesh. Because water is under the purview of state governments, the challenge is to encourage states to adopt the whole reform package.

As a start, the national government recently introduced an incentive program to encourage cost recovery of operations and maintenance costs under the Accelerated Benefits Program by providing central assistance for the completion of "last mile" projects, with Rs95 billion allocated during the Tenth Plan period. So far, Rajasthan, Madhya Pradesh, Orissa, Maharashtra, and Uttar Pradesh have availed of these resources. In 2003 the Government established a task force to look into the feasibility of interlinking rivers as a way of transferring water from surplus to deficit areas.

Power Supply to Agriculture

In 1997/98 about 57% of net irrigated area in India used groundwater. Electric pumps have been critical for expanding groundwater irrigated area, contributing to the growth of agricultural productivity and aggregate output. Studies at the village level found that the use of electric pumps for irrigation increased aggregate output growth by two percentage points (World Bank 2002i). A study on the cost of unserved energy found an estimated loss in crop production of 3.1% of agricultural gross state domestic product in Haryana and 13.3% in Karnataka (Tata Energy Research Institute 2000).

---

[59] The public sector gross capital formation statistics from the national accounts and the capital expenditures based on the government budget differ considerably. The irrigation capital expenditure estimates, which primarily make up the agriculture gross capital formation, exceed the reported agriculture gross capital formation figure, due to differences in definition.

The large subsidy on the price of electricity to farmers, however, has led to the severe financial crises among the State Electricity Boards (SEB): and fiscal crises for state governments because of the need to cover for the huge SEB losses. Because a large part of the power supply to agriculture is unmetered,[60] utilities disguise theft and other commercial losses as consumption of power by agriculture, hiding their inefficiencies and poor governance. A metering study in Haryana showed that the state utility overestimated the electricity consumption by agriculture by a third (World Bank 2001b). State level studies of the incidence of the subsidies find them to be regressive, benefiting larger farmers more. In Karnataka, Howes and Murgai (2002) found that a large farmer received almost 10 times the subsidy received by a marginal farmer.

The financial crisis of the SEBs has had direct repercussions on agriculture sector, reducing their ability to undertake required investments, respond to rising local demand, and maintain reliable day-to-day operations. The results: power rationing, frequent power interruptions, and large voltage fluctuations that led to pump burnouts, reducing the reliability of irrigation water supplies, undermining farm productivity, and lowering farm profits. Farmer dissatisfaction has increased, making them less than willing to pay even the highly subsidized charges. Their delays in paying electricity bills and resistance to tariff increases, in turn, aggravates the financial crises in the SEBs.

Recent farm-level studies in Haryana and Andhra Pradesh found that poor quality of supply imposed additional costs on farmers (World Bank 2001b). Motor burnouts cost about Rs1,000 to Rs4,000 to repair and impose undue burdens on small and marginal farmers, amounting to about 10% of gross farm income for marginal farmers in Haryana and about 8% in Andhra Pradesh (figure 5.2). Simulating the impact of tariff increases with and without improvements in the quality of electricity supply, the study found that improvements in the quality of supply could more than compensate farmers for the increase in tariffs.

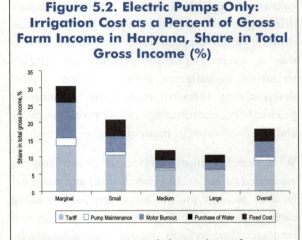

Figure 5.2. Electric Pumps Only: Irrigation Cost as a Percent of Gross Farm Income in Haryana, Share in Total Gross Income (%)

Note: Pump maintenance includes travel costs for repair and other costs. Motor burnout consists of motor rewinding cost. Fixed costs per year cover pump and well investments. Some farmers have zero fixed costs, as pumps are fully depreciated (assuming a 20-year lifespan).

Source: World Bank 2001b.

Current subsidy delivery mechanism is inefficient and ineffective. A large proportion of farmers who are not using electricity for irrigation do not benefit from the subsidies, and those who are connected do not receive adequate electricity services. India should thus move toward adopting a more transparent and targeted mechanism. For such an alternative model, it is indispensable that there is cost recovery of at least operating costs, universal metering of consumption, payment discipline, and more efficient electricity providers.

---

[60] Metered power supply was universal practice in India until the mid-1970s and 1980s. As SEBs faced increasing problems of pilferage, poor collection efficiency, and large numbers of corrupt meter readers, the shift was made to flat tariffs (Kishore and other 2003)

Product and Factor Markets

Trade Policies and Regulations

Economic and trade reforms in the 1990s have improved the incentive framework for agriculture, overregulation of domestic trading activities for major agricultural commodities hampers growth. These include small-scale reservations and controls on storage, transport, processing, credit, and exports and imports under the umbrella of the Essential Commodities Act 1955 is the umbrella for small-scale reservations and controls on storage, transport, processing, credit, and exports and imports (table 5.3). In addition, the Agricultural Product Market Acts of most states restrict the development and operation of wholesale "regulated" markets for agricultural products to the state government and force farmers within a defined area to sell only through these regulated markets. These regulations increase transaction costs and market risks-and hurt the agricultural sector.

The licensing requirements and movement and storage restrictions for rice, wheat, coarse grains, edible oil, oilseeds, and sugar were lifted in 2002. But the continuing uncertainty over their possible re-introduction discourage private sector investments, both local and foreign, in marketing, agro-processing, and industry. And some state governments continue to enforce some controls

Table 5.3. Major Domestic Policy and Trade Regulations, January 2003

Regulation	Rice	Wheat	Sugar	Oilseeds/edible oils	Cotton	Livestock/ products
Central Government						
Movement controls	Lifted	Lifted	Lifted	Lifted	Lifted	
Storage controls	Lifted	Lifted	Lifted	Lifted	Lifted	
Zoning						
Small scale reservation						
Selective credit controls	Lifted	Lifted	Lifted	Lifted	Lifted	
Jute packaging requirement						
Minimum price support						
Consumer price subsidy						
Export/import						
Futures banned						
State Governments						
Mill commodity levy						
Marketing controls						
Storage controls	Lifted	Lifted	Lifted	Lifted	Lifted	
Price support						
Consumer price subsidy						

Note: Shaded cells-commodity regulation exists. Lifted-commodity regulation temporarily not enforced. These commodities account for about two-thirds of agricultural GDP.

Source: World Bank staff estimates.

(cotton marketing controls in Maharasthra). A consensus has emerged, however, on the reform of the state Agricultural Produce Markets Acts to permit greater private sector and cooperative involvement in wholesale market development and to remove the restrictions on farmer marketing options. A government taskforce is currently drafting a model act. So far, only Karnataka has made minor amendments to allow the National Dairy Development Board to set up a fruit and vegetable wholesale market. And Punjab, Haryana, and Madhya Pradesh have allowed farmers under contract farming arrangements to bypass the wholesale markets and sell directly to the private buyer and contractors.

The reduction in manufacturing protection and exchange rate devaluations, started in 1991/92, substantially reduced the overall anti-agriculture bias of the system (Blarel and others 1999). After 1997, however, several major aspects of the external environment changed, with repercussions for India's agricultural trade policies. The quantitative restrictions on agricultural consumer goods imports were abolished in April 2001 when world prices of some major commodities produced by India declined substantially, reinforcing local pressures for protection. And Indian policymakers developed a more pessimistic view of the prospects for world agricultural trade liberalization, especially following the massive new subsidies in the 2001 U.S. Farm Bill. In response, the Government has raised agricultural tariffs, so that they are now above the average nonagricultural tariffs. In 2003/04 the unweighted average rate (including the special additional duty) is 46.8% compared with 30.7% for nonagricultural tariffs. But with only a few exceptions, India is no longer explicitly using taxes, licensing, export bans, or quotas to restrict agricultural exports and depress domestic prices.

Even though Indian agriculture remains internationally competitive, there are dangers given the direction of increasing trade protection. Experience worldwide, especially in agriculture, shows that high protection will sooner or later create high-cost production-as land, labor and capital move to produce products protected by high barriers to imports, at the expense of other products where pro-protection lobbies are less effective. Exporters and exports are typically major losers in this process, since they have to compete in world markets without protection. From this perspective, it would be in India's interests to reduce its World Trade Organization agricultural tariff bindings to much lower levels-constraining domestic lobbies pressing for high protection. As one of the world's largest agricultural economies, India directly influences the world markets of many agricultural products. If it follows open, predictable, noninterventionist trade policies, it can broaden these markets and reduce their instability. But if India intervenes excessively to protect its domestic market against instability in world markets, it is large enough to increase international instability, reinforcing moves for protection and intervention in other countries.

Access to Land

The agrarian structure in India has undergone significant structural transformation since the 1970s, with the distribution of land ownership becoming less skewed (figure 5.3).[61] The trend toward landlessness also appears to have been arrested, with the percentage of landless remaining at around 11% between 1982/83 and 1999/2000. The two main factors driving this process have been the Government's land policies and the demographic pressures (farm breakups through inheritance), though the contribution of each of these is open to some debate.

---

[61] These figures do not account for land quality. The ceiling on land ownership varies across states and depends on the quality of the land (dryland, irrigated land with one or two crops).

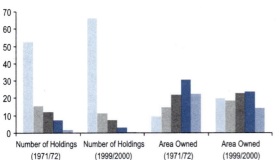

Figure 5.3. Distribution of Number of Owned Holdings and Area Owned by Farm Size (%)

Legend: Marginal, Small, Semi-Medium, Medium, Large

Note: Marginal-0.1 to less than 1 hectare. Small-1 to 2 hectares. Semi-medium-2 to 4 hectares. Medium-4 to 10 hectares. Large-10 or more hectares.

Source: 1971/72 and 1992/93 National Sample Surveys, as cited in Vyas 2002b; 1990/00 National Sample Survey - Deininger 2003.

Under the Constitution, state governments have the responsibility for land reform, and all states completed the passing of land reform legislations in 1972. The legislation focused on abolishing intermediaries between the state and the cultivator, imposing land ownership ceilings and distributing surplus lands to the landless, reforming tenancy to provide security of tenure and regulate fair rent, and consolidating holdings to prevent their further fragmentation. The land ceiling, the redistribution of surplus land, and the purchase of land by tenants contributed to the changing land ownership structure in India. But it appeared to work more through encouraging subdivision rather than selling surplus land to the poor. Government purchases of ceiling surplus land for redistribution to the landless have been very limited in almost all states. Today, because of declining average farm sizes in all states, there is more debate on the land ceiling legislation. Another area of concern is ensuring legal recognition of property rights for women, neglected in earlier land legislations (Saxena 2000b).[62]

Tenancy restrictions vary by state, ranging from a total ban to almost complete freedom of rental.[63] These laws, however, had unintended adverse impacts, including large-scale self-cultivation by landlords and the adoption of wage labor contracts. Appu (1997) estimated that tenancy legislations were associated with the eviction of more than 100 million tenants, causing the rural poor to lose access to about 30% of the total operated area. The legislation has also driven tenancy underground in most states, reducing the scope for greater land access through rental markets and the tenant's bargaining position and ability to enforce contract terms. These restrictions are also limiting the ability of small and marginal farmers to use their labor more productively, whether in farming by renting in land or renting it out to take advantage of higher-paying nonfarm opportunities.

There is a growing consensus about the need to revisit and reformulate tenancy legislation. In considering reform, it would be critical to draw lessons from experience in states that do not have any tenancy restrictions. More important, in some states the benefits from relaxing tenancy laws are likely to be higher than in others, due to the more advanced commercialization of agriculture (and significant amounts of informal leasing) and stronger political commitment to reform. These states could serve as pilots, yielding important insights for the policy debate and serving as a basis for broader implementation of tenancy reform initiatives in other states.

[62] For example, in Haryana, Himachal Pradesh, Jammu and Kashmir, Punjab, Delhi and Uttar Pradesh, a woman can only hold limited tenancy rights on the land and on her death, the holding goes to the heirs of the last male landowner and not to her heirs.

[63] Tenancy is totally banned in Bihar, Gujarat, Karnataka, Kerala, Manipur, Orissa, Rajasthan, Jammu and Kashmir, and Uttar Pradesh, while there is almost complete freedom of rental in Assam, Punjab, and Haryana.

In 1997/98 the Department of Land Resources introduced a centrally sponsored scheme to pilot the computerization of land records in selected districts nationwide. Its objective was to promote greater efficiency through faster information retrieval and transparency. Some states, such as Karnataka and Maharashtra, have scaled-up the program statewide and implemented the program in partnership with the private sector. The initiatives reportedly contribute to more efficient and faster service and reduce the opportunities for corruption. Over the longer term, the focus would need to shift toward improving land administration systems at the state level. To be successful, the land administration system would need to meet several other key standards of performance, including security, cost-effectiveness, fairness, clarity, simplicity, and sustainability. States could draw on the considerable international experience in this area.

Access to Rural Credit

India has a wide network of rural finance institutions (RFIs), but many rural poor remain underserved or completely left out of the formal financial system. There are more than 30,000 commercial bank branches, 14,000 regional rural banks, and 100,000 rural credit cooperatives, in addition to several nonbank financial institutions. This translates to about 4,700 people served by each RFI outlet. But the last available rural household survey found that only about a sixth of rural households borrowed from formal RFIs (RBI 1991). Noninstitutional sources accounted for 52-62% of household outstanding debt. The rural nonfarm sector also faces constraints to getting finance. A recent study covering some 20 million small rural enterprises (in the unorganized sector) found that commercial banks reportedly meet only 4% of the credit needs of this sector, and microfinance sources provide another 3%. Various estimates suggest that India's rural poor rely almost entirely on informal sources (money lenders, traders, commission agents) to meet their consumption credit needs-at annual interest rates ranging from 36% to 120% a year.

A key factor constraining improved access to rural credit relates to inefficiencies in the formal RFIs. Several task forces set up by the Government have concluded that the weak financial health and poor performance of RFIs prevent them from providing credit to rural areas. Most regional rural banks report losses, despite major government efforts to recapitalize and reform them. Cooperative banks in general, and rural credit cooperatives in particular, are also performing poorly, due to governance and management weaknesses, the result of pervasive government control. Rural access to finance is further constrained by the inefficiency of rural financial markets, characterized by interest rate "caps" requiring banks to price small loans within a range of 2% above or below the prime lending rate. These caps have the perverse effect of rationing credit to small rural borrowers, because banks prefer not to lend than lend at these rates. That drives small rural borrowers to borrow from the informal sector, where money lenders charge exorbitant rates.

Both the Government and RFIs can devise market-based solutions to help the rural poor gain access to a larger range of financial services more easily-and on less costly terms. Future priorities for the Government should include:

+ Liberalizing interest rates by removing the existing interest rate "caps" for small loans.

+ Improving credit information on rural households, by designating an agency that could take the lead in collecting and disseminating information on micro borrowers.

+ Facilitating the scaling-up and sustainability of existing low-cost microfinance models, such as the self-help group-bank linkage model, as well as the Grameen Bank replicators, piloted in various parts of India, particularly in the South, to make finance accessible to the poor.

✦ Removing legal and regulatory obstacles to innovations that can help reduce the costs and risks associated with rural finance.

The Government should also aim to improve the performance of the regional rural banks and rural credit cooperatives through:

✦ Enhancing regulatory oversight and supervision based on internationally accepted prudential norms.

✦ Reducing government control and ownership, which, for regional rural banks would require an amendment to the existing law, and for rural credit cooperatives, states to adoption of the recently enacted Model Cooperatives law.

✦ Strengthening corporate governance.

✦ Improving management and staff skills, particularly in credit decisions and risk assessment and management.

✦ Strengthening the legal framework to make it easier for regional rural banks and rural credit cooperatives to recover small loans and to facilitate the use of land as collateral.

Enhancing the Productivity of Public Investments

Greater emphasis on productivity-enhancing investments-such as agricultural research and extension, irrigation, and rural infrastructure-is critical to enhancing agricultural productivity, rural nonfarm growth, and rural poverty reduction. Indeed, Fan, Hazell, and Thorat (2000) estimate that a 10% increase in government expenditures on agricultural research and development, irrigation, and rural roads contributes to increases of 2.6%, 0.4%, and 0.6% in total factor productivity and reductions of 0.6%, 0.1%, and 0.5% reduction in the rural poverty rate.

Agricultural Research and Extension

India's public agricultural research and extension service, primarily under the purview of the central government, is one of the largest in the world. The public agricultural research system overseen by the Indian Council of Agricultural Research (ICAR) alone includes 184 institutes, centers, directorates, and special projects and programs and 29 state agricultural universities with a research staff of more than 30,000. The extension system is primarily under the purview of the state government, though ICAR also operates 261 Krishi Vigyan Kendras (farmer science centers) and 8 trainer training centers (ICAR 2002). The public agricultural and extension services have promoted agricultural productivity and output growth, especially during the green revolution in the 1970s and 1980s. But over time their efficiency and cost effectiveness have since been called to question.

Agricultural research. During the Ninth Plan (1997/98-2001/02), the budget outlay for the public agricultural research system amounted to Rs67 billion, 0.8% of agricultural GDP. Although there is room for increasing budgetary allocations further, there is also an urgent need to first improve the effectiveness of existing expenditures. Critical weaknesses of the ICAR system include:

✦ Crop bias towards rice and wheat.

✦ Inadequate priority to post-harvest, gender-related, and environmental conservation issues.

✦ Inadequate regional emphasis to rainfed areas.

✦ Imbalances in research priorities and resource allocations.

✦ Multiplicity of agencies at times leading to duplication.

✦ Inadequacy of collaborative multidisciplinary research.

✦ Weak interaction among researchers, extension workers, farmers and the private sector.

✦ Excessive centralization of planning and monitoring.

✦ The lack of accountability for performance (Vaidyanathan 2002; ICAR 2002).

Private participation in agricultural research is on the rise in India, especially with biotechnology and recent key policies, including the Plant Variety Protection and Farmer's Rights Act (2002), National Seed Policy (2002), and National Seed Act (in draft) aimed to protect of intellectual property rights. But private participation tends to focus more on higher value crops grown in better endowed areas. Public research still needs to address the problems of poorer farmers in less-endowed regions (Hanumantha Rao 2003). So, what is needed is a more regionally differentiated research strategy. Greater consultation and coordination between the public and private sectors would also minimize duplication of research efforts.

Agricultural extension. The agricultural extension systems at the state level-based on the training and visit system with its top-down, narrow crop-focused approach-has become outmoded and ineffective in meeting the new needs of farmers. In many states, tight fiscal constraints have led to the breakdown of the state extension machinery (Hanumantha Rao 2003). At the same time the private sector is providing more extension to farmers. And cooperatives, input suppliers, traders and private extension providers have become an important source of information for farmers.

In the future, improving the effectiveness of the public extension system would require reforms to make them more demand-driven and address the broad information and technical needs of farmers, taking advantage of major advances in communication technologies and innovative delivery mechanisms. There is also a need to build synergies between public and private extension. The Ministry of Agriculture formulated a new Policy Framework for Agricultural Extension in 2002. The key priorities include the adoption of a farming systems approach through multiagency

(public and private) delivery systems, greater farmer participation (including women) in planning and implementation, greater use of innovative information technologies, and initiatives for increased financial sustainability and cost effectiveness. The challenge lies in promoting the adoption and implementation of this policy framework at the state level.

Rural Roads

India's rural road network faces two major problems. First, about 40% of the rural villages are not yet connected by all-weather roads to market centers or main road networks. These unconnected villages are often cut off from the outside world for long periods during the monsoons. It is estimated that 20-30% of the agricultural, horticultural, and forest produce is wasted due to lack of roads to carry the produce to markets and processing centers. Second, much of the rural road network is poorly maintained, thus severely deteriorated. Due to poor maintenance of bridges and culverts, many rural roads become practically impassable in the rainy season.

Most government programs suffer from the lack of a carefully designed policy and institutional framework to ensure the sustainability of these investments. All India rural road maintenance requires about Rs50 billion a year, but only 20-30% of that is generally available. Politicization of investment decisions bias resource allocation towards investment. And the quality of construction and maintenance work is generally poor, resulting in overall low service lives for the roads. The multiplicity of agencies involved in roads further increases the complexity of rural road development and management.

The Government gives priority to improving the connectivity of villages through several centrally sponsored programs. Rural roads generally received about 50% of funding from various government employment-generation programs. The Government is committed to providing all-weather roads to the remaining unconnected villages, upgrading or constructing about 1.1 million kilometers of rural roads at a cost of Rs1.1 trillion. In 2000 it launched a national program, called "Pradhan Mantri Gram Sadak Yogna" (Prime Minister's Rural Road Program), to provide all-weather road access to all communities with more than 1,000 people by 2003 and those with more than 500 by 2007.[64]

To ensure greater consistency, the Ministry of Rural Development should take the lead in essential policy and institutional changes, and in financing, technology transfer, human resources development, and monitoring of rural road development in different states. The Pradhan Mantri Gram Sadak Yojana can also influence state-level rural road sector reform. If the program is properly structured, it can provide a powerful incentive for change. Panchayat Raj bodies at district, block and village levels are expected to play a pivotal role in the construction and management of rural roads.

Rural Electrification

India's rural electrification program has focused on extending the grid supply to villages and remote areas, covering 85%[65] of the villages and electrifying 13 million irrigation pumps. But access by rural households remains low at 31% (All India household access rate 52%). And electricity-based economic activities in the electrified villages are minimal. About 77% of the rural poor and 31% of the urban poor remain unconnected. During the 1990s the rural electrification program slowed down, and the

supply conditions in rural areas deteriorated. The policy of various states has been to subsidize electricity prices for agriculture and domestic use rather than improving access to the consumers. Often the rural areas face extensive power cuts (scheduled and unscheduled), much more than what urban areas experience.[66] About a tenth of the households reported adverse impact on their livelihood, and among the salaried and business category households by about a fourth (TARU 2001).

The Government plans to accelerate the electrification program, setting targets for covering all the remaining 62,000 unelectrified villages by 2007 and having 100% household connections by 2012. The remaining 18,000 remote villages are to be electrified by 2012 through the use of nonconventional technologies. Funds have been made available under the Prime Minister's Gramadaya Yojna. For strategic and implementation support, the Ministry of Power recently set up a high-level commission for renewable energy.

To facilitate electricity service delivery for agriculture and rural development will require a conducive policy environment:

- Adequate incentives for the service provider.

- At a minimum the agriculture and residential tariffs should cover the operating costs.

- Early subsidy reform to bring subsidies to a fiscally sustainable levels and enable more effective targeting of poorer farmers and rural consumers.

---

[64] The major source of funding of the program is the Central Road Fund with revenues from an earmarked tax on diesel and gasoline. The allocation to rural roads amounted to Rs25 billion in 2001.

[65] In India village electrification is defined as the existence of at least one electricity connection within the revenue boundary of a particular village. A village could just have a single connection to the house, or an agriculture pump and it would be considered as electrified by the utility and planning agencies.

[66] In Kerala a fifth of consumers surveyed in 2000 reported power cuts, 98% of which were from the rural areas. In Haryana (2000), a third of rural households reported frequent power cuts, and in Andhra Pradesh (2001) 40% of the rural households reported dissatisfaction.

+ Encouraging cost-effective technical designs of rural networks and exploiting the scope for reducing the construction and operating cost of rural electrification.

+ Improving affordability of connection charges through subsidized connection charges and financing of the capital subsidy for the service provider through innovative models of subsidy provision.

+ A supportive regulatory regime for rural supply. Decentralized generation should be incorporated into the rural energy service company model to augment power supply, provide voltage support, and reduce transmission losses. These steps to reform need to be put in place in parallel with reforms aimed at more conventional privatization of the commercially viable parts of the sector.

CHAPTER 6

CONCLUSION: DEVELOPMENT PROSPECTS AND RISKS

India's economic growth over the past two decades has been one of the world's fastest for large countries. In an outcome that few might have expected in the late 1970s, it jumped from an entrenched 3.5% a year to close to 6% during the 1980s and 1990s, substantially reducing poverty. Although progress in improving other indicators of living standards has been uneven, there has been real progress in education. Because around a third of the world's poor live in India, these are also achievements of global significance. But India remains far behind its main competitors in East Asia, particularly China. Poverty remains widespread, with average incomes low and social indicators poor. Moreover, a gulf is growing between India's richer and poorer states.

Accelerating development requires improving the delivery of health, water, and sanitation, setting India on a higher growth trajectory. Many of these goals are reflected in the Government's Tenth Five-Year Plan for 2002/03-2006/07, which targets average growth rate of 8% a year and rapid progress across a wide range of living standards. But if the trends of the past decade continue, the goals of the Tenth Plan (and the less ambitious Millenium Development Goals) will not be achieved. Growth has fallen in recent years, to below 6% a year between 1997/98 and 2001/02, and below 5% in 2002/03. Loose fiscal policies and a slowdown in the pace of structural reform have been likely contributors to this growth deceleration. Although a recovery may take place in 2003/04, India's current growth trajectory appears closer to 5%, than to the desired 8%. And the rate of progress in improving social indicators is insufficient to meet the Government's goals. A comprehensive set of reforms, as discussed in this report and summarized in box 6.1, could unleash faster growth and improve delivery of key services.

Outlook

Growth. The Tenth Plan period started with a further deceleration of growth in fiscal 2002/03 to an estimated 4.4%, partly as a result of external shocks. Agricultural output declined by 3% due to flooding in some areas and drought in others. Industrial and services output growth remained above 6%, despite depressed global demand. The degree to which global demand affects domestic output (except information technology (IT) output and exports) remains limited, however. And domestic demand and the policies that affect it are still largely responsible for India's output performance.

Baseline scenario. In the absence of major external or domestic shocks, and despite the expected recovery in 2003/04, the continuation of current policies will translate into a growth slowdown over the Tenth Plan period (table 6.1). Without a major reform impetus, it is unlikely that GDP will average much more than 5% a year between 2002/03 and 2006/07. Agricultural output is expected to recover from the 2002/03 slump and subsequently return to the previous trend. Industrial sector growth is expected to remain at between 5% and 6% a year, although the lagged effect of the contraction in agriculture on industrial output may dampen this recovery in 2003/04. Services, the fastest growing sector over the 1990s, can be expected to continue expanding rapidly throughout the period, albeit at rates slightly lower than those of the past five years, because large civil service wage increases are unlikely to be repeated given the existing fiscal crisis. Although growth in IT-enabled services may expand rapidly, it is also unlikely that the IT sector will continue to expand at rates comparable to those of previous years. The speed of recovery in global demand will be important to continue fuel the growth in services.

Reform scenario. A comprehensive reform program could improve the outlook considerably by providing new impetus to growth and accelerating improvements in social indicators. Although it is unlikely that an average annual growth rate of 8% can be achieved, it would be possible to gradually set growth on a higher trajectory and reach 8% by the end of the Tenth Plan period. Because of the low initial growth rate in 2002/03, this would translate into an average growth rate of 6.5% a year over the Tenth Plan period (table 6.1).

The reforms underpinning the above reform scenario are comprehensive, and would be expected to have an impact across the board-

during and beyond the Tenth Plan period. Reforms to reduce fiscal imbalances at the center and state levels would reduce crowding out and create space for increased private investment. Improvements in the composition of public expenditures-with a lower share spent on civil servants' wages, pensions, and interest, and on covering power sector losses, and a higher share spent on operations and management and investments in key infrastructure-would further "crowd in" private investment. Improvements in the investment climate, through the removal of bottlenecks in product and factor markets and key infrastructure, would increase the productivity of both public and private investment across the economy, including in India's poor rural areas. More foreign direct investment would contribute to technology transfer and increase output. More

Table 6.1. Macroeconomic Projections, Baseline and Reform Scenarios, 1997/98-2006/07

	1997/98-2001/02[a]	2002/03-2006/07 Baseline scenario	2002/03-2006/07 Reform scenario
Real GDP growth at factor cost (% a year)	5.5	5.0	6.5
Agriculture, forestry, and fishing	1.8	1.5	2.2
Industry	4.5	5.3	7.1
Services	8.1	6.4	8.0
Investment (% of GDP)	22.5	20.5	27.7
Public	6.6	6.4	7.3
of which: general government	3.1	3.0	3.7
Private	15.9	14.1	20.4
Consumption (% of GDP)	78.8	80.5	73.5
Public	12.5	12.0	12.4
Private	66.3	68.5	61.1
General government (% of GDP)			
Fiscal deficit	9.3	11.8	10.3
Primary deficit	3.5	3.6	2.2

a.   Ninth Plan.

Source: 1997/98-2001/02-Central Statistical Office. 2002/03-2006/07-World Bank staff estimates.

effective delivery of health, education and safety nets would accelerate progress in social indicators, empowering India's citizens to contribute to and benefit from faster economic growth.

Accelerating growth and poverty reduction in India cannot be achieved without also accelerating growth in India's lagging states. If growth continues to be divergent across states in 2002-07 (with poorer states growing no faster than 5% a year or only slightly better than in 1997-2002), richer states would have to grow at nearly 10% a year on average in 2002-07 to reach an all-India average of 6.5% a year-a rather unlikely scenario. Implicit in the envisaged reform is an acceleration of growth in India's lagging states, which have to implement the reform agenda outlined in this report-reducing fiscal imbalances, realigning the composition of public expenditures, improving the investment climate, and strengthening the delivery of health and education services and social safety nets. The central government has to catalyze and set the pace for reforms at the state level.

Particularly important for reducing poverty and increasing rural incomes are policies to increase productivity of agriculture. In the short run, removing subsidies to foodgrains could reduce agricultural output in the few states that benefit the most from them. But these are also the states where significant agricultural diversification can take place. More important, this reform would release resources for other expenditures, such as research and extension, rural electrification, and rural roads. Simultaneously, faster growth in industry and continuing rapid growth in services can provide jobs for the labor force released from agriculture.

Employment impact. Relative to the baseline scenario, reforms can be expected to have a positive impact on employment. Even though the employment elasticity of GDP is less than one (reflecting increased productivity of labor) and has been declining in India since the 1970s, a higher aggregate growth rate of the economy can be expected to generate higher employment levels (table 6.2). The composition of growth also matters. Agriculture, which employs a large share of the labor force, can be expected to continue expanding output without increasing employment significantly, reflecting underemployment and improvements in labor productivity, and thus increasing agricultural wages. During the 1990s agricultural growth had a zero elasticity of employment, even though it has a strong positive impact on poverty reduction. The estimated elasticities of employment to GDP in services and manufacturing are considerably higher, so accelerating growth in these sectors will have a stronger impact on job creation.

Table 6.2. Elasticity of Employment to GDP, Selected Sectors, 1993/94-1999/2000

	Estimated elasticity
Agriculture	0.00
Manufacturing	0.26
Construction	1.00
Wholesale and retail trade	0.55
Transport, storage, and construction	0.69
Finance, real estate, insurance, and business services	0.73

Source: India, Planning Commission 2001a.

Poverty impact. The continuation of the current growth trajectory is unlikely to make a big dent on poverty. Without efforts to reform the agricultural sector, improve productivity, and direct development expenditures to rural growth, it is unlikely that agricultural growth rates will accelerate beyond 3% a year. This will have direct consequences on the pace of poverty reduction in India over the next five years. Given the strong correlation between agricultural performance and wages and poverty reduction in rural areas, an unbalanced growth pattern-with agriculture continuing to lag behind-will do little to accelerate poverty reduction in India. Part of the rapid progress in reducing poverty in China is due to faster growth in agriculture, fueled by reforms in the sector. The incidence of poverty can be projected to decline by less than 6 percentage points under the baseline scenario between 2002/03 and 2006/07 and by nearly 10 percentage points under the reform scenario.

External sector. The continuation of recent trends would translate into modest growth of merchandise exports over the Tenth Plan period. But recovery in domestic demand, coupled with the Government's planned reduction in import tariffs, could lead to some acceleration in import growth, possibly pushing the current balance into deficit again. This could be reinforced by a renewed rise in domestic interest rates as a result of competition between public and private borrowers, putting further upward pressure on the real effective exchange rate. So part of any crowding out could be reflected in the balance of payments. Without any major policy slippage, however, any renewed current deficit is likely to be moderate. The Tenth Plan envisages a deficit equal to about 3-4% of GDP by 2006/07, albeit with faster growth of both exports and imports.

Financing such a deficit would require a mix of renewed equity inflows and new borrowings from foreign commercial banks and the bond markets. India's attractiveness to direct and portfolio equity investors is likely to require reinvigoration of the Government's privatization program and fresh reforms to enhance domestic industrial prospects. Foreign lenders, in turn, are likely to look for action to tackle the imbalances in the domestic economy, especially the fiscal deficits of the central government and the states. The current high level of reserves provides a cushion against both domestic and external shocks, although a change in sentiment for the rupee-as a result of continued high fiscal deficits or nervousness about the health of parts of the domestic financial sector-could lead to some erosion of reserves.

Risks

Fiscal. India's large fiscal imbalances pose a serious threat to sustained growth and development over the medium term. In the short run, the risk of a speculative attack is reduced by a compliant financial system, a large pool of household savers, the limited convertibility of the current account, and a flexible exchange rate. So, in the absence of a rapid increase in interest rates and weakening growth performance, India is not vulnerable in the short term to the type of collapse suffered by Russia or Argentina. But over the medium term, there are consequences to leaving the current fiscal situation unchecked. Current policies have helped reduce external vulnerabilities, but they have also kept economic growth below potential-with growing interest payments crowding out public investment and high real interest rates constraining private investment. Slower growth, in turn, speeds up the deterioration in debt dynamics. Even though interest rates have declined over the past 18 months, public debt dynamics have continued to worsen. With interest rates can be expected to increase from the current historical lows, the growth-interest rate ratio that has prevented the current fiscal vulnerabilities from translating into a full-blown macroeconomic crisis could deteriorate. The persistence of current fiscal trends will, at best, further limit growth and job creation. If this negative cycle continues, a full-fledged fiscal crisis cannot be ruled out over the medium term.

It is easy politically to downplay this risk, hoping that higher growth and lower interest rates will eventually solve the fiscal problem. But it would be unwise to sit back and wait for such a virtuous circle to emerge. Instead, the central and state governments will have to be active in reducing the fiscal deficit, shifting expenditures to more productive areas, and removing structural impediments to higher private investment and productivity. The sooner the roadmap for these reforms is put in place, and concrete actions taken to show commitment to follow through, the more manageable will be the adjustment path, and the quicker the payoff in higher growth and reduced poverty.

Political. Other risks could threaten India's development prospects. An important risk is that the comprehensive reforms needed to accelerate development will be delayed due to the primacy of political concerns, such as general or state elections. Another is the diversion of policymakers' attention (and public resources) to other issues, such as the tensions with neighboring countries. Political obstacles to the needed hardening of budget constraints between the center and the states, particularly in states that wield considerable political power, threaten to further erode state finances and discourage reforming states.

External. In the short run, developments in the external environment cannot be expected to be strong positive forces. The recovery of the global economy is expected to be slow. There remain weaknesses in demand in the world's largest markets Western Europe, Japan, and North America. This will slow the growth in industry. A slow down in the inflow of remittances is also likely. At least part of the higher inflow of remittances observed in India is likely to have been a one-off episode. The same trends can be observed in other countries, such as Pakistan and Bangladesh. This level of inflows can be expected to weaken, emphasizing India's fiscal vulnerabilities.

Conclusion

India can be proud of its development record over the past two decades. It reflects the emergence of a much wider consensus about the importance of opening the Indian economy to competition. The results in faster growth and poverty reduction are impressive. But India has still fallen behind its main competitors in East Asia-and poverty remains a reality for many Indians, especially those in the poorer states of the North and East. The Government is right to set ambitious targets for growth and social development during the Tenth Plan. The key now is to implement the policy and institutional changes to achieve these goals. Sustained progress will no doubt be difficult, especially in the politically charged areas of labor, power, and agricultural reform. But it also promises high returns by reducing poverty.

Box 6.1. Summary of Priority Reforms

Fiscal Policy

✦ Progressively reduce the primary deficit at the center and in states by completing tax reforms (eliminating exemptions, bringing services into the tax net, and implementing a uniform state value-added tax), reducing power sector losses, and phasing out petroleum subsidies.

✦ Reduce financial sector risks by implementing the new securitization law, linking returns on provident funds and small savings to market benchmarks, and establishing a clear framework for managing state government guarantees.

✦ Improve fiscal management by imposing greater fiscal discipline on state borrowing and transfers, breaking down artificial distinctions between plan and nonplan expenditures, and consolidating centrally sponsored schemes.

✦ Improve the composition of public expenditures, by reducing the share spent on wages, pensions, interest payments, and agricultural subsidies, and increasing investment and operations and maintenance for priority social, infrastructure and agriculture programs.

Delivery of Public Services

✦ Reduce administrative fragmentation and reform civil service pay policy and pensions. Improve the performance of the civil service and quality of service delivery by improving public access to information, strengthening accountability, and reducing political interference.

✦ Refocus health, education, and social safety net programs on outcomes. The central government can be an independent source for measuring progress toward agreed goals.

✦ Improve the private market for health care through training, public information, and accreditation. Priorities for public funds are to provide clean water and sanitation, and to combat communicable diseases (including HIV/AIDS prevention).

✦ Support the education-for-all goals by providing more public resources and improving resource use in elementary education. Schools should be more accountable to communities and have more local autonomy to find the best solutions.

✦ Develop a well-designed fiscal framework for local governments to guarantee their autonomy and accountability. Flows of funds from the center and states should depend on good local fiscal performance and resource mobilization.

Investment Climate for Industry and Services

✦ Speed up trade reform by reducing average import tariffs and phasing out tariff exemptions, specific tariffs, and antidumping duties. Remove other product market distortions by eliminating preferential policies for small players, implementing a full and uniform value-added tax, and phasing out remaining foreign direct investment restrictions.

- Reduce inefficiencies in factor markets by easing restrictions on hiring and firing of workers, improving access to credit for small and medium-scale enterprises, addressing problems in the use and transfer of land, and updating bankruptcy procedures.

- Ensure access to reliable power at reasonable costs by rationalizing power tariffs and improving the financial and operational performance of State Electricity Boards.

- Address capacity and quality constraints in transport by improving public sector performance (for roads and rail), mobilizing private investment (including better cost recovery for roads), phasing out price distortions (for rail), and improving the efficiency of existing capacity (for ports).

Agricultural Policy and Rural Development

- Put in place a market-based foodgrain policy that protects the poor through targeted safety nets, while mitigating drastic supply shocks through a cost-effective and well-managed price stabilization mechanism.

- Reduce input subsidies that are fiscally unsustainable and distorting input use. Savings should be used to fund more productive investments in agricultural research and extension, rural roads, and rural electrification.

- Reduce regulation of domestic trading activities for major agricultural commodities and eliminate remaining trade policy distortions, including subsidized exports of rice and wheat.

- Improve access to land by revisiting current legislation on land tenancy and building on successful initiatives to improve land administration. Devise market-based solutions to improve rural access to a larger range of financial services at lower cost.

REFERENCES

Acharya, Shankar. 2001. "India's Macroeconomic Management in the Nineties." Indian Council for Research on International Economic Relations, New Delhi.

————. 2002a. "Macroeconomic Management in the Nineties." *Economic and Political Weekly,* April.

————. 2002b. "India's Medium-Term Growth Prospects." *Economic and Political Weekly,* July.

————. 2003. "Reform Agenda for Indian Agriculture." Indian Council for Research on International Economic Relations, New Delhi.

Acharya, Shankar, Isher Ahluwalia, K.L. Krishna, and Ila Patnaik. 2002. "Global Research Project: India Case Study." Indian Council for Research on International Economic Relations, New Delhi.

Ahluwalia, Montek S. 2002a. "India's Vulnerability to External Crisis: An Assessment." In Montek Ahluwalia, S.S. Tarapore, and Y.V. Reddy, eds., *Macroeconomics and Monetary Policy: Issues for a Reforming Economy: Essays in Honor of C. Rangarajan.* Oxford: Oxford University Press.

————. 2002b. "Economic Reforms in India: A Decade of Gradualism." *Journal of Economic Perspectives,* forthcoming. World Bank, Washington, D.C.

Aiyar, Shekhar. 2001. "Growth Theory and Convergence Across Indian States: A Panel Study." In Tim Callen, Patricia Reynolds, and Christopher Towe, eds., *India at the Crossroads: Sustaining Growth and Reducing Poverty.* Washington, D.C.: International Monetary Fund.

Anant, T.C.A., and N.L. Mitra. 1998. "The Role of Law and Legal Institutions in Asian Economic Development: The Case of India." Discussion paper 662. Harvard Institute for International Development, Cambridge, Mass.

Appu, P.S. 1997. *Land Reform in India: A Survey of Policy, Legislation and Implementation.* New Delhi: Vikas Publishing House.

Bajpai, Nirupam, and Jeffrey Sachs. 1998. "Strengthening India's Strategy for Economic Growth." *Economic and Political Weekly*, July.

Banerjee, A. V., P. J. Gertler, and M. Ghatak. 2002. "Empowerment and Efficiency: Tenancy Reform in West Bengal." *Journal of Political Economy* 110 (2): 239–80.

Banerjee, Abhijit, and Lakshmi Iyer. 2002. "History, Institutions and Economic Performance: The Legacy of Colonial Land Tenure Systems in India." Paper delivered at World Bank research seminar, March, Washington, D.C.

Bardhan, P. 2002. "Disjunctures in the Indian Reform Process: Some Reflections." Outline presented at Cornell University, April 19–20. Ithaca, New York.

Barro, Robert, and Xavier Sala-I-Martin. 2002. *Economic Growth.* New York: McGraw Hill Inc.

Basu, Priya, Clive Harris, and Stephan Von Klaudy. 2003. "Public Support for Private Infrastructure Projects: Issues and Challenges." Policy Note. World Bank, Washington, D.C.

Besley, T., and R. Burgess. 2000. "Land Reform, Poverty Reduction, and Growth: Evidence from India." *Quarterly Journal of Economics* 115 (2): 389–430.

Bhalla, Surjit S. 2002. "Imagine There's No Country—Poverty, Inequality and Growth in the Era of Globalization." Institute for International Economics, Washington, D.C.

Brandon, C., and K. Hommann. 1995. "The Cost of Inaction: Valuing the Economy-Wide Cost of Environmental Degradation in India." Draft. World Bank, Washington, D.C.

Buiter, Willem, and Urjit Patel. 1992. "Debt, Deficits and Inflation: An Application to the Public Finances of India." *Journal of Public Economics* 47: 171–205.

Burgess, Robin, and R. Pande. 2002. "Do Rural Banks Matter? Evidence from the Indian Social Banking Experiment." Draft.

Cashin, P., N. Olekalns, and R. Sahay. 2001. "Tax Smoothing, Financial Repression and Fiscal Deficits in India." In Tim Callen, Patricia Reynolds, and Christopher Towe, eds., *India at the Crossroads—Sustaining Growth and Reducing Poverty*. International Monetary Fund, Washington, D.C.

Central Statistical Organization. 2002. Ministry of Statistics and Program Implementation, National Accounts Statistics, New Delhi

Chang, Roberto, and Andres Velasco. 1998. *The Asian Liquidity Crisis.* NBER Working Paper 6796. Washington, D.C.: National Bureau of Economic Research.

Chaudhry, M.D. 1966. *Regional Income Accounting in an Underdeveloped Economy: A Case Study of India.* Calcutta: Firma K. L. Mukhopadhyay.

CMIE (Center for Monitoring Indian Economy). 2000. *Agriculture.* Mumbai.

———. 2002. *Agriculture.* Mumbai.

———. 2002. *Energy.* Mumbai.

Comptroller and Auditor General of India. 2000. *Report of the CAG on the Union Government for the Year Ended 1999.* New Delhi.

CRISIL (Credit Rating and Information Services of India Limited). 2002. "Mounting State Government Guarantees—Fiscally Unsustainable." Mumbai.

Deaton, Angus. 2002. "Adjusted Indian Poverty Estimates for 1999–2000." Paper delivered at the India Workshop on Poverty Measurement, Monitoring and Evaluation, January 11–12, New Delhi.

Deaton, A., and Jean Drèze. 2002. "Poverty and Inequality in India, A Re-Examination." *Economic and Political Weekly*, September: 3729–48.

Deininger, Klaus, and D. Umali-Deininger. 2001. "Towards Greater Food Security For India's Poor: Balancing Government Intervention And Private Competition." *Agricultural Economics* 25: 321–35.

———. Forthcoming. "Targeted Public Distribution System: Is it Reaching the Poor?"

Deshpande, R.S. 2003. "Land Issues in India." *Land Reform, Land Settlement and Cooperatives Journal.* Forthcoming.

Dregne, H. E., and N. T. Chou. 1992. "Global Desertifications Dimensions and Costs." In H.E. Dregne, ed., *Degradation and Restoration of Arid Lands*. Lubbock, Texas Tech University.

Drèze, Jean. 2001. "Starving the Poor." *The Hindu*. February 26–27. New Delhi.

Duflo, Esther. 2003. "Scaling Up and Evaluation" Draft paper prepared for the ABCDE Conference, May 23–25, 2003, Bangalore.

Dutta, B., and B. Ramaswami. 2001. "Targeting and Efficiency in the Public Distribution System: Case of Andhra Pradesh and Maharashtra." *Economic and Political Weekly*, May: 1524–32.

Economic and Political Weekly. 2003. "Fertilizers: Revamping Pricing." Editorial, March 15.

EIU (Economist Intelligence Unit). 2002. *India Country Profile 2002*. July. London.

Esrey S., J. Potash, L. Roberts, and C. Shiff. 1991. "Effects of Improved Water Supply and Sanitation on Ascariasis, Diarrhea, Dracunculiasis, Hookworm Infection, Schistosomiasis, and Trachoma." World Health Organization Bulletin 69(5): 609–21.

Expenditure Reform Commission. 2000. "Rationalizing Fertilizer Subsidies, Part I." Mimeo.

Fan, S., P. Hazell, and S. Thorat. 2000. "Government Spending, Growth and Poverty in Rural India." *American Journal of Agricultural Economics* 82(4): 1038–51.

Ferro, M., D. Rosenblatt, and N. Stern. 2002. "Policies for Pro-Poor Growth in India." Paper presented at Cornell University, April 19–20, Ithaca, New York.

FICCI (Federation of Indian Chambers of Commerce and Industry). 2002. "Indian Agriculture Unbound: Making Indian Agriculture Globally Competitive." New Delhi.

Godbole, Madhav. 1997. "Pay Revision: High Cost of Total Surrender." *Economic and Political Weekly*, October.

Goswami, Omkar, and David Dollar. 2002. "Competitiveness of Indian Manufacturing: Results from a Firm Level Survey." Confederation of Indian Industries, New Delhi.

Govinda Rao, M. 2000. "Invisible Transfers in Indian Federalism." *Public Finance*, 52 (3, 4): 429–48.

Gulati, A., and G. Pursell. 2003. "Indian Agriculture During the 1990s, Performance, Policy Environment and Incentives." World Bank Working Paper. Washington, D.C.

Gulati, A., and S. Bathla. 2002. "*Capital Formation in India Agriculture: Trends, Composition and Implications for Growth.*" Occasional Paper 24. National Bank for Agriculture and Rural Development, Mumbai.

Gulati, A., and S. Narayanan. 2002. "Demystifying Fertilizer and Power Subsidies in India." In R. Kapila and U. Kapila, eds., *Indian Agriculture in the Changing Environment*. Vol. 1. New Delhi: Academic Foundation.

Haggblade, Steven, Peter Hazell, and Thomas Reardon. 2001. "Strategies for Stimulating Equitable Growth of the Rural Non-farm Economy in Developing Countries." South Asia Rural Development Unit, World Bank, Washington, D.C.

Hanchate, A., and T. Dyson, 2000. "Trends in the Composition of Food Consumption and Their Impact on Nutrition and Poverty in India." London School of Economics, London.

Hanson, J. 2002. "Improving Indian Banks Performance." Paper presented at the Goa Conference on Adapting India's Financial Sector to a Globalized World, October 31–November 2, 2002, Goa.

Hanson, J., and S. Kathuria, eds. 1999. *India: A Financial Sector for the Twenty-First Century*. New Delhi: Oxford University Press.

Hanumantha Rao, C.H. 2000. "Declining Demand for Foodgrains in Rural India: Causes and Implications." *Economic and Political Weekly*, January 22.

———. 2002. "Agricultural Growth Sustainability and Poverty Alleviation," In R. Kapila and U. Kapila, eds., *Indian Agriculture in the Changing Environment*. Vol. 1. New Delhi: Academic Foundation.

———. 2003. "Reform Agenda for Agriculture." *Economic and Political Weekly*, February 15.

Howes, Stephen, A. Lahiri, and N. Stern (ed.) Forthcoming. "State Level Reforms in India – Towards More Effective Government," Macmillan.

Howes, Stephen, and Rinku Murgai. 2002. "Karnataka: Incidence of Agricultural Power Subsidies: Estimate." *Economic and Political Weekly* 38(16): 1533–35.

Hughes G., K. Lvovsky, and M. Dunleavy. 2000. *Environmental Health in India: Priorities in Andhra Pradesh*. World Bank, South Asia Environment Unit, Washington, D.C.

Hutley S., S. Morris, and V. Pisana. 1997. "Prevention of Diarrhea in Young Children in Developing Countries." World Health Organization Bulletin 75(2): 163–74.

ICAR (Indian Council of Agricultural Research). 2001. *ICAR Now and Ahead*. New Delhi.

———. 2002. *ICAR Vision 2020*. New Delhi.

IMF (International Monetary Fund). 2002. *India: Selected Issues and Statistical Appendix*. IMF Country Report 02/193.

India, 1998. "Report of the High Level Credit Committee on SMEs" (led by S.L. Kapur).

———. 1999. "Report of the Task Force on the Cooperative Credit System (led by Jagdish Capoor)."

———. 2000a. "The Interim Report of the Study Group on Development of Small Enterprises" (led by S.P. Gupta).

———. 2002. *External Debt Status Report*. August. New Delhi.

———. Ministry of Agriculture. 2002a."Agricultural Statistics at a Glance 2002." New Delhi: Directorate of Economics and Statistics.

———. 2000b. "National Agricultural policy." Department of Agriculture and Cooperation.

———. 2002c. "Policy Framework for Agricultural Extension." New Delhi: Department of Agriculture and Cooperation, Extension Division.

India, Ministry of Chemicals and Fertilizers. 1998. "Fertilizer Pricing Policy: Report of the High Powered Review Committee." New Delhi.

India, Ministry of Consumer Affairs, Food and Public Distribution. 2002. *Report of the High Level Committee on Long-Term Grain Policy.* New Delhi: Department of Food and Public Distribution.

India, Ministry of Commerce. 2002a. "Reforming Investment Approval & Implementation Procedures." New Delhi.

———. 2002b. "Report of the High Level Committee for EXIM Policy, 2002–07." Directorate General of Foreign Trade, New Delhi.

India, Ministry of Finance. 1999. *Economic Survey 1998–99.* New Delhi.

———. 2001a. "Budget Speech 2001–02." New Delhi.

———. 2001b. *Economic Survey 2000–01.* New Delhi.

———. 2001c. "Implementation of Budget Announcements." New Delhi.

———. 2001d. "Report of the Joint Committee on Revitalization Support to Cooperative Credit Structure (chaired by Balasaheb Vikhe Patil)." New Delhi.

———. 2002a. "Budget Speech 2002–03." New Delhi.

———. 2002b. *Economic Survey 2001–02.* New Delhi.

———. 2002c. "Implementation of Budget Announcements." New Delhi.

———. 2002d. "Report of the Working Group to Suggest Amendments in the Regional Rural Banks Act (Chaired by M.V.S. Chalapathi Rao)." New Delhi.

———. 2003a. Central Budget Documents 2003–04. New Delhi.

———. 2003b. *Economic Survey, 2002–03.* New Delhi.

———. 2003c. "Implementation of Budget Announcements." New Delhi.

India, Ministry of Rural Development. 2001. *Annual Report 2000–2001.* New Delhi.

India, Office of the Registrar General. 1981. Census of India. New Delhi.

———.1991. Census of India. New Delhi.

———.2001. Census of India. New Delhi.

India, Planning Commission. 1997. *Report of the Abid Hussain Committee on Small Scale Enterprises.* New Delhi.

———. 1999. *Report of the S.P. Gupta Committee on Small Scale Industry.* New Delhi.

———. 2001a. "Approach Paper to the Tenth Five Year Plan 2002–2007." New Delhi.

———. 2001b. "Report of the Task Force on Employment Opportunities." New Delhi.

———. 2002a. "Annual Report on the Working of SEBs and Electricity Departments." New Delhi.

———. 2002b. "Report of the Steering Committee on Foreign Direct Investment." New Delhi.

———. 2002c. *Planning Commission Reports on Labour and Employment.* New Delhi: Economica India Info-Services, Academic Foundation.

————. 2003. *Tenth Five-Year Plan 2001–02 to 2006–07.* New Delhi.

India, Prime Minister's Economic Advisory Council. 2001. "Report of the Prime Minister's Economic Advisory Council." New Delhi.

————. 2002a. "Economic Reforms: A Medium-Term Perspective." New Delhi.

————. 2002b. "Report of the Prime Minister's Economic Advisory Council." New Delhi.

ILO (International Labour Organization). 2001. "Life at Work in the Information Economy." *World Employment Report.* Geneva.

Infrastructure Development Finance Company Ltd. 2001. "India Infrastructure Report." Mumbai.

————. 2002. "India Infrastructure Report." Mumbai.

Irwin, Timothy. 2002. "Deciding When to Offer Guarantees, Out-based Subsidies, or other Forms of Fiscal Support for Private Infrastructure Services." World Bank, Washington, D.C.

Irwin, Timothy, Michael Klein, Guillermo E. Perry, and Mateen Thobani. 1997. "Dealing with Public Risk in Private Infrastructure." World Bank, Washington, D.C.

Jalan, J., and M. Ravallion. 2001. "Does Piped Water Reduce Diarrhea for Children in Rural India?" Policy Research Working Paper 2664. World Bank, Washington, D.C.

Jha, Shikha, and P.V. Srinivasan. 2001. "Taking the PDS to the poor: Directions for further reform." *Economic and Political Weekly*, September 29: 3779–86.

Joshi, P. K., and D. Jha. 1991. "Farm-Level Effects of Soil Degradation in Sharda Sahayak Irrigation Project." Working Papers on Future Growth in Indian Agriculture No. 1. Indian Council of Agricultural Research, Central Soil Salinity Research Institute, New Delhi, and International Food Policy Research Institute, Washington, D.C.

Kalirajan, K.P., and R. T. Shand. 1997. "Sources of Output Growth in India Agriculture." *Indian Journal of Agricultural Economics* 52(4): 693–706.

Kapur, Devesh, and Urjit R. Patel. 2003. "Large Foreign Currency Reserves: Insurance for Domestic Weakness and External Uncertainities?" *Economic and Political Weekly* 38(11): 1047–53.

Kelkar, V.J. 2002. *Report of the Task Force on Direct-Indirect Taxes.* New Delhi: Akalank Publications.

Kharas, Homi J., Brian Pinto, and Sergei Ulatov. 2001. "An Analysis of Russia's 1998 Meltdown: Fundamentals and Market Signals." *Brookings Papers on Economic Activity* Issue 1.

Kishore, A., A. Sharma, and C. Scott. 2003. "Power Supply to Agriculture, Reassessing Options." Water Policy Research Highlight 7. IWMI-Tata Water Policy Program, Ahmedabad, India.

Kochar, Anjini. 1997. "An Empirical Investigation of Rationing Constraints in Rural Credit Markets in India." *Journal of Development Economics* 53(2): 339–71.

Krueger, A., ed. 2002. *Economic Policy Reforms and the Indian Economy.* New Delhi: Oxford University Press.

Kumar, P. 2002. "Economic Analysis of Total Factor Productivity of Crop Sector in the Indo-Gangetic Plain of India by District and Region." *Agricultural Economics Research Report 2002–02.* New

Delhi: Indian Agricultural Research Institute, National Agricultural Technology Project Irrigated Ago-Ecosystem Research.

Kumar, Praduman, and Mark W. Rosegrant. 1994. "Productivity and Sources of Growth for Rice in India." *Economic and Political Weekly* 29(52): A183–88.

Lahiri, Ashok, and R. Kannan. 2002. "India's Fiscal Deficits and Their Sustainability in Perspective." In "India–Fiscal Policies to Accelerate Economic Growth." Green Cover Report 2473-IN. World Bank, South Asia Region, Poverty Reduction and Economic Management Unit, Washington, D.C.

Lanjouw, P. 2000. "Poverty in Karnataka: Profiles and Emerging Issues." World Bank, Washington, D.C.

Lanjouw, P., and G. Feder. 2001. "Rural Non-Farm Activities and Rural Development, from Experience Towards Strategy." *Rural Strategy Background Paper* 4. World Bank, Rural Development Department, Washington, D.C.

Mahal, A., and others. 2001. "Who Benefits from Public Health Spending in India." Health Nutrition and Population Working Paper. World Bank, Washington, D.C.

Majumdar, Grace, and J. L. Kapoor. 1980. "Behavior of inter-state income inequalities in India." *Journal of Income and Wealth* 4(1): 1–8.

Mattoo, Aaditya, and Arvind Subramanian. 2003. "India and the Multilateral Trading System Post-Doha: Defensive or Proactive?" In Aaditya Mattoo and Robert Stern, eds. *India and the WTO.* Washington D.C.: Oxford University Press and World Bank.

McKinsey and CII (Competitiveness of India Inc.). 2002. "Learning from China to Unlock India's Manufacturing Potential." New Delhi.

McKinsey Global Institute. 2001. "India: The Growth Imperative, Understanding the Barriers to Rapid Growth and Employment Creation." New Delhi.

Mohan, Rakesh. 2003. "Transforming Indian Banking: In Search of a Better Tomorrow." *Reserve Bank of India Bulletin.* Mumbai.

Mussa, Michael. 2002. "Argentina and the Fund: From Triumph to Tragedy." Institute for International Economics, Washington, D.C.

Nair, K.R.G. 1985. "A Note on Inter-State Income Differentials in India 1970–71 to 1979–80." In G.P. Misra, ed., *Regional Structure of Growth and Development in India.* Vol. 1. New Delhi: Ashish Publishing House.

NABARD (National Bank for Agriculture and Rural Development). Various years. *Annual Report.* Mumbai.

———. Various years. "Statistical Statements Relating to The Cooperative Movement in India." Mumbai.

———. 2001a. "Regional Rural Banks: Key Statistics, 2001." Mumbai.

———. 2001b. "Report of the Expert Committee on Rural Credit, Chaired by VS Vyas." Mumbai.

Nelson, Howard. 1994. "International Comparisons of Teachers Salaries and Conditions of Employment." In *Developments in School Finance.* Washington, D.C.: U.S. Department of Education, National Center for Education Statistics.

Parikh, K., J. Parikh, and T. L. Raghu Ram. 1999. "Air and Water Quality Management: New Initiatives Needed." In Kirit S. Parikh, ed., *India Development Report 1999–2000*. New Delhi: Oxford University Press.

Paul, Samuel, and Sita Shekhar. 1999. "The Second Report Card on Bangalore's Public Services." Public Affairs Center, Bangalore.

Perry, Guillermo, and Luis Serven. 2002. "The Anatomy of a Multiple Crisis: Why Was Argentina Special and What Can We Learn from It." World Bank, Washington, D.C.

Peters, D., A. Yazbeck, R. Sharma, G. Ramana, L. Pritchett, and A. Wagstaff. 2002. "Better Health Systems for India's Poor." World Bank, Washington, D.C.

Pinto, Brian, and Farah Zahir. 2003. "India: Why Fiscal Adjustment Now?" World Bank, Washington, D.C.

Pursell, Garry, B. Blarel, A. Gupta, and D. Rosenblatt. 1999. "Anti-Agricultural Bias in India." World Bank, Washington, D.C.

Radhakrishna, R., and K. Subbarao. 1997. "India's Public Distribution System: A National and International Perspective." World Bank Discussion Paper. World Bank, Washington, D.C.

Rao, M., R.T. Shand, and K.P. Kalirajan. 1999. Convergence of Incomes Across Indian States: A Divergent View." *Economic and Political Weekly* 34: 769–78.

Ravallion, Martin, and Gaurav Datt. 1995. "Is Targeting through a Work Requirement Efficient? Some Evidence for Rural India." In D. van de Walle and K. Nead, eds., *Public Spending and the Poor: Theory and Evidence*. Baltimore, MD: Johns Hopkins University Press.

———. 1996. "How Important to India's Poor Is the Sectoral Composition of Growth?" *World Bank Economic Review* 10(1): 1–25.

———. 1998a. "Farm Productivity and Rural Poverty in India." *Journal of Development Studies*, 34(4): 62–85.

———. 1998b. "Why Have Some Indian States Done Better Than Others at Reducing Rural Poverty?" *Economica* 65 (257): 17–38.

———. 2001. "Why Has Economic Growth Been More Pro-Poor in Some States of India Than Others?" *International Monetary Fund Seminar Series*, 2001–59.

———. 2002a. "Growth and Poverty in India: What Have We Learnt from the NSS?" India Workshop on Poverty Measurement, Monitoring and Evaluation, January 11–12, New Delhi.

———. 2002b. "Is India's Economic Growth Leaving the Poor Behind?" *Journal of Economic Perspectives* 16 (3): 89–108.

Rawal, V. 2001. "Agrarian Reform and Land Markets: A Study of Land Transactions in Two Villages of West Bengal, 1977–1995." *Economic Development and Cultural Change* 49(3): 611–29.

Ray, T. 1999. "Share Tenancy as Strategic Delegation." *Journal of Development Economics* 58(1): 45–60.

RBI (Reserve Bank of India). 1991. *All India Debt and Investment Survey*. Mumbai.

———. 2002a. *Annual Report 2001–02*. Mumbai.

———. 2002b. *Report on Trends and Progress of Banking in India 2001–02*. Mumbai.

———. 2002c. *Report on Currency and Finance 2000–01*. Mumbai.

———. *Report on Trend and Progress of Banking in India,* various years.

———. 2001a. *Annual Report 2000–01*. Mumbai.

———. 2001b. *Handbook of Statistics of Indian Economy 2001*. Mumbai.

———. 2001c. Reserve Bank of India Monthly Bulletin January 2002. Mumbai.

———. 2003a. *Report on Currency and Finance 2001–02*. Mumbai.

———. 2003b. "Accretion to Foreign Exchange Reserves in India: Sources, Arbitage and Costs." Press Release January. Mumbai.

———. 2003c. *Monthly Bulletin.* January. Mumbai.

———. 2003d. *State Finances: A Study of Budgets of 2002–03*. February. Mumbai.

———. 2003e. *Report of the Group to Assess the Fiscal Risk of State Government Guarantees.* July. Mumbai.

Reynolds, Patricia. 2001. "Fiscal Adjustment and Growth Prospects in India." In Tim Callen, Patricia Reynolds, and Christopher Towe, eds., *India at the Crossroads: Sustaining Growth and Reducing Poverty*. Washington, D.C.: International Monetary Fund.

Sachs, Jeffrey, Ashutosh Varshney, and Nirupam Bajpai. 1999. *India in the Era of Economic Reforms*. New Delhi, New York: Oxford University Press.

Sachs, Jeffrey, Nirupam Bajpai, and Ananthi Ramiah. 2002. "Understanding Regional Economic Growth in India." Working Paper 88. Harvard University, Center for International Development, Cambridge, Mass.

Sattar, Zaidi, and Garry Pursell. 2003. "South Asian Trade Policies: An Overview." Draft. World Bank, Washington, D.C.

Saxena, N.C. 2000a. "Tenancy Reforms vs Open Market Leasing—What Would Serve the Poor Better?" Planning Commission Discussion Paper. Government of India, New Delhi.

———. 2000b. "Theme Paper on Enhancement of Property Rights Including Land Rights of Women." Planning Commission Discussion Paper. Government of India, New Delhi.

Sharma, A. 2002. "The Agricultural Sector." In *Economic and Policy Reforms in India*. New Delhi: National Council of Applied Economic Research.

Shariff, Abusaleh, Prabir Ghosh, and Samir Mondal. 2002. "Indian Public Expenditures on Social Sector and Poverty Alleviation Programmes during the 1990s." ODI Working Paper 169. Overseas Development Institute, London.

Shariff, Abusaleh, and Ananta C. Mallick. 1999. "Dynamics of Food Intake and Nutrition by Expenditure Class in India." *Economic and Political Weekly*, July 3–9.

Shekhar, S., and S. Balakrishnan. 1999. *"Voices from the Capital: A Report Card on Public Service in Delhi."* Public Affairs Center, Bangalore.

Singh, Nirvikar. 2002. "Information Technology and India's Economic Development." Paper presented at the Cornell University Conference on the Indian Economy, April, Ithaca, New York.

Smith K. R. 2000. "National Burden of Disease in India from Indoor Air Pollution." PNAS 97: 13286–93. Proceedings of the National Academy of Sciences, Washington, D.C.

Smith K. R., and S. Mehta. 2000. "The Burden of Disease from Indoor Air Pollution in Developing Countries: Comparison of Estimates." Prepared for the USAID/WHO Global Technical Consultation on the Health Impacts of Indoor Air Pollution and Household Energy in Developing Countries, May 3–4, Washington, D.C.

Srinivasan, T.N. 2001. "India's Fiscal Situation: Is a Crisis Ahead?" Working Paper 92. Stanford University, Center for Research on Economic Development and Policy Reform, Palo Alto, Ca.

———. 2002. "China and India, Growth and Poverty, 1980–2000." June.

Stern, N. 2002. "Public Finance and Policy for Development: Challenges for India." NIPFP (National Institute of Public Finance and Policy) Silver Jubilee Lecture, January 10, New Delhi.

Sundaram, K., and S. Tendulkar. 2002. "Recent Debates on Database for Measurement of Poverty in India: Some Fresh Evidence." Paper presented at the Workshop on Poverty Measurement, Monitoring and Evaluation, January 11–12, New Delhi.

Sundararajan, V. and S. Thakur. 1980. "Public Investment, Crowding Out, and Growth: A Dynamic Model Applied to India and Korea." *International Monetary Fund Staff Papers* 27: 814–88.

Sur and Umali-Deininger. 2003. "The Equity Consequences of Public Irrigation Investments: The Case of Surface Irrigation Subsidies in India," Contributed paper for the 25th International Conference of Agricultural Economists, August 16–22, Durban, South Africa.

Taimin, B.K. 2001. *Food Security in the 21st Century, Perspective and Vision.* New Delhi: Konark Publishers Pvt. Ltd.

Tanzi, Vito, and Howell Zee. 2002. "Tax Policies for Emerging Markets." International Monetary Fund Working Paper 00/35. Washington, D.C.

TARU Leading Edge. 2000. "Socio Economic Impact Assessment Study for Haryana." New Delhi.

———. 2001. "Socio Economic Impact Assessment Study for Andhra Pradesh." New Delhi.

Tata Energy Research Institute. 2000. "Cost of Un-served Energy." New Delhi.

[RTF bookmark start: OLE_LINK1]———.[RTF bookmark end: OLE_LINK1] 2002. "Cost of Un-served Energy." New Delhi.

———. 2000. "Survey on India's Power Sector." New Delhi.

Vaidyanathan, A. 2002. "India's Agricultural Development Policy." In R. Kapila and U. Kapila, eds., *Indian Agriculture in the Changing Environment.* Vol. 1. New Delhi: Academic Foundation.

Venkatasubramanian, K. 2000. "Land Reforms Remain an Unfinished Business." Planning Commission Discussion Paper. Government of India, New Delhi.

Virmani, A. 2002. "A New Development Paradigm: Employment, Entitlement and Empowerment." Paper presented at the Conference on the Politics and Economics of Liberalisation in India, April 11–13, RG Institute for Contemporary Studies, New Delhi.

Vyas, V.S. 2002a. "Agriculture The Second Round of Reforms." In R. Kapila and U. Kapila, eds., *Indian Agriculture in the Changing Environment.* Vol. 1. New Delhi: Academic Foundation.

———. 2002b. "Changing Contours of Indian Agriculture." In R. Kapila and U. Kapila, eds., *Indian Agriculture in the Changing Environment.* Vol. 1. New Delhi: Academic Foundation.

———. 2003. "Market Reforms in Indian Agriculture." Institute of Development Studies, Jaipur.

Williamson, J., and R. Zagha. 2002. "From Slow Growth to Slow Reform?" Paper presented at Stanford University, June 3–4, Palo Alto, Ca.

World Bank. 1998a. "India: Report on Rural Finance." Washington, D.C.

———. 1998b. "Reducing Poverty in India: Options for more Effective Public Services." World Bank Country Study. Washington, D.C.

———. 1998c. "Report on Rural Credit Cooperatives Draft." Washington, D.C.

———. 1999a. "India Foodgrain Marketing Policies: Reforming to Meet Food Security Needs." Report 18329-IN. Washington, D.C.

———. 1999b. "India: Towards Rural Development and Poverty Reduction." Washington, D.C.

———. 1999c. "Special Infrastructure Financing Facilities–Cross-Country Experience." Washington, D.C.

———. 2000a. *India: Reducing Poverty, Accelerating Development.* World Bank Country Study. New Delhi: Oxford University Press.

———. 2000b. Rural Development Report. Washington, D.C.

———. 2000c. *World Business Environment Survey.* Washington, D.C.

———. 2001a. *"India Improving Household Food and Nutrition Security."* Report No. 20300-IN. Washington, D.C.

———. 2001b. *"India: Power Supply to Agriculture Vol I-IV."* Report 22171-IN. South Asia Energy and Infrastructure Unit, Washington, D.C.

———. 2001c. "India: The Challenges of Development." OED Country Assistance Evaluation. Operations Evaluation Department, Washington, D.C.

———. 2001d. "India: Country Assistance Strategy." June. Washington, D.C.

———. 2002a. "Poverty in India: The Challenge of Uttar Pradesh." South Asia Region, Poverty Reduction and Economic Management Sector Unit, Washington, D.C.

———. 2002b. *India: CAS Progress Report.* 2002. Washington, D.C.

———. 2002c. *Report on the Transport Sector Strategy for India*, 2002. Washington, D.C.

———. 2002d. *Report on the Financial Sector Strategy for India*, May 2002. Washington, D.C.

World Bank-CII. 2002e. "Improving India's Investment Climate." March. Washington D.C.

———. 2002f. "India: Fiscal Policies to Accelerate Economic Growth." Green Cover Report 2473IN. South Asia Region, Poverty Reduction and Economic Management Unit, Washington, D.C.

———. 2002g. "Micro-finance in India: Issues, Constraints, and Potential for Sustainable Growth." Report No. 22531-IN. Washington, D.C.

———. 2002h. "Sustainability of Micro-finance Self Help Groups in India: Would Federating Help?" Washington, D.C.

———. 2002i. "Improving Rural Access to Electricity Services in India." South Asia Energy and Infrastructure Unit, Washington, D.C.

———. 2002j. "India: Power Sector Reforms and the Poor." South Asian Energy and Infrastructure Unit, World Bank, Washington, D.C.

———. 2002k. "Maharashtra: Reorienting Government to Facilitate Growth and Reduce Poverty." Washington, D.C.

———. 2002l. "India Household Energy, Indoor Air Pollution and Health." Report 261/02. Washington, D.C.

———. 2002m. "Review of ICT Developments in South Asian Countries and Lessons from the Indian IT Service Industry Experience." Concept paper. South Asia Financial and Private Sector Development Division, Washington, D.C.

———. 2002n. "Challenges for India's Transport Sector, Final Report, February 25, 2002. Washington, D.C.

———. 2002o. "Development Policy Review: Rationale, Content and Process." Poverty Reduction and Economic Management Economic Policy, Washington, D.C.

———. 2002p. "Power for India: A Strategy for Sustained Reform in the State Power Sectors." draft report, October 24. Washington, D.C.

———. 2002q. "Country Assistance Strategy Progress Report of the World Bank Group for India." November 4. Washington, D.C.

———. 2002r. "India: Agricultural Policy Framework for Growth and Sustained Rural Poverty Reduction: Recent Achievements and Challenges Ahead." draft concept note, November 13. Washington, D.C.

———. 2002s. *World Development Indicators.* Washington, D.C.

———. 2003a. "Access of the Poor to Clean Household Fuels in India." Washington, D.C.

———. 2003b. Doing Business Database. Washington, D.C.

———. 2003c. "Global Development Finance." Washington, D.C.

———. 2003d. "Strategy for Sustained Reforms in the State Power Sector." Draft discussion paper. South Asia Region, Energy and Infrastructure Unit, Washington, D.C.

———. Forthcoming. *World Development Report 2004: Making Services Work for Poor People*. Washington, D.C.: Oxford University Press.

———. Forthcoming. "Wage Differentials Between the Public and Private Sectors in India." Washington, D.C.

World Economic Forum. 2002/03 and previous years. Global Competitiveness Report. Oxford University Press: USA.

World Health Organization. 1999. *World Health Report 1999: Making a Difference*. Geneva.

———. 2002. *Polio News Eradication*, Newsletter 17. Global Polio Eradication Initiative, Geneva.

Young, A. 1993. "Land Degradation in South Asia: Its severity, causes, and effects upon the people." Final report prepared for submission to the Economic and Social Council of the United Nations, ECOSOC. Rome: Food and Agriculture Organization of the United Nations, United Nations Development Programme, and United Nations Environment Programme.

STATISTICAL ANNEX

	1993/94	1994/95	1995/96	1996/97	1997/98	1998/99	1999/2000	2000/01	2001/02
A. Shares of Gross Domestic Expenditure at Market Prices									
1. Final consumption	78.3	76.3	75.3	76.7	75.8	77.7	78.6	77.7	77.9
a) Public sector	11.4	10.7	10.8	10.7	11.3	12.3	13.0	13.1	12.8
b) Private sector	66.9	65.6	64.5	66.0	64.5	65.4	65.6	64.6	65.0
2. Gross capital formation	21.3	23.4	26.5	21.8	22.6	21.4	23.7	22.5	22.4
a) Gross fixed capital formation	21.4	21.9	24.4	22.8	21.7	21.5	21.8	21.8	21.7
i) Public sector	8.0	8.8	7.7	6.9	6.4	6.5	6.2	6.1	5.9
ii) Private sector	13.4	13.2	16.7	15.9	15.3	15.1	15.6	15.8	15.7
b) Change in inventories	-0.2	1.4	2.2	-1.0	0.9	-0.1	1.9	0.7	0.8
3. Total absorption (1+2)	99.5	99.7	101.8	98.5	98.4	99.1	102.3	100.2	100.3
4. Resource balance	0.0	-0.3	-1.2	-1.2	-1.3	-1.7	-2.0	-0.8	-0.7
a) Exports of goods and services	10.0	10.0	11.0	10.6	10.9	11.2	11.8	13.8	13.3
b) Imports of goods and services	10.0	10.3	12.2	11.8	12.1	12.9	13.7	14.5	13.9
5. Gross domestic product	100.0	100.0	100.0	100.0	100.0	100.0	100.0	100.0	100.0
6. Net income from abroad	-1.4	-1.3	-1.1	-1.0	-0.9	-0.9	-0.8	-0.8	-0.6
7. Gross national income (5+6)	98.6	98.7	98.9	99.0	99.1	99.1	99.2	99.2	99.4
8. Net current transfers from abroad	1.9	2.5	2.4	3.2	2.9	2.5	2.7	2.8	2.5
9. Gross national disposable income (7+8)	100.5	101.2	101.3	102.3	102.0	101.6	101.9	102.0	102.0
10. National savings (9-1)	22.2	24.9	26.0	25.6	26.2	23.9	23.3	24.2	24.1
a) Public sector	0.6	1.7	2.0	1.7	1.3	-1.0	-1.0	-2.3	-2.5
b) Private sector	21.6	23.2	23.9	23.9	24.9	24.9	24.4	26.5	26.6
B. Shares of GDP by Industrial Origin									
1. Agriculture	28.2	27.5	25.5	26.5	25.4	25.4	23.9	22.7	22.8
2. Industry	23.9	24.5	25.4	24.9	24.9	24.3	23.5	24.2	23.6
Construction	4.7	4.6	4.6	4.6	5.1	5.3	5.4	5.5	5.5
Gas, electricity, and water	2.2	2.4	2.3	2.2	2.3	2.5	2.2	2.2	2.2
Mining and quarrying	2.3	2.2	2.1	2.0	2.2	2.0	2.1	2.2	2.0
Manufacturing	14.6	15.3	16.3	16.1	15.2	14.5	13.8	14.3	13.9
3. Services	38.9	38.5	39.4	39.5	41.0	42.0	43.6	44.2	44.8
4. Statistical discrepancy	-1.0	0.0	0.0	0.0	0.0	0.0	0.0	0.0	0.0
5. Total value added at basic prices	90.9	90.5	90.3	90.9	91.3	91.8	91.0	91.1	91.2
6. Taxes less subsidies on products	9.1	9.5	9.7	9.1	8.7	8.2	9.0	8.9	8.8
7. GDP at market prices	100.0	100.0	100.0	100.0	100.0	100.0	100.0	100.0	100.0
Memo Item (billions of rupees)									
Gross domestic product at market prices	8,592	10,128	11,880	13,682	15,225	17,409	19,369	21,043	22,960

Source: Central Statistical Organization, National Accounts Statistics.

Table A2. Gross Domestic Expenditure and Product
(billions of rupees at current prices)

	1993/94	1994/95	1995/96	1996/97	1997/98	1998/99	1999/2000	2000/01	2001/02
A. GDP by Expenditure									
1. Final consumption	6,725	7,728	8,946	10,494	11,539	13,534	15,227	16,353	17,879
a) Public sector	977	1,086	1,288	1,457	1,722	2,140	2,511	2,759	2,950
b) Private sector	5,748	6,642	7,658	9,037	9,817	11,394	12,716	13,594	14,929
2. Gross capital formation	1,826	2,368	3,152	2,979	3,437	3,722	4,583	4,736	5,151
a) Gross fixed capital formation	1,843	2,222	2894	3,119	3,304	3,743	4,219	4,598	4,973
i) Public sector	689	889	916	943	971	1,123	1,204	1,277	1,357
ii) Private sector	1,154	1,334	1978	2,175	2,333	2,620	3,015	3,321	3,616
b) Change in inventories	-17	145	258	-140	133	-21	364	138	178
3. Total absorption (1+2)	8,551	10,096	12,098	13,472	14,976	17,257	19,809	21,089	23,030
4. Resource balance	1	-31	-142	-162	-191	-295	-380	-159	-158
a) Exports of goods and services	861	1,016	1,307	1,449	1,652	1,953	2,277	2,902	3,045
b) Imports of goods and services	860	1,047	1,450	1,610	1,843	2,247	2,657	3,061	3,202
5. Gross domestic product	8,592	10,128	11,880	13,682	15,225	17,409	19,369	21,043	22,960
6. Net income from abroad	-121	-131	-135	-131	-132	-150	-154	-174	-127
7. Gross national income (5+6)	8,471	9,997	11,745	13,551	15,093	17,260	19,215	20,869	22,834
8. Net current transfers from abroad	165	254	285	439	440	432	531	585	578
9. Gross national disposable income (7+8)	8,637	10,251	12,030	13,990	15,533	17,692	19,746	21,454	23,412
10. National savings (9-1)	1,912	2,523	3,084	3,497	3,994	4,158	4,519	5,101	5,533
a) Public sector	54	168	241	229	203	-172	-200	-480	-577
b) Private sector	1,857	2,355	2,843	3,267	3,792	4,329	4,720	5,581	6,110
B. GDP by Industry of Origin									
1. Agriculture	2,420	2,788	3,031	3,626	3,870	4,425	4,620	4,785	5,226
2. Industry	2,052	2,485	3,018	3,411	3,785	4,235	4,557	5,099	5,417
Construction	406	466	550	628	778	920	1,053	1,166	1,256
Gas, electricity, and water	190	238	277	300	353	436	423	466	500
Mining and quarrying	201	227	253	277	334	357	413	454	463
Manufacturing	1,255	1,554	1,938	2,207	2,320	2,522	2,668	3,014	3,199
3. Services	3,342	3,897	4,684	5,398	6,246	7,320	8,443	9,293	10,297
Transportation	511	611	707	836	975	1,125	1,243	1,403	1,545
Trade	994	1,192	1,463	1,717	1,945	2,208	2,460	2,727	3,025
Dwellings	484	529	590	655	728	855	1,015	1,204	1,370
Banking	417	501	661	720	840	956	1,191	1,185	1,302
Public administration	436	486	573	652	800	996	1,167	1,240	1,331
Other	500	577	690	817	958	1,180	1,367	1,535	1,726
4. Statistical discrepancy	0	0	0	0	0	0	0	0	0
5. Total value added at basic prices	7,813	9,171	10,733	12,435	13,901	15,981	17,619	19,177	20,940
6. Taxes less subsidies on products	779	957	1147	1,247	1,324	1,429	1,750	1,866	2,020
7. GDP at market prices	8,592	10,128	11,880	13,682	15,225	17,409	19,369	21,043	22,960

Source: Central Statistical Organization, National Accounts Statistics.

114

Table A3. National Income and Product at Constant Prices
(annual growth rates, %)

	1994/95	1995/96	1996/97	1997/98	1998/99	1999/2000	2000/01	2001/02
A. GDP by Expenditure and Income								
1. Final consumption	4.2	6.5	7.4	3.8	7.4	7.1	2.3	6.1
a) Public sector	1.2	8.0	4.5	11.1	12.9	13.2	0.6	7.2
b) Private sector	4.6	6.2	7.9	2.6	6.4	6.0	2.6	5.9
2. Gross capital formation	12.8	19.3	1.6	2.2	8.6	8.6	9.4	3.0
Gross fixed capital formation	11.8	19.3	1.5	2.1	8.7	8.6	4.7	3.0
i) Public sector	18.0	-6.5	-5.9	-2.8	9.4	4.9	10.9	3.0
ii) Private sector	8.1	36.1	4.8	4.1	8.4	10.0	2.4	3.0
3. Total absorption	6.0	9.4	6.0	3.4	7.7	7.5	4.0	5.3
4. Exports of goods and services	13.1	31.4	6.3	-2.3	13.9	18.0	23.4	6.0
5. Imports of goods and services	22.7	28.0	-2.5	13.2	20.8	7.0	6.5	3.5
6. Capacity to import[a]	18.9	19.0	-2.7	12.8	17.2	5.5	17.8	3.8
7. Gross domestic income at market prices	8.0	6.4	6.3	6.3	6.4	5.5	3.0	5.1
8. Gross national income	7.4	7.8	7.7	4.5	5.9	7.2	3.9	5.8
9. Gross national disposable income	8.1	7.7	8.5	4.2	5.5	7.5	3.9	5.5
10. Gross national savings	21.8	11.4	11.6	5.6	0.5	8.5	8.7	4.0
B. GDP by Industrial Origin								
1. Agriculture	5.0	-0.9	9.6	-2.4	6.2	0.3	-0.4	5.7
2. Industry	10.2	11.6	7.1	4.3	3.7	4.8	6.6	3.3
Construction	5.5	6.2	2.1	10.2	6.2	8.0	6.9	3.7
Gas, electricity, and water	9.4	6.8	5.4	7.9	7.0	5.2	5.0	4.3
Mining and quarrying	9.3	5.9	0.5	9.8	2.8	3.3	2.4	1.0
Manufacturing	12.0	14.9	9.7	1.5	2.7	4.0	7.3	3.4
3. Services	7.1	10.5	7.2	9.8	8.4	10.1	5.6	6.8
4. Total value added at basic prices	7.3	7.3	7.8	4.8	6.5	6.1	4.4	5.6
5. GDP at market prices	7.5	7.6	7.4	4.5	6.0	7.1	3.9	5.5

a.   Exports deflated by import price index.
Source: Central Statistical Organization, National Accounts Statistics.

	1993/94	1994/95	1995/96	1996/97	1997/98	1998/99	1999/2000	2000/01	2001/02
A. GDP by Expenditure and Income									
1. Final consumption	6,725	7,004	7,458	8,012	8,313	8,924	9,561	9,780	10,378
a) Public sector	977	989	1,069	1,116	1,240	1,400	1,584	1,593	1,709
b) Private sector	5,748	6,015	6,389	6,896	7,073	7,524	7,977	8,186	8,669
2. Gross capital formation	1,826	2,061	2,458	2,496	2,551	2,772	3,010	3,294	3,394
a) Gross fixed capital formation	1,843	2,061	2,458	2,495	2,548	2,769	3,008	3,148	3,244
i) Public sector	689	813	759	715	695	760	798	885	911
ii) Private sector	1,154	1,248	1,698	1,780	1,853	2,009	2,210	2,264	2,333
b) Change in inventories	141	378	252	189	343	140	493	304	150
3. Total absorption (1+2)	8,551	9,065	9,916	10,509	10,864	11,696	12,571	13,074	13,772
4. Resource balance	1	-82	-71	43	-163	-290	-144	149	210
a) Exports of goods and services	861	974	1,280	1,361	1,329	1,514	1,786	2,204	2,336
b) Imports of goods and services	860	1,055	1,351	1,318	1,492	1,803	1,930	2,054	2,125
5. Gross domestic product	8,592	9,233	9,939	10,674	11,152	11,820	12,664	13,163	13,881
6. Trading gains or losses	0	50	-61	-175	8	53	-132	-256	-315
7. Gross domestic income (5+6)	8,592	9,284	9,878	10,499	11,161	11,874	12,532	12,907	13,566
8. Net income from abroad	-121	-132	-126	-107	-106	-120	-116	-124	-84
9. Gross national income (7+8)	8,471	9,101	9,813	10,567	11,046	11,700	12,548	13,039	13,798
10. Net current transfers from abroad	165	232	238	339	322	293	345	362	345
11. Gross national disposable income (9+10)	8,637	9,333	10,052	10,906	11,368	11,994	12,892	13,401	14,143
12. Gross national savings (11-1)	1,912	2,329	2,594	2,894	3,056	3,069	3,332	3,621	3,765
Memo Item									
Capacity to import	861	1,024	1,219	1,185	1,337	1,567	1,654	1,948	2,021
B. GDP by Industrial Origin									
1. Agriculture	2,420	2,541	2,519	2,761	2,694	2,861	2,870	2,859	3,021
2. Industry	2,052	2,261	2,524	2,702	2,818	2,923	3,064	3,266	3,375
Construction	406	428	455	465	512	544	587	628	652
Gas, electricity, and water	190	208	222	234	252	270	284	298	311
Mining and quarrying	201	220	233	234	257	264	273	279	282
Manufacturing	1,255	1,405	1,614	1,770	1,797	1,846	1,920	2,061	2,131
3. Services	3,342	3,579	3,953	4,238	4,654	5,043	5,551	5,862	6,259
Transportation	511	562	623	674	730	789	876	983	1,066
Trade	994	1,100	1,259	1,355	1,458	1,569	1,682	1,751	1,906
Dwellings	484	499	527	550	580	613	659	719	761
Banking	417	452	501	550	648	705	800	790	816
Public administration	436	442	472	491	562	622	704	722	743
Other	500	525	571	617	676	744	829	897	966
4. Statistical discrepancy	0	0	0	0	0	0	0	0	0
5. Total value added at basic prices	7,813	8,380	8,996	9,701	10,166	10,827	11,484	11,987	12,654
6. Taxes less subsidies on products	779	853	944	974	987	993	1,179	1,177	1,227
7. GDP at market prices (5+6)	8,592	9,233	9,939	10,674	11,152	11,820	12,664	13,163	13,881

Source: Central Statistical Organization, National Accounts Statistics.

116

Table A5. Exchange Rates and Prices

	1993/94	1994/95	1995/96	1996/97	1997/98	1998/99	1999/2000	2000/01	2001/02
Exchange Rates (rupees per U.S. dollar)									
Nominal official average exchange rate	31.37	31.40	33.45	35.50	37.16	42.07	43.33	45.68	47.69
Real effective exchange rate (1985=100)	61.59	66.0	63.6	63.8	67.0	63.4	63.3	66.5	68.4
Price Indices									
Wholesale Price Index (1993-94=100)	100.0	112.5	121.6	127.2	132.8	140.7	145.3	155.7	161.3
Consumer Price Index (1993-94=100)	100.0	107.6	118.3	129.4	138.3	156.4	161.6	168.0	173.1
Consumer Price Index (% change)	5.0	7.6	10.0	9.4	6.8	13.1	3.3	3.9	3.1
Manuf. Exp. Unit Value Index (1990=100)	106.7	110.5	117.0	111.3	103.5	99.6	99.4	97.3	95.9
Implicit Deflators (1993=100)									
Real gross domestic product	100.0	109.7	119.5	128.2	136.5	147.3	153.0	159.9	165.4
Exports of goods and services	100.0	95.9	97.9	93.9	80.4	77.5	78.4	75.9	76.7
Imports of goods and services	100.0	100.8	93.2	81.8	81.0	80.2	72.6	67.1	66.4
Terms of Trade Index	100.0	95.1	105.0	114.8	99.4	96.6	108.0	113.1	115.6

Source: IMF; RBI; India, Ministry of Industry; World Bank staff estimates.

Table A6. Central Government Finances Summary
(billions of rupees at current prices)

	1991/92	1992/93	1993/94	1994/95	1995/96	1996/97	1997/98	1998/99	1999/00	2000/01	2001/02	2002/03[a]	2002/03[b]	2003/04[a]
Revenue	660	741	755	911	1,101	1,263	1,339	1,495	1,815	1,926	2,014	2,451	2,369	2,539
Tax revenue	501	540	534	675	819	937	957	1,047	1,283	1,367	1,337	1,730	1,642	1,842
Customs[c]	223	238	222	268	358	429	402	407	484	475	403	452	455	494
Union excise[c]	160	164	172	211	222	235	255	286	349	685	726	914	874	968
Income tax[c]	16	18	14	35	43	47	36	58	91	318	320	425	373	441
Corporate tax	79	89	101	138	165	186	200	245	307	357	366	486	447	515
Other	23	32	26	23	32	41	64	51	375	49	29	61	72	71
Nontax revenue	160	201	220	236	282	326	382	448	532	559	678	721	728	698
Interest receipts	109	125	151	158	184	221	253	301	339	328	355	414	406	392
Other	50	76	69	78	98	105	129	148	193	231	323	307	322	306
Expenditure[d]	999	1,120	1,307	1,447	1,618	1,828	2,080	2,449	2,880	3,136	3,461	3,926	3,858	4,208
Nonplan expenditure	750	817	932	1,037	1,219	1,368	1,572	1,888	2,219	2,429	2,613	2,968	2,899	3,178
Interest payments	266	310	367	440	500	595	656	779	946	993	1,075	1,174	1,160	1,232
Defense	163	176	218	232	269	295	353	399	471	496	543	650	560	653
Subsidies	123	108	116	119	127	155	185	236	245	268	312	399	446	499
Other nonplan expenditure	198	223	230	245	324	323	378	474	558	672	683	746	733	794
Plan expenditure	310	367	437	474	464	535	591	668	762	827	1,012	1,135	1,141	1,210
Less: recovery of loans	60	64	62	63	65	75	83	106	101	120	164	177	183	180
Gross fiscal deficit	339	379	552	536	517	565	741	954	1,064	1,210	1,446	1,475	1,488	1,668
Financed by:														
Disinvestment of PSEs	30	20	0	51	4	4	9	59	17	21	36	120	34	132
Domestic borrowing (net)	254	306	502	450	510	531	721	876	1,035	1,113	1,354	1,348	1,590	1,501
External borrowing (net)	54	53	51	36	3	30	11	19	12	75	56	8	-135	36
Memo														
GDPmp	6,531	7,484	8,592	10,128	11,880	13,682	15,225	17,409	19,369	21,043	22,960	25,571	24,655	27,435
Fiscal Deficit / GDP	5.2	5.1	6.4	5.3	4.3	4.1	4.9	5.5	5.5	5.7	6.3	5.8	6.0	6.1
Revenue / GDP	10.1	9.9	8.8	9.0	9.3	9.2	8.8	8.6	9.4	9.2	8.8	9.6	9.6	9.3
Expenditure / GDP	15.3	15.0	15.2	14.3	13.6	13.4	13.7	14.1	14.9	14.9	15.1	15.4	15.6	15.3

a. Budget estimates.
b. Revised estimates.
c. Until 1999-2000 net of state's share. After that, gross receipts.
d. Net of loan recoveries and loans on small savings.
Source: Ministry of Finance union budget documents; World Bank staff estimates

Table A7. Budgetary Classification of Central Government Finances
(billions of rupees at current prices)

	1985/86	1986/87	1987/88	1988/89	1989/90	1990/91	1991/92	1992/93	1993/94	1994/95	1995/96	1996/97	1997/98	1998/99	1999/00	2000/01	2001/02	2002/03	2002/03[b]	2003/04[a]
Revenue receipts	280	331	370	436	500	550	660	741	755	911	1,101	1,263	1,339	1,495	1,815	1,926	2,014	2,451	2,369	2,539
Tax revenue	211	243	280	338	383	430	501	540	534	675	819	937	957	1,047	1,283	1,367	1,337	1,730	1,642	1,842
Nontax revenue	69	88	90	98	116	120	160	201	220	236	282	326	382	448	532	559	678	721	728	698
of which: Interest from states	19	28	32	38	44	52	65	78	96	112	130	152	178	212	254	270	296	279	301	308
Revenue expenditure (A+B+C+D)	339	409	462	541	642	735	823	927	1,082	1,221	1,399	1,589	1,803	2,165	2,491	2,778	3,016	3,405	3,416	3,662
A. Developmental	86	103	114	140	184	196	198	209	244	301	356	400	460	585	607	726	823	974	1,073	1,124
1. Social services	13	17	19	22	25	28	31	34	41	47	66	84	106	131	156	156	185	193	179	203
2. Economic services	74	86	95	118	159	168	168	174	203	254	290	315	354	454	451	570	638	781	894	921
B. Nondevelopmental	176	220	245	288	335	391	450	522	613	708	817	943	1,101	1,303	1,580	1,654	1,746	1,926	1,876	1,995
Defense services	70	92	89	96	102	109	114	121	150	164	188	210	262	299	352	372	381	436	411	443
Interest payments	75	92	112	143	178	215	266	310	367	440	500	595	656	779	946	993	1,075	1,174	1,160	1,232
C. Grants-in-aid and contributions	72	79	93	102	109	134	160	181	211	205	218	238	232	264	290	384	432	487	450	524
of which: Grants to states	67	74	91	100	86	132	157	178	208	200	213	232	297	251	290	368	415	468	430	501
D. Revenue expenditure of UTs	6	7	9	11	13	14	15	16	14	7	8	9	10	12	14	14	16	17	18	20
Net current balance	-59	-78	-91	-105	-142	-186	-163	-186	-327	-310	-297	-327	-464	-670	-676	-852	-1002	-954	-1047	-1123
Capital expenditure (A+B+C+D)	131	160	151	165	180	191	176	193	225	226	219	239	277	285	388	357	444	521	441	545
A. Developmental	59	76	57	60	71	69	58	74	56	74	50	47	73	76	108	93	84	172	135	188
1. Social services	2	4	3	4	3	2	2	3	3	7	5	7	6	10	11	8	-34	11	10	11
2. Economic services	57	72	54	57	68	67	56	71	52	67	45	40	67	67	97	85	118	161	125	177
B. Nondevelopmental	16	15	33	41	45	50	52	59	74	73	88	93	100	109	129	136	178	232	165	232
of which: Defense services	10	13	31	38	42	46	49	55	69	68	80	85	91	100	119	124	162	214	149	210
C. Capital expenditure of UTs	1	2	3	2	2	3	3	4	3	2	2	2	2	3	4	5	3	3	3	3
D. Loans and advances (net)	54	68	58	62	62	69	62	57	93	77	78	97	101	96	148	123	179	115	138	123
to states & UTs	26	22	28	25	22	28	39	44	51	46	48	69	76	75	117	88	105	118	135	107
to others	28	46	30	37	40	41	23	12	42	31	30	28	25	21	31	35	74	-3	3	16
Gross fiscal deficit (World Bank definition)	190	238	242	270	322	376	339	379	552	536	517	565	741	954	1,064	1,209	1,446	1,475	1,488	1,668
Financed by instruments																				
Disinvestment of equity in PSEs	0	0	0	0	0	0	30	20	0	51	4	4	9	59	17	21	36	120	34	132
Market loans	49	55	59	84	74	80	75	37	289	203	331	200	325	690	703	729	877	959	1,000	1,072
Small savings	44	34	39	58	86	91	66	57	91	166	128	153	245	330	90	83	88	80	0	0
Provident funds	4	8	9	10	11	12	13	16	18	20	23	23	44	57	66	49	42	100	85	75
External loans	14	20	29	25	26	32	54	53	51	36	3	30	11	19	12	75	56	8	-135	36
Other (includes T-bills)	78	121	107	93	125	161	100	196	104	61	29	155	107	-201	177	251	347	209	505	354

a. Budget estimates.
b. Revised estimates.

Source: Ministry of Finance, Union budget documents; India, Department of Expenditure, Finance Accounts; World Bank staff estimates.

Table A8. Budgetary Classification of State Government Finances
(billions of rupees at current prices)

	1985/86	1986/87	1987/88	1988/89	1989/90	1990/91	1991/92	1992/93	1993/94	1994/95	1995/96	1996/97	1997/98	1998/99	1999/00	2000/01	2001/02 B.E.	2001/02 R.E.	2002/03 B.E.
Revenue receipts	334	382	440	504	565	665	805	911	1,056	1,223	1,368	1,528	1,703	1,764	2,072	2,380	2,831	2,709	3,034
Tax revenue	218	251	290	331	391	446	526	604	688	806	929	1,061	1,216	1,284	1,467	1,687	2,015	1,885	2,116
Direct taxes	15	17	20	24	30	34	40	42	50	70	81	84	94	100	115	132	165	162	186
Indirect taxes	131	150	173	200	230	270	318	356	415	487	558	627	718	790	911	1,048	1,247	1,169	1,305
State share in central taxes	73	84	97	107	131	142	168	206	224	249	290	350	404	394	441	507	603	554	625
Nontax revenue	116	131	150	173	174	219	279	306	367	417	439	467	487	480	605	692	816	824	918
of which: Grants from center	63	70	83	97	85	126	152	178	212	200	210	232	242	239	306	378	486	507	541
Revenue expenditure [A+B+C]	328	381	452	522	602	718	866	962	1,094	1,285	1,450	1,689	1,866	2,201	2,611	2,915	3,327	3,314	3,552
A. Developmental (1+2)	231	269	318	362	408	489	589	635	708	790	893	1,062	1,138	1,319	1,515	1,685	1,840	1,861	1,911
1. Social services	134	152	177	206	240	280	315	346	390	450	536	603	683	820	963	1,045	1,185	1,174	1,207
2. Economic services	97	117	141	157	168	209	274	289	319	340	357	458	455	498	552	640	654	687	704
B. Nondevelopmental	93	107	128	154	188	221	267	315	374	482	542	609	699	847	1,051	1,181	1,430	1,400	1,575
of which: Interest payments	34	44	53	63	76	92	115	139	165	201	230	269	316	376	463	532	671	664	747
To center	17	27	31	37	44	52	65	78	95	112	131	152	175	209	254	274	311	297	310
To others	17	17	21	26	32	40	50	60	70	90	99	117	140	167	209	258	360	367	436
C. Other expenditure^c	4	4	5	6	6	8	10	12	12	13	15	19	30	35	45	50	57	53	66
Net current balance	7	1	-12	-18	-37	-53	-61	-51	-38	-62	-82	-161	-163	-436	-539	-536	-496	-605	-518
Capital expenditure [A+B+C]	85	94	101	99	118	135	132	158	168	208	232	213	279	311	377	360	480	461	546
A. Developmental (1+2)	57	61	64	69	77	90	99	103	121	171	178	168	218	223	244	302	388	365	415
1. Social services	10	10	11	11	12	13	16	17	18	23	26	30	34	42	43	58	85	82	94
2. Economic services	46	51	54	57	66	77	82	87	102	148	152	139	184	181	201	245	303	283	322
B. Nondevelopmental	1	2	2	2	2	3	2	3	4	4	7	7	10	8	11	9	15	18	22
C. Loans and advances (net)	27	32	35	28	38	43	32	51	43	33	47	38	51	80	122	48	77	77	109
Gross fiscal deficit	78	93	113	117	154	188	193	209	206	270	314	374	442	748	916	895	977	1,066	1,064
Financed by instrument:																			
Market loans	14	14	18	22	26	26	33	39	42	41	64	65	79	122	142	130	122	175	137
Loans from center (net)	58	48	58	67	79	100	94	89	95	148	148	175	237	311	124	84	168	148	187
Small savings and provident funds	10	10	16	20	23	31	29	36	43	48	49	54	62	120	179	131	132	118	115
Other	-3	21	20	7	26	32	37	45	25	33	53	80	64	195	471	551	554	624	624

Source: RBI bulletins on state finances; World Bank staff estimates.

Table A9. Budgetary Classification of General Government (Center and States) Finances
(billions of rupees at current prices)

	1985/86	1986/87	1987/88	1988/89	1989/90	1990/91	1991/92	1992/93	1993/94	1994/95	1995/96	1996/97	1997/98	1998/99	1999/00	2000/01	2001/02[a]
Revenue receipts	535	617	695	805	937	1,039	1,252	1,396	1,501	1,821	2,132	2,408	2,653	2,806	3,320	3,670	3,901
Tax revenue	432	495	569	668	776	879	1,030	1,144	1,221	1,480	1,751	1,999	2,205	2,328	2,743	3,066	3,201
Non tax revenue	103	122	126	137	162	160	221	252	280	341	381	410	448	478	576	604	699
Revenue expenditure [A+B+C]	583	689	790	926	1,114	1,269	1,467	1,632	1,872	2,194	25,05	2,896	3,197	3,906	4,557	5,052	5,619
A. Developmental	317	372	432	503	592	685	787	843	952	1,091	1,249	1,461	1,598	1,903	2,122	2,411	2,684
1. Social services	146	169	196	228	265	307	346	380	431	497	602	688	789	951	1,118	1,201	1,359
2. Economic services	171	204	236	275	327	377	442	463	521	594	646	774	809	953	1,003	1,210	1,325
B. Nondevelopmental	250	300	341	404	480	561	652	759	891	1,078	1,229	1,400	1,622	1,938	2,377	2,565	2,850
C. Other revenue expenditure	16	17	17	19	42	24	28	30	29	24	28	35	-22	64	59	75	85
Net current balance	-48	-72	-95	-121	-177	-230	-215	-236	-371	-372	-373	-488	-544	-1,100	-1,237	-1,382	-1,718
Capital expenditure [A+B+C+D]	189	233	225	238	275	297	269	306	342	388	403	383	479	520	649	629	800
A. Developmental (1+2)	115	136	121	129	148	159	157	177	176	245	229	215	292	299	352	396	449
1. Social services	12	14	14	15	15	15	19	19	22	30	32	36	40	52	54	66	49
2. Economic services	103	122	107	114	133	144	138	158	154	215	197	179	251	247	297	330	401
B. Nondevelopmental	17	17	36	43	48	52	55	62	78	77	95	100	109	117	140	145	196
C. Loans and advances (net)	55	77	65	65	77	83	54	64	85	64	77	66	76	101	153	83	151
D. Capital disbursements of UTs	1	2	3	2	2	3	3	4	3	2	2	2	2	3	4	5	3
Gross fiscal deficit	237	305	320	359	452	527	484	542	713	760	776	870	1,024	1,621	1,886	2,010	2,518
Financed by Instrument:																	
Disinvestment of equities in PSEs	0	0	0	0	0	0	30	20	0	51	4	4	9	59	17	21	36
Market Loans	70	80	85	111	106	115	122	87	343	254	450	344	513	959	1,008	1,132	1,318
Small savings and provident funds	58	52	64	88	120	134	108	109	152	234	199	230	351	507	334	263	248
External loans	14	20	29	25	26	32	54	53	51	36	3	30	11	19	12	75	56
Others (including T-bills)	95	153	142	135	199	246	169	273	167	186	120	263	140	76	515	519	860

a. Actuals for center and revised estimates for states.

Source: Union budget Documents; RBI bulletin on state finances; World Bank staff estimates.

121

Table A10. Transfers between Center and States

Billions of rupees	1985/86	1986/87	1987/88	1988/89	1989/90	1990/91	1991/92	1992/93	1993/94	1994/95	1995/96	1996/97	1997/98	1998/99	1999/00	2000/01	2001/02	2002/03ᵃ	2002/03ᵇ	2003/04ᵃ
States' share in central taxes	75	85	96	107	132	145	172	205	222	248	293	351	435	391	435	517	528	612	561	638
Grants to states	67	74	91	100	86	132	157	178	208	200	213	232	297	251	290	368	415	468	430	501
Loans to states	92	75	87	99	109	136	123	121	140	188	193	231	294	385	193	173	206	252	249	242
of which: on small savings	29	28	31	42	57	70	55	43	50	97	100	107	151	230	0	0	0	0	0	0
Loan repayments by states	27	29	36	33	34	47	38	46	52	45	48	65	71	95	98	117	140	155	149	155
Interest payments by states	19	28	32	38	44	52	65	78	96	112	130	152	178	212	254	270	296	279	301	308
Gross transfers (center to states)	234	233	274	306	328	413	452	505	571	637	699	813	1,027	1,027	918	1,058	1,149	1,333	1,240	1,381
Net transfer (center to states)	188	177	207	235	250	315	349	381	423	480	521	596	777	720	565	672	713	899	790	918
Gross transfers (center to states) without small savings	205	205	243	264	271	343	397	462	521	540	599	706	876	797	918	1,058	1,149	1,333	1,240	1,381
Net transfers (center to states) without small savings	159	149	176	193	193	244	294	338	373	383	421	490	627	489	565	672	713	899	790	918
Percent of GDP																				
States' share in central taxes	2.7	2.7	2.7	2.5	2.7	2.6	2.6	2.7	2.6	2.5	2.5	2.6	2.9	2.2	2.2	2.5	2.3	2.4	2.3	2.3
Income tax	0.7	0.7	0.7	0.7	0.8	0.7	0.8	0.8	0.9	0.8	0.9	1.0	0.9	0.8	0.9	..	..	..	..	..
VDIS	..	..	..	..	..	..	..	..	..	..	..	..	0.5	..	..	..	..	..	..	..
Estate duty	0.0	0.0	0.0	0.0	0.0	0.0	0.0	0.0	0.0	0.0	0.0	0.0	0.0	0.0	0.0	..	..	..	..	..
Union excise duties	2.0	2.0	2.0	1.9	1.9	1.8	1.9	1.9	1.7	1.6	1.5	1.6	1.5	1.4	1.4	..	..	..	..	..
Grants to states	2.4	2.4	2.6	2.4	1.8	2.3	2.4	2.4	2.4	2.0	1.8	1.7	2.0	1.4	1.5	1.7	1.8	1.8	1.7	1.8
Loans to states	3.3	2.4	2.5	2.4	2.2	2.4	1.9	1.6	1.6	1.9	1.6	1.7	1.9	2.2	1.0	0.8	0.9	1.0	1.0	0.9
of which: on small savings	1.0	0.9	0.9	1.0	1.2	1.2	0.8	0.6	0.6	1.0	0.8	0.8	1.0	1.3	0.0	0.0	0.0	0.0	0.0	0.0
Loan repayments by states	1.0	0.9	1.0	0.8	0.7	0.8	0.6	0.6	0.6	0.4	0.4	0.5	0.5	0.5	0.5	0.6	0.6	0.6	0.6	0.6
Interest payments by states	0.7	0.9	0.9	0.9	0.9	0.9	1.0	1.0	1.1	1.1	1.1	1.1	1.2	1.2	1.3	1.3	1.3	1.1	1.2	1.1
Gross transfers (center to states)	8.4	7.5	7.7	7.3	6.7	7.3	6.9	6.7	6.6	6.3	5.9	5.9	6.7	5.9	4.7	5.0	5.0	5.2	5.0	5.0
Net transfer (center to states)	6.8	5.7	5.8	5.6	5.1	5.5	5.3	5.1	4.9	4.7	4.4	4.4	5.1	4.1	2.9	3.2	3.1	3.5	3.2	3.3
Gross transfers (center to states) without small savings	7.4	6.6	6.9	6.3	5.6	6.0	6.1	6.2	6.1	5.3	5.0	5.2	5.8	4.6	4.7	5.0	5.0	5.2	5.0	5.0
Net transfers (center to states) without small savings	5.7	4.8	5.0	4.6	4.0	4.3	4.5	4.5	4.3	3.8	3.5	3.6	4.1	2.8	2.9	3.2	3.1	3.5	3.2	3.3
GDPmp (billions of rupees)	2,780	3,112	3,543	4,216	4,862	5,687	6,531	7,484	8,592	10,128	11,880	13,682	15,225	17,409	19,369	21,043	22,960	25,571	24,655	27,435

a. Budget estimates.
b. Revised estimates.
Source: Union budget documents; RBI bulletins on state finances; Finance Accounts; World Bank staff estimates.

Table A 11: Outstanding Debt (Center and States)
(billions of rupees at current prices)

	1990/91	1991/92	1992/93	1993/94	1994/95	1995/96	1996/97	1997/98	1998/99	1999/00	2000/01	2001/02
Outstanding Liabilities of Central Government												
Internal debt	1,540	1,728	1,991	2,457	2,665	3,079	3,445	3,890	4,597	7,143	8,037	9,091
Of which:												
Market loans	705	780	817	1,106	1,309	1,640	1,841	2,166	2,854	3,559	4,288	5,171
91 T-bills	70	88	206	326	323	438	565	16	15	15	19	19
182/364 T-bills	11	40	88	84	82	19	82	162	102	160	163	195
Small savings, deposits and provident funds	618	697	770	879	1,064	1,214	1,390	1,678	2,065	664	1,048	1,488
Other accounts	453	518	598	725	858	920	1,001	1,241	1,268	1,344	1,440	1,579
Reserve funds and deposits	219	235	238	246	290	337	379	421	416	475	585	586
Total domestic liabilities	2,830	3,177	3,597	4,306	4,877	5,550	6,214	7,230	8,346	9,626	11,108	12,741
External liabilities (at historical exchange rates)	315	369	423	473	509	512	542	553	573	584	659	679
External liabilities (at current exchange rates)	929	1,259	1,631	1,688	1,792	1,792	1,754	1,812	1,928	2,004	2,019	2,077
Outstanding Liabilities of State Government												
Internal debt	192	230	263	303	352	432	516	594	771	986	1,220	1,459
Market loans	156	189	224	261	301	360	425	498	603	729	855	1,013
Compensation and other bonds	0	0	0	0	0	0	0	0	0	0	0	0
WMA from RBI	7	9	7	7	-12	0	6	-13	29	55	41	41
Loans from banks and other institutions	29	32	32	35	63	72	84	108	139	201	324	456
Loans and advances from central government	741	835	924	1,019	1,167	1,315	1,491	1,727	2,038	2,162	2,244	2,376
Special securities issued to NSSF	..	..	..	..	..	..	..	..	..	264	592	926
Total provident funds	170	199	235	278	326	375	429	491	611	789	928	1060
State provident funds	140	164	193	230	268	310	356	408	508	656	772	887
Insurance and pension fund trust and endowments	30	35	41	48	58	65	73	83	102	133	157	173
Total liabilities	1,103	1,263	1,422	1,601	1,845	2,122	2,435	2,812	3,420	4,201	4,979	5,882
Outstanding Liabilities of General Government												
Domestic liabilities	3,192	3,606	4,094	4,888	5,555	6,357	7,159	8,314	9,727	11,665	13,843	16,246
External liabilities (at current exchange rates)	929	1,259	1,631	1,688	1,792	1,792	1,754	1,812	1,928	2,004	2,019	2,077
Total liabilities (with external debt at current exchange rates)	4,121	4,864	5,726	6,575	7,347	8,149	8,913	10,127	11,655	13,669	15,862	18,323
Domestic liabilities (% of GDP)	56.1	55.2	54.7	56.9	54.8	53.5	52.3	54.6	55.9	60.2	65.8	70.8
External liabilities (% of GDP) at current exchange rates	16.3	19.3	21.8	19.6	17.7	15.1	12.8	11.9	11.1	10.3	9.6	9.0
Total liabilities (% of GDP)	72.5	74.5	76.5	76.5	72.5	68.6	65.1	66.5	66.9	70.6	75.4	79.8

Source: Central Budget, RBI; World Bank staff estimates.

Table A12. Banking Survey and Interest Rates

	1993/94	1994/95	1995/96	1996/97	1997/98	1998/99	1999/00	2000/01	2001/02
I. Banking Survey									
A) Billions of Rupees, End Year Stock									
Net foreign assets	423	650	647	889	1,109	1,373	1,663	1,966	2,603
Domestic credit	4,375	5,083	5,929	6,533	7,434	8,692	9,942	11,415	12,819
Claims on public sector	2,141	2,344	2,739	2,952	3,343	3,877	4,397	4,986	5,689
Claims on private sector	2,10	2,611	3,057	3,455	3,945	4,621	5,319	6,256	6,974
Claims on nonbank financial institutions	124	128	133	126	147	193	226	174	156
Total assets (= total liabilities)	4,798	5,733	6,576	7,422	8,543	10,065	11,605	13,381	15,422
Liquid liabilities	4,798	5,733	6,577	7,422	8,543	10,065	11,605	13,381	15,422
of which: money + quasimoney	4,106	5,025	5,657	6,578	7,746	9,122	10,345	12,077	13,821
Money market instruments	0.0	0.0	0.0	0.0	0.0	0.0	0.0	0.0	0.0
Long term foreign liabilities	0.0	0.0	0.0	0.0	0.0	13.7	12.9	13.5	0.0
All other net	0.0	0.0	0.0	0.0	0.0	0.0	0.0	0.0	0.0
B) Shares of GDP (%)									
Net foreign assets	4.9	6.4	5.4	6.5	7.3	7.9	8.6	9.3	11.3
Domestic credit	50.9	50.2	49.9	47.7	48.8	49.9	51.3	54.2	55.8
to public sector	24.9	23.1	23.1	21.6	22.0	22.3	22.7	23.7	24.8
to private sector	24.6	25.8	25.7	25.3	25.9	26.5	27.5	29.7	30.4
Liquid liabilities	55.8	56.6	55.4	54.2	56.1	57.8	59.9	63.6	67.2
Long term foreign liabilities	0.0	0.0	0.0	0.0	0.0	0.1	0.1	0.1	0.0
C) Real annual growth rates (%)									
Net foreign assets		43.0	-9.5	25.5	16.8	9.5	17.2	13.7	28.5
Domestic credit		8.0	6.1	0.7	6.5	3.4	10.7	10.5	9.0
to public sector		1.8	6.3	-1.5	6.0	2.5	9.8	9.1	10.7
to private sector		15.0	6.5	3.3	6.9	3.6	11.4	13.2	8.2
Liquid liabilities		11.1	4.3	3.1	7.7	4.1	11.6	11.0	11.8
Long term foreign liabilities		..	..	..	..	..	-9.3	0.8	..
II. Interest rates (%)									
Money market rate (call money rates)	6.99	9.4	17.7	7.8	8.7	7.8	8.9	9.2	7.3
Yield on Government of India securities (1-5 years)	11.86-12.86	9.75-11.76	6.00-14.28	5.21-16.21	5.50-17.69	4.45-17.73	3.18-14.30	4.94-16.66	—
Deposit rate (1-3 years)	10	11.0	12.0	11.0-12.0	10.5-11.0	9.0-11.0	8.5-9.5	8.5-9.0	8.0-8.5
Lending rate (minimum lending rate)	14	15.0	16.5	14.5-15.0	14	12.0-13.0	12.0-12.5	11.0-12.0	11.0-12.0
Real deposit rate[a]	5.0	3.4	2.0	1.6-2.6	3.7-4.2	-4.1 - -2.1	5.2-6.2	4.6-5.1	4.9-5.4
Real lending rate[a]	9.0	7.4	6.5	5.1-5.6	14.0	-1.0 - -0.1	8.7-9.2	7.1-8.1	7.9-8.9

a. Nominal rate less Inflation.
Source: IFS; RBI.

Table A13. Balance of Payments
(millions of U.S. dollars)

	1993/94	1994/95	1995/96	1996/97	1997/98	1998/99	1999/00	2000/01	2001/02
Current Account									
Exports of goods and services	27,947	32,990	39,657	41,607	45,109	47,484	53,251	63,764	65,201
Exports of goods	22,683	26,855	32,311	34,133	35,680	34,298	37,542	44,894	44,915
Exports of services	5,264	6,135	7,346	7,474	9,429	13,186	15,709	18,870	20,286
Imports of goods and services	31,468	41,437	51,213	55,696	59,297	58,565	67,028	75,656	73,705
Imports of goods, f.o.b.	26,739	35,904	43,670	48,948	51,187	47,544	55,383	59,264	57,618
Imports of services	4,729	5,533	7,543	6,748	8,110	11,021	11,645	16,392	16,087
Net trade in goods and services	-3,521	-8,447	-11,556	-14,089	-14,188	-11,081	-13,777	-11,892	-8,504
Income receipts	395	886	1,429	1,073	1,561	1,935	1,931	2,366	2,749
Income payments	3,665	4,317	4,634	4,380	5,082	5,479	5,490	6,187	5,403
Net income from abroad	-3,270	-3,431	-3,205	-3,307	-3,521	-3,544	-3,559	-3,821	-2,654
Private current transfer receipts	5,287	8,112	8,539	12,435	11,875	10,341	12,290	12,873	12,192
Private current transfer payments	22	19	33	68	45	61	34	75	67
Net private current transfers	5,265	8,093	8,506	12,367	11,830	10,280	12,256	12,798	12,125
Current account balance	-1,526	-3,785	-6,255	-5,029	-5,879	-4,345	-5,080	-2,915	967
Capital and Financial Account									
Net official capital grants	368	416	345	410	379	307	382	336	384
Net total private investment inflows	4,235	4,807	4,805	6,153	5,390	2,412	5,191	5,102	5,925
Net direct investment inflows	668	983	2,057	2,841	3,562	2,473	2,165	2,342	3,905
Net portfolio investment inflows	3,567	3,824	2,748	3,312	1,828	-61	3,026	2,760	2,020
External assistance, net	1,901	1,526	883	1,109	907	820	901	427	1,204
Commercial borrowings, net	607	1,030	1,275	2,848	3,999	4,362	313	4,011	-1,147
Rupee debt service	-1,053	-983	-952	-727	-767	-802	-711	-617	-519
NRI deposits, net	1,205	172	1,103	3,350	1,125	960	1,540	2,317	2,754
Other capital	2,800	2,604	-2,425	-1,321	-643	508	3,866	-2,805	2,189
Reserves, net change (negative sign indicates increase)	-8,724	-4,644	2,936	-5,818	-3,893	-3,829	-6,142	-5,830	-11,757
Other Series									
Foreign exchange reserves (end of period, including gold)	19,254	25,186	21,687	26,423	29,367	32,490	38,036	42,281	54,106
Reserves (as months of imports of goods and services)	7.3	7.3	5.1	5.7	5.9	6.7	6.8	6.7	8.8
GDP (billions of U.S. dollars)	273.9	322.6	355.2	385.4	409.7	413.8	447.0	460.6	481.4

Source: RBI.

	1993/94	1994/95	1995/96	1996/97	1997/98	1998/99	1999/00	2000/01	2001/02
A. EXPORTS									
A1. Exports (f.o.b., U.S. dollars)									
Total primary commodities	4,916	5,214	7,257	8,035	7,687	6,928	6,524	7,126	7,065
Oil meals	741	573	702	985	924	462	378	448	474
Marine products	814	1,126	1,011	1,129	1,207	1,038	1,183	1,396	1,218
Ores and minerals	888	988	1,175	1,172	1,061	893	916	1,155	1,214
Other primary commodities	2,473	2,527	4,369	4,749	4,495	4,535	4,048	4,127	4,159
Manufactures	16,657	20,404	23,747	24,613	26,547	25,792	29,714	34,391	33,241
Gems and jewelry	3,996	4,500	5,275	4,753	5,346	5,929	7,502	7,384	7,306
Readymade garments	2,586	3,282	3,676	3,753	3,876	4,365	4,765	5,578	5,004
Other manufactures	10,075	12,622	14,797	16,107	17,325	15,497	17,447	21,429	20,930
Total 22,683	26,855	32,311	34,133	3,5680	34,298	37,542	44,894	44,915	
A.2 Exports (constant 1993/94 prices)									
Total primary commodities	4,916	4,907	7,868	7,694	6,676	7,904	7,171	7,877	8,546
Oil meals	741	579	687	770	685	633	490	453	493
Marine products	814	935	922	1,033	1,030	994	1,141	1,231	1,288
Ores and minerals	888	1,136	1,386	1,181	1,043	910	1,070	1,104	1,094
Other primary commodities	2,473	2,258	4,874	4,711	3,918	5,367	4,469	5,090	5,671
Manufactures	16,657	20,388	23,207	27,003	23,891	21,907	23,988	38,427	41,061
Gems and jewelry	3,996	4,339	5,283	5,622	5,700	6,452	7,898	8,857	8,116
Readymade garments	2,586	2,978	3,285	4,562	5,711	6,415	7,090	81,46	8,637
Other manufactures	10,075	13,071	14,639	16,819	12,481	9,040	9,000	21,424	24,308
Total	22,683	25,769	33,739	36,290	34,007	35,638	40,711	49,681	52,391
B. IMPORTS									
B.1 Imports (c.i.f., U.S. dollars)									
Food 327	1,144	970	1,214	1,483	2,524	2,417	1,443	2,044	
Consumer goods	3,032	4,249	5,819	5,115	5,143	4,307	4,618	3,722	4,209
POL and other energy	5,754	5,928	7,526	10,036	8,164	6,399	12,611	15,650	14,000
Intermediate goods	7,951	9,696	12,031	12,845	16,898	19,094	21,059	20,780	21,519
Pearls, precious and semiprecious stones	2,635	1,630	2,106	2,925	3,342	3,760	5,436	4,808	4,622
Organic and inorganic chemicals	1,371	2,137	2,566	2,661	2,956	2,684	2,866	2,444	2,771
Other intermediate goods	3,946	5,929	7,359	7,260	10,600	12,650	12,757	13,528	14,126
Capital goods	6,243	7,638	10,330	9,922	9,796	10,064	8,966	8,941	9,315
Total	23,306	28,654	36,675	39,132	41,485	42,389	49,671	50,536	51,087
B.2 Imports (constant 1993/94 prices)									
Food 327	858	641	1,002	1,276	2,085	1,768	2,078	1,542	
Consumer goods	3,032	3,603	4,606	3,812	4,171	3,551	4,133	3,215	4,202
POL and other energy	5,754	5,775	6,832	7,614	7,793	8,504	9,533	9,207	9,978
Intermediate goods	7,951	4,212	12,073	13,196	18,108	22,794	24,873	25,326	24,709
Pearls, precious and semiprecious Stones	2,635	1,493	1,550	2,337	2,875	3,656	5,518	4,161	4,600
Organic and inorganic chemicals	1,371	1,898	2,319	2,784	2,881	5,986	7,480	5,419	2,773
Other intermediate goods	3,946	821	8,204	8,075	12,352	13,152	11,875	15,745	17,337
Capital goods	6,243	14,413	12,286	10,584	8,438	8,635	9,559	9,598	11,091
Total	23,306	28,861	36,438	36,208	39,786	45,568	49,865	49,424	51,523
C. INDICES (1993=100)									
C1. Volume indices									
Merchandise exports	100.0	113.7	149.2	159.9	149.9	155.0	179.0	221.7	274.7
Merchandise imports	100.0	124.1	156.4	155.5	170.8	195.7	214.2	212.1	210.0
C2. Price Indices									
Merchandise export price index	100.0	104.2	95.8	94.1	104.9	96.2	92.2	90.4	86
Merchandise import price index	100.0	99.3	100.7	108.1	104.3	93.0	99.6	102.3	99
Merchandise terms of trade	100.0	105.0	95.1	87.0	100.6	103.5	92.6	88.4	86

Source: RBI.

Table A15. External Debt and Debt Service

	1993/94	1994/95	1995/96	1996/97	1997/98	1998/99	1999/00	2000/01	2001/02
I. (millions of U.S. dollars)									
A. Debt outstanding and disbursed									
Total long term	85,676	93,907	87,040	85,427	88,606	93,021	94,354	95,971	94,120
Public and public guaranteed	83,906	87,480	80422	78,045	79,398	84,611	86,410	83,491	82,446
Private nonguaranteed	1,770	6,427	6,618	7,382	9,208	8,409	7,944	12,480	11,674
Short term	3,626	4,264	5,049	6,726	5,046	4,329	3,933	3,462	2,951
IMF 5,041	4,312	2,374	1,313	664	288	26	0	0	
Total DOD	94,342	102,483	94,464	93,466	94,317	97,637	98,313	99,433	97,071
B. Debt service									
Interest	4,178	4,633	4,918	4,364	4,864	5,120	3,782	4,182	3,817
Amortizations	4,033	5,144	6,929	6,644	6,936	6,574	6,062	6,661	5,465
IMF repurchases	134	1,174	1,719	972	613	390	262	25	0
Total 8,345	10,951	13,566	11,981	12,413	12,084	10,107	10,868	9,282	
II. Ratios (%)									
Total DOD to GDP	34.4	31.8	26.6	24.3	23.0	23.6	22.0	21.6	20.2
Total DOD (% total exports)	280.5	244.1	190.4	169.6	161.1	163.4	145.7	125.9	121.1
Debt service (% total exports)	24.8	26.1	27.3	21.7	21.2	20.2	15.0	13.8	11.6

Source: Global Development Finance, 2003.

Table A16. Financial Sector Indicators

	1996/97	1997/98	1998/99	1999/00	2000/01	2001/02
A. Banking System						
1. Depth and structure						
Total domestic credit (%of GDP)	47.7	48.8	49.9	51.3	54.2	55.8
of which private credit (% of GDP)	25.3	25.9	26.5	27.5	29.7	30.4
Number of banks						
Public sector	27	27	27	27	27	27
Private banks						30
Foreign banks						23
2. Efficiency and strength						
Spread over LIBOR	10.4	8.1	8.0	7.1	5.8	8.3
Nonperforming loans as % of total						
Public sector banks(27)	17.8	16.0	15.9	14.0	12.4	11.1
Private banks (34)	8.5	8.7	10.8	8.2	8.4	9.7
Foreign banks (45)	4.3	6.4	7.6	7.0	6.8	5.4
B. Stock Market						
Market capitalization (% of GDP)	32.0	31.4	25.4	41.5	32.4	23.1
Value Traded (% of GDP)	25.06	38.64	35.80	62.63	111.56	52.20
Number of listed companies					5795	
S&P/IFC investable index (annual % change)	-2.0	5.8	-23.0	81.0	-31.1	-19.9

Source: RBI and World Development Indicators.

Table A17. Investment Climate

	Year	India	Income Group Average	Regional Average	Middle-Income Average
Private Investment Environment					
Private investment/gross domestic fixed investment (%)	1995-1999	61.0	53.7	71.8	74.8
Domestic credit to private sector (stock, % GDP)	2001	29.1	24.1	28.8	57.8
Real lending rate	2001				
Highest marginal corporate tax rate (%)	2002	36.0			
Euromoney credit rating	Sep-02	55.1	28.4	38.7	46.5
ICRG composite risk rating	Oct-02	65.8	58.8	69.5	69.8
Institutional investor risk rating	Sep-02	47.3	18.0	36.4	39.0
Governance					
ICRG corruption rating (1-6, bad to good)	Feb-03	1.5			
ICRG bureaucratic quality rating (1-6)	Feb-03	3.0			
ICRG law and order (1-6)	Feb-03	4.0			
Openness					
Trade (imports+exports)/GDP (%)	2001	19.5	37.6	23.4	50.2
FDI inflows (% GDP)	2001	0.6	1.7	0.6	3.9
WTO member?		Y			
Weighted mean tariff (%)	2001	28.2			
Infrastructure					
Paved roads (% of total)	1995-2001	45.7	16.1	36.9	52.7
Motor vehicles (per 1,000 persons)	2000	8	10	8	65
Cost of calls to United States (U.S. dollars per 3 min)	2001	4.20	..	3.60	..
Internet users (thousands)	2001	5,000	9,337	5,413	87,311
Electricity consumption (kWh per capita)	2000	355	350	323	1,391
GDP per unit energy use (PPP dollars per kilogram oil equivalent)	1999	4.6	3.6	4.9	4.0
Wages and Productivity					
Minimum wage (U.S. dollars per year)	1995-99	408			
Labor cost per worker in manufacturing (U.S. dollars per year)	1995-99	1,192			
Value added per worker in manufacturing (U.S. dollars per year)	1995-99	3,118			
R&D expenditure (% of GNI)	1989-2000	0.62	..	0.62	..

Source: World Bank, World Development Indicators Database, 2003.

Table A18. Vulnerability Indicators

	1996/97	1997/98	1998/99	1999/00	2000/01	2001/02
A. Market Indicators						
Annual percent change in average exchange rate (%)	6.1	4.7	13.2	3.0	5.4	4.4
Annual change in T-Bill rates (short-term)						
Average spread on Eurobonds (basis points)						
Annual change in stock market index (%)	-2.0	5.8	-23.0	81.0	-31.1	-19.9
B. Risk Ratings						
ICRG composite (1-100, bad to good)	68.1	69.2	65.2	63.3	63.8	65.0
Euromoney (1-100, bad to good)						
Institutional Investor (1-100, bad to good)						
C. Financial						
Annual growth in real domestic credit (%)	0.7	6.5	3.4	10.7	10.5	9.0
Foreign currency to total deposits (%)	15.4	16.4	17.0	18.1	18.6	21.9
Nonperforming loans of commercial banks (% of total)						
Public sector	17.84	16.0	15.89	13.98	12.37	11.09
Private banks	8.49	8.7	10.81	8.17	8.37	9.65
Foreign banks	4.29	6.4	7.59	6.99	6.84	5.38
D. Reserve Cover Indicators						
Reserve cover of imports (months of imports)	5.7	5.94	6.7	6.8	6.7	8.8
Reserves to short term debt	3.9	5.8	7.5	9.7	12.2	18.3
Reserves/M2 (%)	12.2	13.2	13.7	14.8	15.3	18.0
E. Prices						
Annual change in terms of trade (%)	-8.5	15.6	2.8	-10.5	-4.5	-2.2
Annual depreciation REER (%)	0.3	5.0	-5.3	-0.2	5.1	2.9
F. External						
Current account balance (% of GDP)	-1.3	-1.4	-1.0	-1.1	-0.6	0.2
External debt (% of GDP)	24.3	23.0	23.6	22.0	21.6	20.2
G. Fiscal Sustainability Indicators (General Government)						
Total public debt (% of GDP)	65.1	66.5	66.9	70.6	75.4	79.8
Fiscal deficit (% of GDP)	6.4	6.7	9.3	9.7	9.6	11.0
Primary deficit (% of GDP)	1.2	1.5	3.9	3.8	3.6	4.7

Sources: IFS, WDI, Reserve Bank of India and World Bank Staff Estimates.

Table A19. Millennium Development Goals Indicators

	1990	1994	1999	2001
1. Eradicate extreme poverty and hunger 2015 target = halve 1990 $1 a day poverty and malnutrition rates				
Population below $1 a day (%)	..	44	..	..
Poverty gap at $1 a day (%)	..	12	..	..
Poverty rate (%)		36		28.6
Percentage share of income or consumption held by poorest 20%	..	..	8	..
Prevalence of child malnutrition (% of children under age 5)	64	53	47	..
Population below minimum level of dietary energy consumption (%)	25	..	23	..
2. Achieve universal primary education 2015 target = net enrollment to 100				
Net primary enrollment ratio (% of relevant age group)	..	51	77	..
Percentage of cohort reaching grade 5 (%)	..	55	60	..
Youth literacy rate (% ages 15-24)	64	68	72	73
3. Promote gender equality 2005 target = education ratio to 100				
Ratio of girls to boys in primary and secondary education (%)	68	70	75	..
Ratio of young literate females to males (% ages 15-24)	74	78	81	81
Share of women employed in the nonagricultural sector (%)	..	..	..	..
Proportion of seats held by women in national parliament (%)	8	..	48	..
4. Reduce child mortality 2015 target = reduce 1990 under 5 mortality by two-thirds				
Under-five mortality rate (per 1,000)	..	94	95	..
Infant mortality rate (per 1,000 live births)	..	79	68	..
Immunization, measles (% of children under 12 months)	..	35	42	..
5. Improve maternal health 2015 target = reduce 1990 maternal mortality by three-fourths				
Maternal mortality ratio (per 100,000 live births)	..	424	540	..
Births attended by skilled health staff (% of total)	..	34	42	..
6. Combat HIV/AIDS, malaria and other diseases 2015 target = halt, and begin to reverse, AIDS, etc.				
Prevalence of HIV, female (% ages 15-24)	..	..	0.6	..
Contraceptive prevalence rate (% of women ages 15-49)	..	40.6	48.2	..
Number of children orphaned by HIV/AIDS	..	..	..	..
Incidence of tuberculosis (per 100,000 people)	..	467	544	..
Tuberculosis cases detected under DOTS (%)	..	..	6	..
7. Ensure environmental sustainability 2015 target = various (see notes)				
Forest area (% of total land area)	21.4	..	..	21.6
Nationally protected areas (% of total land area)	..	4.8	4.8	
GDP per unit of energy use (PPP dollar per kilogram oil equivalent)	3.3	4	4.7	..
CO_2 emissions (metric tons per capita)	0.8	1	1.1	..
Access to an improved water source (% of population)	..	68	78	..
Access to improved sanitation (% of population)	21	..	..	31
Number of households with toilet facility (%)	..	30	36	..
Access to secure tenure (% of population)	..	..	..	..
8. Develop a Global Partnership for Development 2015 target = various (see notes)				
Youth unemployment rate (% of total labor force ages 15-29)		10.1	..	12.1
Fixed line and mobile telephones (per 1,000 people)	5.9	13	26.5	32
Personal computers (per 1,000 people)	0.3	1.3	3.3	4.5

Note: In some cases the data are for earlier or later years than those stated.
Source: World Development Indicators database, April 2003; National Family Health Survey (NFHS); National Sample Survey (NSS); Planning Commission, Government of India.

Table A20. Development Indicators, India and Comparator Countries

Indicator	Unit	Year	India	China	Brazil	Indonesia	Pakistan
Per capita Income	U.S. dollars	2000	450	840	3,580	570	440
PPP Per capita income	U.S. dollars	2000	2,340	3,920	7,300	2,830	1,860
Population	Million	2000	1,016	1,262	170	210	138
Male literacy rate	Percent	2001	76	92	85	92	57
Female literacy rate	Percent	2001	54.3	76	85	82	28
Population below the poverty line[a]	Percent	Survey year in brackets	26.1 (2000)	6 (1996)	17.4 (1990)	15.7 (1996)	34 (1991)
Population below $1/day	Percent	Survey year in brackets	44.2 (1997)	18.8 (1999)	11.6 (1998)	7.7 (1999)	31 (1996)
Number of poor	Million	1999/2000	312.6	75.7	29.6	33	47
Infant mortality rate	Per 1000 live births	2000	69	32	32	41	83
Life expectancy at birth	Years	2000	63	70	68	66	63
Access to improved sanitation facilities[b]	Percent	2000	31	38	77	66	61

Note: Data on male and female literacy rate for countries other than India is for the year 2000.
a.   An alternate methodology used by Deaton and Drèze estimated the poverty headcount to be 28.6% in 1999/2000.
b.   Access to improved sanitation facilities refers to percent of population with at least adequate excreta disposal facilities (private or shared, but not public) that can effectively prevent contact with excreta.
Source: World Development Indicators, 2002, The World Bank; Poverty data on India (1999/2000) sourced from India, Planning Commission.

Unemployment Rates	Usual Principal Status	Usual Principal and Subsidiary Status	Current Weekly Status	Current Daily Status
All-India				
1987/88	3.8	2.6	4.8	6.1
1993/94	2.6	1.9	3.6	6.0
1999/00	2.8	2.2	4.4	7.3
Urban				
1987/88	6.6	5.3	7.1	9.4
1993/94	5.2	4.5	5.8	7.4
1999/00	5.2	4.6	5.9	7.7
Rural				
1987/88	3.1	2.0	4.2	5.3
1993/94	1.8	1.2	3.0	5.6
1999/00	2.0	1.4	3.9	7.2

Table A21. Unemployment Rates: Alternative Measures